This ground-breaking study reveals an unorganized and previously unacknowledged religion at the heart of American culture. Nature, Catherine Albanese argues, has provided a compelling religious center throughout American history. In a book of remarkable originality and vision, Albanese charts the multiple histories of American nature religion and explores the moral and spiritual responses the encounter with nature has provoked throughout American history. Tracing the connections between movements and individuals both unconventional and established, Albanese treats figures from popular culture, such as the nineteenth-century Hutchinson Family Singers and almanac-version Davy Crockett, as well as historically prominent culture brokers, including Thomas Jefferson, Ralph Waldo Emerson, Henry David Thoreau, and John Muir.

Just as there are variant understandings of what nature is, there are diverse nature religions. Moving beyond Algonkian Indians, Anglo-American Puritans, and Revolutionary War patriots, Albanese argues persuasively for a classic American double vision of nature, notably articulated by Emerson and Thoreau. On the one hand, nature was real, and Americans should live in harmony with it; on the other, nature was illusory, and they should master it with the power of mind. The conceptual crack between nature real and nature illusory dogged later Americans: Albanese explores nineteenth-century wilderness preservation and mind cure and turns her attention, too, to physical forms of nature healing in movements such as water cure, homeopathy, and chiropractic. She goes on in the twentieth century to find that the quantum provides a powerful metaphor to fill the crack between contrary views of nature. And she discovers old and new together in politically organized Greens and feminist followers of the Goddess, who also share a common landscape with nature writer Annie Dillard and Bear Tribe founder Sun Bear, with Reiki initiate healers and practitioners of macrobiotics.

Throughout *Nature Religion in America,* Albanese emphasizes those who have not been formally trained as theologians, ceremonial leaders, or ethical guides. She demonstrates that nature religion in America has flourished among a cadre of people who have thought and acted for themselves. The first of its kind, this study is a preliminary guide to a vast and previously uncharted religious world. It will become essential reading for all students of American religion and for general readers who themselves look to nature as the site of the sacred.

Nature Religion in America

Nature Religion in America
FROM THE ALGONKIAN INDIANS
TO THE NEW AGE ❧ ❧ ❧ ❧

Catherine L. Albanese

Chicago History of American Religion,
a Series Edited by Martin E. Marty

THE UNIVERSITY OF CHICAGO PRESS
CHICAGO AND LONDON

Frontispiece: Portrait of Ninigret II, Son of Ninigret I, Chief of the Niantic Indians, unknown American artist, ca. 1681. Oil on canvas; 33″ × 30″. (Courtesy, Museum of Art, Rhode Island School of Design. Gift of Mr. Robert Winthrop.) The Niantics were a small Algonkian-speaking (Pequot) nation, but the painting adumbrates many of the themes explored in this book.

The University of Chicago Press, Chicago 60637
The University of Chicago Press, Ltd., London
© 1990 by the University of Chicago
All rights reserved. Published 1990
Printed in the United States of America

99 98 97 96 95 94 93 92 91 90   5 4 3 2 1

Library of Congress Cataloging-in-Publication Data

Albanese, Catherine L.
    Nature religion in America : from the Algonkian Indians to the new age / Catherine L. Albanese.
        p.   cm. — (Chicago history of American religion)
    Includes bibliographical references.
    1. Nature worship—United States—History.   2. United States—Religion.   I. Title.   II. Series.
BL435.A43   1990   89-39561
291.2′12′0973—dc20   CIP
ISBN 0-226-01145-3 (alk. paper)

∞ The paper used in this publication meets the minimum requirements of the American National Standard for Information Sciences—Permanence of Paper for Printed Library Materials, ANSI Z39.48-1984.

For Samantha

Contents

Illustrations

Foreword ✿ BY MARTIN E. MARTY

At the risk of intruding too far on Catherine Albanese's page space, let me use a personal anecdote because it frames her story. Some Japanese scholars whose company included some Christian theologians, rarities in that land, asked for a lecture on the concept of "covenant" in America. I lectured on "America's Two Covenants and Its Countercovenant." Covenant One is biblical, mediated through Jewish and Christian sources and resources. Christopher Columbus lived by it, and so did Puritans and revivalists, synagogue goers and churchgoers, Bible believers and Bible readers. Covenant Two is enlightened, mediated through the Founders and Framers and their documents and through our free institutions. George Washington lived by it, and so did early republicans and democrats, frequenters of public school and public square, liberal and conservative custodians of our culture.

Both of these covenants—or compacts, or bondings—were religious in that they were sealed by a sense that evoked a transcendent order of Being. In both cases, citizens who lived by the covenants even invoked a transcendent Being. Whether the God of Abraham and Jesus or the God of Nature and Reason, this God at least metaphorically gave promises and exacted responses. Citizens often grasped these covenants through institutions—churches, courthouses, and the like—but they also often avoided the necessity of transacting through formal institutions. They produced do-it-yourself or à la carte versions of both.

In those two parts of the Japanese lecture, I had described first what the public calls "organized religion" and then what the scholars call "civil religion" and what the present scholar, Professor Albanese, calls "republican religion." Neither of these is the topic of her book. These two covenants, I told the Japanese, tend to be highly male and masculine; their God was usually "He." Few women got their names in print as keepers of the covenants or as leaders of the institutions, even if they made up more than half of the constituencies. The covenants produced many effects most of us would cheer, values and virtues off which we live. They were also marked by very productive, almost obsessive notions of contract, production, and achievement. On occasion, their side effects for participants have included compulsiveness, ulcers, heart attacks, endocrine disturbances, alcoholism, and other diseases that come when people oversubscribe to such notions.

So America needed and had a countercovenant. This countercovenant also had its transcendental tinge, and some of its keepers even called themselves Transcendentalists. They might be—but often were not—theists or deists, and they spoke more easily of human spirit than of Holy Spirit. They urged that we keep contracts only with nature, produce only what harmonizes with it, achieve without grim competition, and live with a natural and human universe. Of course, to make their views known, they had to assert them with power, embody the values associated with them, and seek to persuade others. In sum (and as Catherine Albanese shows), they were themselves eager to acquire power to effect their ways, even if the means for doing so seemed subtle. The countercovenanters include, along with Transcendentalists, many Native Americans, women, poets, healers, folksingers, humorists, naturalists, publicists, persuaders, and not a few pragmatic politicians who have found advantage in appealing to the devotees of nature religion.

When America-in-power is too sure of its mission, this company sings songs to raise questions. When it is too confident of the present forms of asserting the power, they write poems to praise vulnerability. When it is too productive, they ask good-natured questions about the point of productivity. (Listen, for instance, to Henry David Thoreau's questions.) When the covenant is too harsh, they soften it without being weak. Thus ended the lecture.

Whereupon a Christian theologian who had survived the bomb in the environs of Nagasaki asked: "Why could this countercovenant not be more prominent in your country's thinking and acting? Better, can you think what a great nation you would have if what you call the countercovenant became part of the covenants themselves and did not merely counter them? If America could be vulnerable while carrying on its mission, thoughtful while being productive, soft when it is asserting itself, wouldn't it become a wonderful nation?" (Leaving aside for now the issue whether Japan could not also learn such things from a countercovenant, let us instead stay on the American theme.)

This book is not about church religion. It is not about civil religion or, finally, about "republican religion." It is not simply about privatized religion. Instead, Catherine Albanese deals with a loose construct that she calls "nature religion," which has some things in common with the outlook described by the Japanese questioner. Since this religion has no Curia, Sanhedrin, or Supreme Court, no apostolic succession or General Assembly, no committees of canon law or liturgical revision, it is necessarily constructed loosely, both in reality, whatever that is, and in the reality imposed by a historian who writes about its development. In this book the reader confronts nature religion as one scholar invents it. But we remember that, in the dictionary, *invent* means both to conceive or fashion something new and also to find something.

Albanese has found a strain of nature religion that softens the aggressive and pragmatic covenants and then has imposed her form on its substance. Other scholars would do it differently, would cover other subjects and discover other meanings. But she deserves a patent for disclosure of this protean, enduring, viscous form of spirituality and religion. One hopes that other scholars will refine her necessarily open definitions and will continue in encyclopedic detail what she has set forth here as a very sophisticated primer on the subject.

My opening story having taken several paragraphs, I hasten to get off stage and out of the way. Rather than anticipate any portion of Albanese's plot, I comment only on some elements of her genre and approach. To do so may help readers who are newcomers feel more at home from the beginning. Here are several:

The genre has to include elements of both formal academic scholarship and an essayist's feel for popular culture. The experts whose footnotes have footnotes are not likely to find much to quibble about so far as accuracy is concerned. Yet they have to be ready, from line one, for notice of vulgar phenomena such as the Hutchinson family, folksy celebrators of nineteenth-century nature religion. On the other hand, devotees of popular culture who look for the earth and ordinary people will find them here, in much of their wondrous variety, but will then have to step with Albanese into the precincts of academic disciplines.

A second overlapping of interests occurs when the author moves with ease between zones that others had marked with boundaries between nonreligious and religious, between scientific and supernatural, between secular and sacred, between—we have to be frank about this, too—people seen in mainstream culture as "nutty" and "nonnutty," and between religions that look eccentric to some and centric to others, and vice versa. Mesmerism, water cures, early chiropractic, and old nostrums coexist here with Emersonianism, holistic healing, and new (and therefore momentarily respectable) nostrums.

Albanese tends to withhold judgment where many of us would issue labels and stamps marked "Fake!" or "Exploitative!" or, also, "Salutary!" She has confidence in her chosen story, in her part of the larger story, and in the genre and approach she uses. She asks the reader to suspend some disbelief about the worth of the subject in order to let the kinds of credibility she seems to find in it work their effect. Albanese would be the first to note in that sentence that her editor here has assumed a certain kind of "the reader." There are other kinds, and this book should appeal to them. For Albanese also writes for those who find organized and civil religions eccentric and incredible.

Rarely do the camps of covenanters and countercovenanters receive such tantalizing invitations to enter each other's company, to engage each other, and to learn together—all of which can begin to happen herewith, to the many sorts of readers who now turn the page and share the descriptions and discoveries of American nature religion.

Acknowledgments

This book began once in daydreams and began again in earnest when Martin Marty allowed himself to be persuaded that I should write on nature religion for the Chicago History of American Religion and not on another theme he had in mind. Since then, he has waited patiently—and so have a series of Chicago editors—for a manuscript that did not come with quite the speed that he and they (and I) had anticipated.

Meanwhile, a National Endowment for the Humanities Fellowship for Independent Study and Research allowed me time to study the symbolic world, with nature at its center, shared by Transcendentalism and a series of popular religious and healing movements. Even more than I initially anticipated, the 1981–82 fellowship year convinced me that the New England Transcendentalists did not so much create a mentality as reflect and articulate one. The year convinced me, as much, that popular movements, tinged often with Swedenborgianism and mesmerism, had more to do with the shape of things than I had previously guessed. A Samuel Foster Haven Fellowship from the American Antiquarian Society enabled me to return to the society's holdings during the summer of 1983 for continued research. There the serendipity of circumstance brought me into contact with Dale Cockrell, the musicologist who introduced me to the Hutchinson Family Singers and shared his edition-in-progress of their journals with me. Subsequently, a research grant from the University of California, Santa Barbara, assisted me in the completion of the manuscript.

Much of the material in the present chapter 2 was published as "Whither the Sons (and Daughters)? Republican Nature and the Quest for the Ideal," in Jack P. Greene, ed., *The American Revolution: Its Character and Limits* (New York and London: New York University Press, 1987): 362–87. In turn, material taken from chapters 3 and 4 was used in another form in my essay "Physic and Metaphysic in Nineteenth-Century America: Medical Sectarians and Religious Healing," published in *Church History* 55 (December 1986): 489–502.

J. Baird Callicott, Robert S. Ellwood, Jr., and Stephen J. Stein read an earlier draft of the manuscript with attentiveness and insight and offered extended commentary that led me to say more and to sharpen. I did not take all of their advice (perhaps foolishly), but I did address each of the problems they pointed to. Jeffrey Burton Russell, my colleague at the University of California, Santa Barbara, also read the manuscript and offered helpful comments, as did students in a graduate seminar in religious studies in the fall of 1988. I remain grateful for the critical acumen and enthusiasm of all of these readers even as I acknowledge that I alone am responsible for any errors that remain.

Beyond these, other debts abound. I continue to be grateful to Charles H. Long, who many years ago taught me to think in terms of both ordinary and extraordinary religion, a distinction crucial to the substance of this book. I am grateful, too, to the generous librarians at numerous institutions who worked over the years to make available to me the materials I needed. My gratitude extends to those who supplied photographs for the book and granted me permission to use them. And in a related debt, I owe special thanks to Christopher Vecsey and to Lynne Williamson, who helped me to find suitable illustrations among the sparse Algonkian materials. Finally, I acknowledge a huge debt to my parents, Louis and Theresa Albanese, who, as always, have unflaggingly supported and encouraged my efforts. And I own my debt to Samantha, who—as the outcome of feline leukemia during the summer of 1985—decided to stay and keep on gracing my life. Her animal wisdom and perspective continue to teach me about nature and about the other-than-human persons of the Algonkians and other peoples.

Introduction ❧ THE CASE FOR NATURE RELIGION

The Tribe of Jesse consisted of the eleven grown sons and two grown daughters of Jesse Hutchinson and Mary (Polly) Leavitt of Milford, New Hampshire. Three more Hutchinsons did not survive to adulthood, but David, the oldest who did, had been born in 1803. Abigail Jemima (Abby), the youngest, lived until 1892 but was outlived by her brother John Wallace. Together the Hutchinsons spanned the nineteenth century.

The Tribe of Jesse are better known in American cultural history as the Hutchinson Family Singers, the first popular singing group in the United States. Playing and singing in cities and towns on the East Coast and into the New West, the Hutchinsons followed a pattern of itinerancy already mapped by revival preachers and lyceum speakers. They were signs of a new time in an industrializing, urbanizing America, expressing a nostalgic longing for old and enduring places as well as a seemingly scatter-gun involvement in a variety of contemporary causes and concerns. In various combinations of family members and, most remembered, as a quartet of John, Asa, Judson, and Abby ("a nest of brothers with a sister in it"), the Hutchinsons captivated mass audiences in well-filled houses and, apparently as often, appeared, like nineteenth-century Pete Seegers or Joan Baezes, at antislavery and temperance rallies.[1]

N. P. Rogers, editor of the abolitionist *Herald of Freedom*, reviewed their early (1842) singing as "simple and natural." The Hutchinsons, he said, possessed a "woodland tone" and enjoyed "perfect freedom from all affectation and stage grimace." A year and a half later, Rogers hailed their singing at a Boston antislavery convention, acclaiming a particularly excited moment that "was life—it was nature, transcending the musical staff, and the gamut, the minim and the semi-breve, and leger lines." Similarly, George P. Braddock, who participated in the Brook Farm experiment, many years afterward recalled the Hutchinsons' visit to the farm and the "wild freshness" of their song.[2] Meanwhile, appearing on temperance platforms with Lyman Beecher and others and continuing to sing elsewhere, the Hutchinsons charmed listeners with their

Hutchinson Family Quartet, 1846. "A nest of brothers with a sister in it." By an unidentified artist, from John Wallace Hutchinson, *Story of the Hutchinsons*, vol. 1 (Boston: Lee & Shepard, 1896), opposite page 142. (Courtesy, American Antiquarian Society.)

family song, "The Old Granite State." It became, in the parlance of the twentieth century, a hit, the perennial favorite of their audiences.

> We have come from the mountains,
> We've come down from the mountains,
> Ho, we've come from the mountains,
>   Of the Old Granite State.
>   We're a band of brothers,
>   We're a band of brothers,
>   We're a band of brothers,
>   And we live among the hills.
>
>   . . . .
>
> David, Noah, Andrew, Zephy, Caleb, Joshua, Jesse, Benny, Judson,
>   Rhoda, John and Asa and Abby are our names;
> We're the sons of Mary, of the tribe of Jesse,
>   And we now address you in our native mountain song.
>
>   . . . .
>
>   Oh, we love the rocks and mountains,
>   Oh, we love the rocks and mountains,

> Oh, we love the rocks and mountains
> Of the Old Granite State.
>> Pointing up to heaven,
>> Pointing up to heaven,
>> Pointing up to heaven,
>>> They are beacon lights to man.[3]

Interspersed among the verses evocative of place and permanence in New Hampshire's granite hills were the Hutchinsons' moral and political commitments. The Hutchinsons were "the friends of emancipation," and they proclaimed to hearers "That the tribe of Jesse / Are the friends of equal rights." They sang that "Every man's a brother, / And our country is the world." As time passed, they included a verse to "Shout 'Free Suffrage' evermore." And, in a striking millennial affirmation, they foretold musically of "the good time's drawing nigher," when "our nation, tried by fire, / Shall proclaim the good Messiah, / Second coming of the Lord."[4]

Nor was this the whole of the Hutchinsons' remarkable catalog of affirmations and commitments. They worshiped Theodore Parker and Henry Ward Beecher, Parker somewhat more. They also made an idol of Horace Greeley, radical editor of the *New-York Tribune,* and, in addition to their trip to Brook Farm, visited his North American Phalanx in Monmouth County, New Jersey. Their millennialism extended well beyond the lyrics of "The Old Granite State," for they had heard William Miller preach in Philadelphia in 1844; and, although never Millerites, they shared the general millennial expectancy of their age. They sang "maddening Second Advent tunes" in the antislavery cause; and, indeed, the verses of "The Old Granite State" were even set to a second-Advent melody. Moreover, the millennial theme continued to be part of Hutchinson consciousness well after the 1840s, so that the post–Civil War suffrage song composed by John Wallace pronounced his "loving, waiting, watching, longing, for the millennial day of light."[5]

Beyond their millennialism, the Hutchinsons as a family epitomized the spiritual trajectory of many New Englanders of their time. Their parents had begun married life in Milford as members of the First Congregational Church, but when still young they turned instead to Baptist preaching. According to church records,

John was "saved" during the revival of 1831; but in time some of the younger Hutchinsons withdrew from the church as come-outers, while almost all of the older brothers and some of the younger became spiritualists. In fact, with Horace Greeley and his wife, probably eight of the brothers had attended a seance given by the Fox sisters in 1851. The Hutchinsons knew Andrew Jackson Davis, the celebrated spiritualist and "Poughkeepsie seer," and he had visited their home. And, at least for Judson, John Wallace, and Jesse Jr., various forms of precognition had manifested themselves at key moments in their lives.[6]

Still further, the Hutchinsons embraced a series of the health-reform movements of the era. The brothers were familiar with various hydropathic (water-cure) institutes, and at least Judson and Jesse Jr. had entered them as patients, Jesse on his deathbed. Moreover, the Hutchinsons' song "Cold Water," written by Jesse Jr. and sung in the temperance cause, was also a clever proclamation of the gospel of hydropathy.

> Oh! if you would preserve your health
>   And trouble never borrow,
> Just take the morning shower bath,
>   'Twill drive away all sorrow.
> And then instead of drinking rum,
>   As doth the poor besotter;
> For health, long life, and happiness,
>   Drink nothing but cold water.
>
>   .   .   .   .
>
> Yes, water'll cure most every ill,
>   'Tis proved without assumption;
> Dyspepsia, gout, and fevers, too,
>   And sometimes old consumption.
> Your head-aches, side-aches, and *heart-aches* too,
>   Which often cause great slaughter;
> Can all be cured by drinking oft
>   And bathing in cold water.[7]

The Hutchinsons knew Dr. William Beach, who had initiated a "reform system of medicine on botanic principles." Asa observed in his journal that he loved *Beach's Family Physician* and found "plain truth with in its covers." And Beach had liked the Hutchinsons well enough too, telling them he enjoyed their song "Calomel"—an unsubtle attack on orthodox medical practice with its universal remedy of (poisonous) chloride of mercury.

Physicians of the highest rank,
To pay their fees we need a bank,
Combine all wisdom art and skill
Science and sense in Calomel.

. . . .

When Mr. A or B. is sick
Go call the docter [sic] and be quick
The docter comes with much good will
But ne'er forgets his Calomel.

. . . .

The man in death begins to groan,
The fatal job for him is done,
He dies alas, but sure to tell,
A sacrifice to Calomel.[8]

Likewise, the brothers used the Thomsonian system of natural herbal healing, taking Thomsonian powders and the perennial Thomsonian cure-all, tincture of lobelia. When Judson lay sick, Asa expressed his gratitude for the ministrations of the Thomsonian physician: "Blessed be his name for it is the helpmeat [sic] of our whole Family and ought to be that of the whole Human Family. May its Cause flourish."[9]

In New York, the Hutchinsons ate at (Sylvester) Graham House, which served only vegetarian food. Jesse must have been vegetarian during part of his life, for once, on the Fourth of July, he made a speech in favor of brown bread. Judson was certainly a committed vegetarian, speaking of the sinfulness of eating flesh or wearing garments that demanded for their construction the slaughter of animals. He himself eventually wore neither boots nor shoes and walked clad only in stockings, and his diet consisted of fruits, cereals, and honey. Meanwhile, Asa pondered the question of vegetarianism and confessed in his private journal: "I eat animal food some of the time." He had formerly abstained, and he thought his health was as good during his vegetarian experiment as later when he abandoned it.[10]

Asa also became absorbed in the works of Orson S. Fowler, the phrenologist, and thought phrenology—the reading of one's character on the basis of various protrusions of the skull—a "true science." He knew Fowler personally and considered him a friend. And Judson became heavily involved with animal magnetism, displaying mesmeric powers and, more often, falling easily into trances induced by others. In fact, the brothers worried about

Judson's magnetic susceptibility, for the magnetic state unnerved the moody and temperamental Hutchinson in frightening ways.[11]

What are we to make of this absorbing list of commitments and concerns by a band of nineteenth-century popular entertainers who sang to common folk and presidents alike? The Hutchinsons surely demonstrated their mass appeal—and, by implication, the appeal of their commitments—even though audiences hedged at times with regard to the group's radical politics. And they certainly presage twentieth-century involvement by entertainment groups in the fads and fancies of their moment. But can we say more about the Hutchinson Family Singers and their unorthodox catalog of affirmations? Are these affirmations merely odd pieces of cultural flotsam strung together by chance and circumstance? Are they a group of ideas and predilections united only by the restlessness of their holders, signals of bored revolt against formal and commonplace culture? Are they simply a celebration of nonnormativeness, a declaration of sociological independence? Or is there some intrinsic relationship between the items in the series, some logic of the symbol that, throughout the list, we can grasp?

This study rejects the thesis of cultural flotsam. It also brackets social scientific explanations (restlessness and nonnormativeness) and, if the qualifiers "only" and "simply" are retained, disclaims the judgments. The book's concerns lie, rather, with the final question. In what follows, I suggest that the Hutchinsons offer one prominent example of a way of organizing reality and relating to it that is consistent and encompassing. Moreover, I call this way of organizing reality and of relating it to a *religion,* and I identify it further as *nature religion.*

Definitions of religion are probably as numerous as the scholars who hold them, and this is not the place to engage in definitional debate. Suffice it to say that I understand religion as the way or ways that people orient themselves in the world with reference to both ordinary and extraordinary powers, meanings, and values. Ordinary powers, meanings, and values are found within the boundaries of human society. They are what cultures are built from—abilities and intuitions that are principles out of which cultural practice comes. Extraordinary power, meanings, and values are harder to name. They are what a given group or society sees, in important ways, as outside the boundaries of its own community. Extraordinary powers, meanings, and values are what the group owns as objective realities—standing in judgment on its project and practice and also inviting its members across an invisible line to a place of transcendence.[12]

Existing on the boundary as well as in the center, religion points in two directions. It is the ways—the systems of symbols—that orient people inward toward the societal center or, conversely, out toward the less known geography beyond the line. So religion includes belief systems, ritual forms, and guides for everyday living, all working in concert to express relationship to the ordinary and to the extraordinary, as a culture construes them. Nor are ordinary and extraordinary ever completely separated. Looked at one way, what people believe and do reinforces the bonds of their own society. But, looked at another way, what they believe and do is generated by the kind of "center beyond" that Mircea Eliade has called the sacred.[13] And, like the nucleus of an atom, this sacred center fixes the orbit of the more partial symbols that surround it.

Throughout the history of Western culture, at least, religious reflection has been preoccupied with three great symbolic centers, two of them more persistently, especially in certain forms of Protestantism. The three are the familiar trinity—God, humanity, and nature—and it is, of course, God and humanity that have been more pondered and nature that has formed the third and less noticed center among them. Within the theological speculation that forms the Judeo-Christian tradition, God has been clearly named as the sole and monotheistic claimant to the religious throne. But humans and nature, as creatures of God and objects of loving providence, have shone in borrowed light. Thus, within the structure of the symbols, the way always lay open not so much for a rejection of the monotheistic God as for a more emphatic turn in another direction.

American nature religion, in unlikely and surprising ways, has done just that. First, I must be clear that the term *nature religion* is my own name for a symbolic center and the cluster of beliefs, behaviors, and values that encircles it. If some prescient nineteenth-century person had cornered a Hutchinson and asked him whether he were a follower of nature religion, he probably would have looked astounded and heartily demurred. Like the term *civil religion,* which has become part of our academic language in religious

studies since 1967, *nature religion* is a contemporary social construction of past and present American religion.[14] It is a useful
construct, I believe, because it throws light on certain aspects of
our history that we have only haphazardly seen—or even failed to
see—religiously. By thinking of these manifestations as nature religion, we begin to discover the links and connections among them,
we gain a sense of their logic, and we come to a sense of their power.

Here I should add that when I speak of nature religion I do not
mean a religious genre that is divorced from human history or society. It is, of course, tempting to subsume the material of this book
into familiar comparative categories, to view the practice of nature
religion as an example, on American terrain, of the "cosmic" opposite to the Judeo-Christian religions of history. But that is hardly
what I have in mind. Nature, in American nature religion, is a reference point with which to think history. Its sacrality masks—and
often quite explicitly reveals—a passionate concern for place and
mastery *in society*.[15] Indeed, if the book has a "plot," it is how early,
inchoate bids for historic and personal dominance are played out
with greater clarity and precision as several centuries pass.

Allow me to return briefly to the Hutchinson Family Singers, to
explain what I mean by way of example. The critical acclaim for
the naturalness of the Hutchinsons' performance style is easy
enough to acknowledge. So is their proclamation of natural wholeness in their song, "The Old Granite State," far and away the favorite of their audiences. Here, combining metaphors of nature
and fixedness with the familial and biblical piety of the "band of
brothers" from the "tribe of Jesse," the Hutchinsons wove in whole
cloth a nature religion that celebrated innocence, permanence, and
purity. The power of these metaphors for a people undergoing the
pain of cultural transition cannot be doubted.

Similarly, temperance and antislavery involvements suggest the
moral urgency of an ethic of purity. Drunkenness and enslavement
were social sins that brought corruption and death to the nation,
destroying the vital connection with home and land. Drunkenness
eroded families, and slavery obstructed the natural relation of men
and women to the land in wholesome agricultural work. Besides,
slavery obliterated the democratic principle of equality, found in
the ideology of the new republic and also found, for American republicans, in nature. As they saw it, the natural world signified the

intrinsic equality of each form or species, displayed in a creation unburdened by rank or privilege. And a "natural" America had moral claims over Europe precisely because it had rejected artificial lineage claims to choose the innate nobility of democracy.

Nature, in fact, offered a model of societal harmony to many pre-Darwinian Americans, who forgot the violence of storm and tornado in the spectacle of nature's grand cooperation. Like the singing style of the Hutchinsons, in which individual voices were said to merge in an ordered harmony of the whole,[16] forms of social harmony would blend Americans who wanted order for themselves and their relationships. The call to natural concert was also a search for mastery, enabling communities to pursue their goals of control unaware. Thus, utopian communities expressed both the innocence of an Edenic world and its natural, but ordered, harmonies and rhythms. And thus, Hutchinson interest in Brook Farm (which became Fourierist only after their visit) and the Fourierist North American Phalanx was of a piece with their other commitments. Indeed, the Fourierist motto of Universal Unity evoked a central value of nature religion.

The come-outer style of some of the Hutchinsons and the spiritualism of many of them may, at first glance, appear to belong to different worlds of meaning entirely. Signing off from the churches is, of course, predominately a negative expression of one's values, the statement that I do *not* agree. But, in another sense, signing off complemented values of freedom and spontaneity that were associated with a physical separation from human society—a flight away to nature—but also a "natural" freedom, a dominance over social forms, within it. Likewise, nineteenth-century spiritualism belied its name in some of its theology. It was true that spiritualists sought contact with the departed. But many of them, with Andrew Jackson Davis, grounded their faith in religious materialism, seeing spirit as a higher and more refined form of matter.[17] From this perspective, spiritualists were true lovers of nature, exploring its further reaches and bringing its benefits back to rule disturbances on the present plane. That spiritualists also experienced precognition in dreams and visions only heightened their sense of mastery through the connectedness between this world and the other. One could see into the future because all things and all times were really one. Clairvoyance testified to the unknown powers of nature.

Even millennialism, the hallmark of nineteenth-century evangelicalism, fed freely into the stream of nature religion. Eliade has told us that millennial myths are inverted myths of origin, that in millennialism the paradise of the beginning is transposed to the end.[18] Thus, in millennialism, the locus of nature moves from the settled past to the active pull of the time to come. Significantly, the innocence and perfection of the first creation are posited in a future time; natural and Edenic bliss become the promise of the advent, when lion and lamb will lie down together, universal harmony will prevail, and—in the American version—humans will be in charge.

The various health reforms pursued by the Hutchinsons probably need little exegesis as symbolic and behavioral expressions of the religion of nature. "Cold water" evokes pure and crystalline mountain streams—significantly, the site of many of the water-cure establishments and the legacy of the granite hills of New Hampshire. Drinking water and bathing in it bespeak a preference for nature in place of artifice, i.e., chemically altered substances such as rum or calomel. They also suggest a confidence in one's ability to control the wayward body when it is ill through the power that nature gives. In the same way, William Beach's botanic principles and Samuel Thomson's herbal remedies used the means that nature provided for healing, refusing to be deceived by the synthetic chemical compounds of the orthodox physicians. And vegetarianism, on Grahamite principles, extolled brown bread because of its composition of unbolted (whole) wheat flour, coarse and unrefined, as nature made the grain. For Grahamites, animal flesh was associated with heavy grease and rich condiments, with overcooked and stimulating foods, with pollution of body and mind and the violation of physiological laws that led to the surrender of strength to disease.

Judson Hutchinson's stocking feet carried the prohibition of animal products as far as it would go. His commitment to the raw was near total, for even the wearing of shoes or boots would bring him too close to the cooked, and then overcooked (rotten—and powerless), state of civilization.[19] Judson would walk au naturel, a perpetual child in the Edenic garden. As that perpetual child, Judson was open to magnetic energies, ready to use or to be used by them. In effect, he was subscribing to the belief system of mesmerism, an essentially physical explanation for the power that one human being could hold over another, with its theory of the ebb and surge of invisible "fluid." Indeed, mesmerism became one of the controlling metaphors of American nature religion, and it reappeared in numerous forms as the decades passed.

Similarly, Asa's interest in phrenology signaled the value he put on nature. In essence, O. S. Fowler's phrenological popularizations presented a physical explanation for character. People were "amative" or "avaricious" because they were born that way, and the bumps on their skulls conformed to the specific character traits they displayed. One could read a person's soul by looking at the shape of the head, much as a twentieth-century handwriting analyst claims to detect personality traits through graphological scrutiny. And one could master one's own character, dominate its weaknesses, if one had a clear sense of the harmony between physical shape and metaphysical bent.

Hence, a second look at the various cultural badges the Hutchinsons wore reveals a good deal of continuity among them. The Tribe of Jesse exhibited consistency in the structure of their beliefs, finding power, meaning, and value in nature and in natural forms. They created ritual expression for their natural creed, positively in their songs and negatively in a series of food and medical taboos. And they stood by an ethic of democratic equality that arose from their beliefs, putting themselves on the line in radical causes and ever eager to evangelize their audiences for them. Meanwhile, in more private moments they pursued interests such as spiritualism and phrenology, which enacted and applied their intellectual commitments. Throughout, even as they sought harmony, they struggled for mastery, for a place of freedom and control, within the context of their society.

The Hutchinson Family Singers offer us one coherent example of nature religion. But there are others, and it will be my task in this book to delineate major forms and moments, describing them chronologically insofar as that is possible and showing the complex interweaving and development of motifs among variants. For there *were* variants to nature religion, just as there were variant understandings of nature and variant degrees of intensity with which a particular form of nature religion was held. Indeed, as we trace the

evolution and (to use a more exact term) convolutions of nature religion in the United States, we come to find that in truth there
were nature religions. There were not only particular expressions
of the religion of nature but even opposing tendencies within the
symbolic cluster.

For some, nature meant the physical world, the "cosmic environmentalism"—to borrow a phrase from Clarence J. Glacken—of
all that was not fashioned by human skill.[20] For others, nature became an abstract principle, an environmentalism so far extruded
into the starry skies that it lost the familiar touch of matter. In
a related distinction, for some, nature meant the truly real. For
others, it became the emblem of the higher spirit.

Similarly, adherence to nature as a central religious symbol
could lead to different—though related—injunctions for living.
On the one hand, nature religion seemed to encourage the pursuit
of harmony, as individuals sought proper attunement of human society to nature and thus mastery over sources of pain and trouble
in themselves and others. And yet, nature religion fostered more
ambivalent themes of fear and fascination for wildness and, at the
same time, an impulse toward its dominance and control. As we
will see, this complicated rhetoric of the symbol is most clearly
expressed in the alliance of nature religion with the politics of
nationalism and expansion. In still another change, the impulse
toward dominance expressed itself in movements teaching the
power of mind to order—and, some would say, to manipulate—nature. But the impulse to dominate was, in fact, everywhere in
nature religion, and the story told here cannot escape the theme.

This book seeks to tell, however, not only how nature was identified and what moral responses it prompted. The book aims to acknowledge also that nature religion had different histories in the
land. For some, such as American Indians, primary religious relation to nature was a legacy, a traditional heritage requiring neither
deliberate choice nor special comment. For others, such as the
New England Transcendentalists, nature religion included a self-
conscious quality, an element of chosenness and even contrivance
that suggested it was a spin-off of modernity. Still further, as in
the case of the Hutchinsons, for many the centrality of the symbol
of nature was indisputable. But for other Americans nature sup-

plied a weaker, more diffuse background, offering one kind of religious horizon for thought and act. Certainly in the latter case it is more correct to speak of the natural *dimension* of religion than to speak of nature religion. In any event, the failure of nature religionists to institutionalize well, if at all, means that—for all our longing for precision—we will find them in a somewhat murky world. In many cases spectrums and continuums will be apter maps of their religious landscapes than precise identification.

My book, then, tries to follow a chronology and to suggest a developmental matrix. But the book also tries, era by era, to attend to differences. At one period, I explore one version of the religion of nature; at a second period, another. Unavoidably, I have not been able to trace each theme through all of American history. That said, however, I understand my project as the encouragement of a conversation that I hope will continue, and so my hope is that others will chart paths that I have not been able to track from end to end.

Perhaps as important, I understand what I do here as a version of what Michel Foucault has called "history of the present."[21] As faithful historian, I try to report the past in terms that respect its integrity. As citizen of my own time and society, I see a past that helps to explain us to ourselves. This stance should be especially clear in the final chapter, where different forms of nature religion from the American past resonate with themes in contemporary society. And this stance should be especially important when, in the final chapter, new twentieth-century developments seem to bring harmony and mastery into easier, more graceful religious partnerships than at any time before.

But this is to get ahead of the story. In the chapters that follow, we look, first, at two juxtaposed forms of nature religion; the one clear and coherent, the other far more ambiguous. Native North Americans and Anglo-American Puritans set the limits of our inquiry, as, separated by distances of space and time and, still more, by fundamental culture, they stand as classic studies in religious difference. Next, in chapter 2, we examine the ideology of nature in the revolutionary era, as nature is subsumed into philosophical construct and political strategem. We pursue the republican ideology of nature into the nineteenth century, finding paradoxically, amid manifest destiny and natural law, an ecstatic religion for hunters and warriors, wild men who desert their haunts in European myth for new American frontiers.

Chapter 3 leaves the field of battle for what are seemingly more peaceful landscapes. Here, in the writings of the New England Transcendentalists, it finds the definitive expression of the principal theories—and confusions—that informed so much of later nature religion. Following the Transcendental legacy, we encounter the metaphysical version of nature religion, watching it become so entangled with notions of Mind and Reason that in the end it loses the material base with which it began. Meanwhile, in an opposite and seemingly more "natural" evolution, we follow the physical trajectory of nature religion in movements for conservation and wilderness preservation.

Chapter 4 studies nature religion as physical religion through movements for natural health and healing, tracing metaphors of mesmerism and Swedenborgianism as they were linked to republican and Transcendental themes. Christian physiology, mesmeric healing, Thomsonian herbal medicine, homeopathy, hydropathy, osteopathy, and chiropractic all make their appearance here, most of them being, at first scrutiny, surprising candidates for religious treatment. Then, in chapter 5, we think through themes regarding the complexity of nature religion and its relationship to a pluralistic American culture. We find familiar patterns from the past, but we find, too, the insistent mark of newness. We consider a Native American syncretism that works to heal the earth and an enduring Calvinist ambivalence that honors its violent mysteries. We find a politics of "natural" democracy that seeks the greening of America and, as well, a politics of feminism that celebrates the Goddess in a marriage of nature and mind. We notice religious perspectives on nature that arise within the holistic health movement, with its inherited nineteenth-century legacy and its fresh encounter with Eastern forms of healing. Throughout we explore some of the many ways in which contemporary Americans express at least partial affiliation with the meanings and values of nature religion.

Finally, throughout this chapter and all of the others, we look not for the differences between elite Americans and ordinary people but instead for the common that is shared. What I have in mind here is less the democracy of the elite with the unintelligent or the unattentive than the democracy of those who, sociologically speaking, have not been formally trained to be theologians, ceremonial leaders, or ethical guides for their generation. Nature religion in America has flourished among a cadre of people who, largely without systematic "seminary" exposure to a high religious or academic tradition, have thought and acted for themselves.

I once heard it said that the task of humanities scholarship was to make the strange familiar and the familiar strange. The phrase is apt, and it is a good description of what I hope to accomplish in this book. If, just as Christianity is the religion of the Christ and his followers and Buddhism is the religion of the Buddha and his disciples, nature religion is the religion of nature and its devotees, then we need an uncommon set of glasses to glimpse the analogy. But the framework itself—the category of nature religion—is, in another sense, the set of glasses, lighting up what we might not otherwise have seen. The estrangement is strategic, and if it is successful it holds the promise of fuller vision. The glasses—and the outline—are preliminary guides to a vast and largely uncharted religious world. Putting on the glasses—following the paths staked out by the study—may introduce us to a dynamic in American culture that surprises in its power and pervasiveness. By coming to terms with nature as religion, we may gain a sense of the more-than-rational force that shapes and orients so much of American life. And that knowledge, in its own way, is a form of power.

1 / Native Ground ✻ NATURE AND CULTURE
IN EARLY AMERICA

In 1634 the Jesuit Paul le Jeune completed a report on his Quebec mission for his provincial in Paris, including in it a long account of his sojourn—and difficulties—among the Montagnais Indians. In one reconstructed conversation with a native, the Jesuit supplied details of his evangelical effort.

"When thou seest the beauty and grandeur of this world,—how the Sun incessantly turns round without stopping, how the seasons follow each other in their time, and how perfectly all the Stars maintain their order,— thou seest clearly that men have not made these wonders, and that they do not govern them; hence there must be some one more noble than men, who has built and who rules this grand mansion. Now it is he whom we call God, who sees all things, and whom we do not see; but we shall see him after death, and we shall be forever happy with him, if we love and obey him." "Thou dost not know what thou art talking about," he answered, "learn to talk and we will listen to thee." [1]

Le Jeune's catechesis is instructive. In an episodic flash it provides a short tour of the European mind in attempted communication with native North Americans. Implicit in the discourse were French assumptions about thought and world as well as about human response and cultural dynamics. For le Jeune and his missionary fellows, the order built into the universe and revealed in its motions led inevitably to reflections on its creator. Nature pointed the way to the cultural apprehension of God and, in le Jeune's reckoning, to an assurance of the afterlife. Even more, reflection on nature suggested a creaturely response of love and obedience.

That the Montagnais Indian strenuously disagreed was clear. His "learn-to-talk" intimated that, from the native point of view, at the most basic level of discourse le Jeune was stumbling hopelessly.[2] Nor was the perception one-sided. Most European men and women could not fathom the "savage" mind and found its expression in belief, ritual, and life-style generally reprehensible. Writing nearly fifty years later of a forced residence among the Narrangansett Indians of southern New England, Mary Rowlandson's response to her captors was typical.

16

Now away we must go with those Barbarous Creatures, with our bodies wounded and bleeding, and our hearts no less than our bodies. . . . I asked them whither I might not lodge in the house that night to which they answered, what will you love English men still? this was the dolefullest night that ever my eyes saw. Oh the roaring, and singing and danceing, and yelling of those black creatures in the night, which made the place a lively resemblance of hell. And as miserable was the wast that was there made, of Horses, Cattle, Sheep, Swine, Calves, Lambs, Roasting Pigs, and Fowl (which they had plundered in the Town) some roasting, some lying and burning, and some boyling to feed our merciless Enemies; who were joyful enough though we were disconsolate.[3]

   Shocked profoundly by the first violence of slaughter and sei-zure, Rowlandson found the Narrangansett ceremonial jubilee at once incomprehensible and demonic. The ritual singing and danc-ing and the spendthrift appropriation of animal flesh provoked hor-ror and repudiation. As her narrative progressed, Rowlandson's later perceptions of the Narrangansetts made common cause with her initial one. Cast on the interpretive grid of biblical mythology, the Indians emerged, fixed in ideological certainty, as familiars of the devil. In spite of her cultural immersion in Narrangansett life, Rowlandson learned little of their different human vision: her long misadventure made sense only as temptation and trial according to biblical canon.[4]

   Between these juxtaposed incidents—the nature narrative of Father le Jeune with its blanket rejection by the Montagnais and the ritual performance of the Narrangansetts with its condem-nation by Rowlandson—lies an unwritten story regarding the place of nature in early American symbol making and experience. In the contact situation, Amerindian and European confronted each other warily, neither comprehending the religious and ideo-logical power that found expression in the lifeways of the other. For both, to be sure, the term *nature religion* is inexact. For Amer-indians, nature as such did not exist but rather dissolved in a uni-verse of persons and personal relations. For American Puritans, to whom the Euro-American discussion will be confined, nature reli-gion dissolved in the ambiguities attendant on a complex Christian vision. Even so, for both the term provides a convenient shorthand to describe religious belief and behavior. The concept throws light on the two sides of the cultural divide, illuminating especially the

A
N A R R A T I V E

OF THE

CAPTIVITY, SUFFERINGS AND REMOVES

OF

Mrs. *Mary Rowlandson,*

Who was taken Prifoner by the INDIANS with feveral others,
and treated in the moft barbarous and cruel Manner by thofe
vile Savages : With many other remarkable Events during her
TRAVELS.

Written by her own Hand, for her private Ufe, and now made
public at the earneft Defire of fome Friends, and for the Benefit of the afflicted.

B O S T O N :

Printed and Sold at JOHN BOYLE's Printing-Office, next Door
to the *Three Doves* in Marlborough-Street. 1773.

Title page of the tenth edition of Mary Rowlandson, *A Narrative of the Captivity,
Sufferings and Removes of Mrs. Mary Rowlandson* (1773). (Courtesy, American Antiquarian Society.) The original edition, with a lengthy title beginning *The Sov-
eraignty & Goodness of God,* was published in 1682.

disparities between them—the pervading differences that complicated and, in the end, confuted human relationship.

In the pages that follow, we examine, first, Amerindian nature
religion as it can be reconstructed largely from late-nineteenth-
and twentieth-century data. The chronological jump is helpful—
and even necessary—because it was during the period beginning
a century and less ago that ethnologists and anthropologists collected much of the repertoire of native myth and custom on which
a full account must depend. Then, supported by this reconstruction, we approach the Algonkian cultures of seventeenth-century
southern New England. Reading in shards and snippets, mostly
from uncomprehending missionaries such as Roger Williams and
Daniel Gookin, and in archaeological remains, we discover a nature religion alive and strong, if threatened by severe cultural
disorientation. Finally, we turn to the disorienters, the familiar
New England Puritans who had so great an impact on the later
cultural trajectory of the nation. We explore their ambivalent
reading of physical nature, and we conclude by watching the Puritans move, in the shadow of the European Enlightenment, from a
wilderness sense of the concept to a more abstract and philosophical one.

Before Amerindians and Europeans encountered one another in
the sixteenth and seventeenth centuries, anywhere from less than
four to more than twelve million native North Americans dwelled
in the area north of the Rio Grande River.[5] Using perhaps 550 languages (as different from one another as, say, Chinese from English) and their dialects, Amerindians spoke in tongues that could
be traced to nine linguistic stocks, each worlds apart from the
other.[6] Even when scholars attempt to reduce this cultural diversity to manageable proportions, they confront a plethora of Indian
nations, each with separate governance and self-understanding expressed in myth, custom, and ritual. Hence, in one way, to speak
collectively of native North American tribal cultures is to do violence to the subjective sensibility of many different peoples. On
the other hand, cast beside the European invaders, Amerindians
and their religious ways shared much in common. Indeed, in southern New England, where Puritan and Amerindian met face-to-
face, the underlying unity among a series of Indian cultures was

reflected in their common Algonkian heritage of related language, social structure, and religious mentality.

However, before we examine the nature religion of the southern New England Algonkians, we need to pursue the more general understanding. We need to be clear about how Indians perceived what we, today, call nature, and we need to reflect on major characteristics of Amerindian religions.

Regarding the first, it is fair to say that the sense of nature as a collective physical whole—an ordered cosmos comprising the animal and vegetable kingdoms on earth as well as the stars and other heavenly bodies—is a product of the European heritage. Filtered through the lens of the eighteenth-century Enlightenment, as we shall see in chapter 2, this understanding of nature grew more systemic and more mechanistic, providing an overarching frame within which humans could comprehend themselves and their cultural pursuits and activities. Amerindian peoples, on the other hand, recognized the nurturing (natural) matrix of their societies, but they sensed at once a more plural and more personal universe. Instead of the abstract and overarching "nature" of Europe, they saw a world peopled with other-than-human persons, often of mysterious powers and dispositions. Not all of what we name nature was identified by the Indians in personal terms, but the presence of persons animating "nature" radically grounded their nature religion. "Are *all* the stones we see about us here alive?" the anthropologist A. Irving Hallowell asked one old Ojibwa man in the 1950s. After reflecting a long time, the man replied, "No! But *some* are." [7]

If native North Americans saw nature, as we know it, as inhabited by natural persons, that fact already opens the way to a survey of major themes in Amerindian religions. For Amerindians' view of their world was fundamentally relational. Bound to the sacred by ties of kinship, they could speak of preterhuman beings as Thunder Grandfathers or Spider Grandmothers or Corn Mothers. The Tewa remembered that in the beginning they had lived beneath Sandy Place Lake with the animals and the first mothers, "Blue Corn Woman, near to summer" and "White Corn Maiden, near to ice." But even beyond their relationship to individual nature beings, the Tewa—as other Amerindian peoples—understood that their relationship was with the earth itself. Sacred origin accounts of native North Americans told, in imaginative language, of their emergence from the womb of earth. Or they detailed how an earth-diving animal had plunged into the waters to come up with a speck of dirt that grew into the world. In the Tewa origin myth, the world above was still "green" and "unripe," but after an elaborate and ritualized migration the people emerged upon a ground that hardened. Expressing the strength of their relationship to the earth in the way they named themselves, ordinary Tewa were the Dry Food People, not unripe like the early earth but mature like the hardened grains of corn that nourished them.[8]

For the Algonkians in the region of the Great Lakes, the animals embodied the power of the earth. A Great Hare had supervised the creation of the world, floating on a wooden raft with the other animals and taking the grain of sand, which the diving muskrat had found, to form from it the earth. When the first animals finally died, "the Great Hare caused the birth of men from their corpses, as also from those of the fishes which were found along the shores of the rivers which he had formed in creating the land." So the Algonkians derived "their origin from a bear, others from a moose, and others similarly from various kinds of animals."[9] The Winnebago, in turn, could recall the antics and foibles of the Trickster/culture hero Coyote, from the remnants of whose mutilated penis came the crops. And numbers of Amerindian peoples acknowledged a "keeper" of the game, a spirit animal who long ago had made a pact pledging the members of his species to sacrifice themselves that the Indians might eat and survive.[10]

For native North Americans the numinous world of nature beings was always very close, and the land itself expressed their presence. Indian peoples created religious geographies in which specific sites were inhabited by sacred powers and persons. Thus, the Eastern Cherokee knew that the spirit Little People had left their footprints within a cave behind a waterfall close to the head of the Oconaluftee River. And they located the game preserve of Kanati, the husband of the corn mother, in a cave on the northern side of Black Mountain, some twenty-five miles from Asheville, North Carolina. The Kiowa recalled the sinister Devil's Tower of the Black Hills, where a Kiowa boy playing with his seven sisters had unaccountably been turned into a bear, run after his terrified

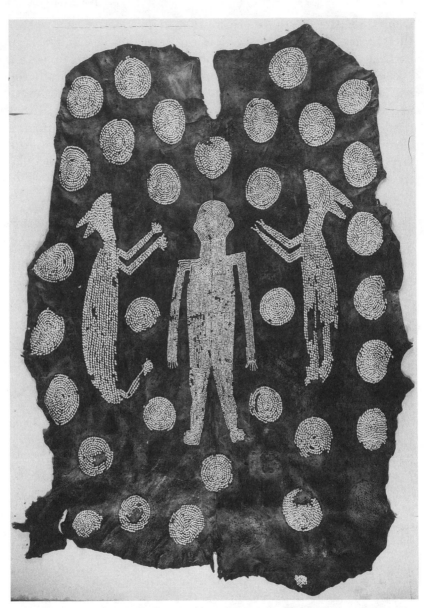

Powhatan's Mantle. Woodlands, Algonkian. (Courtesy, Ashmolean Museum, Oxford.) Made of deerhide and sinew and 2.13 meters long, the mantle belonged to Powhatan, chief of the Algonkian nations in Tidewater Virginia in the early seventeenth century. With motifs suggestive for the study of nature religion among the Algonkians, the mantle is the earliest example, for which documentation exists, of Native American art from the historic period.

siblings, and scored the bark of a great tree they climbed as he chased them. The sisters had escaped, becoming the stars of the Big Dipper; the remnant of the tree was Devil's Tower.[11]

The sense of continuity with the sacred—and natural—world that was revealed in this language had its counterpart in a mythic sense of time, in which what we call history was conflated, for Amerindians, with events that had occurred outside of ordinary time. In the Indian view, the present replicated the past, and one could discern the shape of contemporary events by reflecting on the message gleaned from the time of beginning. So the Kiowa, or "coming-out" people, are today a small tribe because once, at the origins of their earthly life, a pregnant woman became stuck while the people were emerging from a hollow log. Fertility had gotten "hung up," and only those who had come out before it was stopped could constitute the Kiowa nation.[12]

Similarly, in one twentieth-century Hopi account that also includes the founding of the village of Hotevilla, the narrative begins as Hopi Birdmen perform their corn ceremony to help the quarreling people emerge to the earth. In the twentieth century, Hopis had quarreled again—this time about educating their children in United States government schools—and one group, evicted from the ancestral village of Oraibi, made their encampment at the site of Hotevilla. The twentieth-century tale of hostility evokes the time of origins, with conflict a recognized part of Hopi past and present. Ceremony, ordering the tribal life to the natural world, in each case fosters equilibrium.[13]

As this relational view suggests, the well-being of Amerindian peoples depended in large measure on a correspondence between themselves and what they held sacred. The material world was a holy place; and so harmony with nature beings and natural forms was the controlling ethic, reciprocity the recognized mode of interaction. Ritual functioned to restore a lost harmony, like a great balancing act bringing the people back to right relation with the world.

What we, today, would call an ecological perspective came, for the most part, easily—if unselfconsciously—among traditional tribal peoples. Typically, one apologized to the guardian spirit of an animal or plant species for taking the life of the hunted animal or gathered vegetable crop. One paid attention, ceremonially, to the cardinal directions, orienting existence literally by placing oneself in space with reference to all of its beings and powers. A person lived by a ritual calendar in which the naming of months and times centered on growing and hunting seasons. And in disease or other illness, a person sought the cause in relational disharmony with a natural form or person—like a Navajo who encountered lightning in the sheepfold and then got sick or like a Cherokee who knew that overpopulation and overkilling of the animals had brought disease. Similarly, one found cure through the healer's— and patient's—identification with natural forms and through the healer's knowledge of herbal lore.[14]

Meanwhile, healers, as shamans and seers, worked out of their sense of correspondence with natural forms. They were leaders in communication with other-than-human persons who dwelled in nature, sharers in the mysterious power that made things happen— the wakan of the Sioux, the orenda of the Iroquois, the manitou of the Algonkians.[15] From this point of view, what we call magic and miracle were simply cases of like affecting like or of part affecting whole. United to natural forces and persons, Amerindians thought that all parts of the world—and their own societies—were made of the same material. Since everything was, in fact, part of everything else, it followed that one piece of the world could act powerfully on another, affecting change and transformation.

Such transformation often meant the shape-shifting of animals to human form and, likewise, the change of humans into animals. Amerindian myths are filled with accounts of encounters between humans and the other-than-human world. The Oglala Sioux received their sacred pipe and their full ceremonial panoply of seven rites when a strange wakan woman appeared among them with her gift, then moved around "in a sun-wise manner" and turned into a red and brown buffalo calf and subsequently into a white and a black buffalo. "This buffalo then walked farther away from the people, stopped, and after bowing to each of the four quarters of the universe, disappeared over the hill."[16] Encouraged by her widowed mother, a Cherokee girl married her suitor, but when he failed to bring home a substantial hunt she followed him and found that, away from her, he changed into a hooting owl. Two Penobscots, in a contest with some Iroquois who had discovered them, changed themselves into a bear and a panther and got away.[17]

In this world of animal/human transformations, Tricksters such as Coyote or Raven assumed human or animal form as they chose. Amerindians, who delighted in Trickster tales, also transformed themselves ritually by ceremonial clowning. These ritual clowns were deadly serious figures, like the *heyoka* among the Sioux, contorting the natural and accustomed order by doing things completely backward, saying yes when they intended no, and generally overturning canons of normalcy the more to underline them. In still other ritual transformations, Amerindians, like the Tewa healing Bears, portrayed the animal spirits by their clothing, accouterments, and even behavior.[18]

In visions and dreams, too, natural persons appeared to guide Indian peoples. Expressed most explicitly in rituals of seeking for a guardian spirit, the naturalness of sacred things dominated the inner as well as the outer world. In his account of "crying for a vision" given to Joseph Epes Brown, Black Elk explained unequivocally how the powers came. The "lamenter" was required to "be alert to recognize any messenger which the Great Spirit may send to him, for these people often come in the form of an animal, even one as small and as seemingly insignificant as a little ant." "Perhaps," Black Elk continued, "a Spotted Eagle may come to him from the west, or a Black Eagle from the north, or the Bald Eagle from the east, or even the Red-headed Woodpecker may come to him from the south."[19]

In short, Amerindian peoples lived symbolically with nature at center and boundaries. They understood the world as one that answered personally to their needs and words and, in turn, perceived themselves and their societies as part of a sacred landscape. With correspondence as controlling metaphor, they sought their own versions of mastery and control through harmony in a universe of persons who were part of the natural world. Nature religion, if it lived in America at all, lived among Amerindians.

Apparently, for all the changes history wrought, this picture drawn mostly from late nineteenth- and twentieth-century accounts applies as well to earlier times. There was a good deal of likeness between later and earlier expression; and, with only fragmentary—and often hostile—evidence from which to reconstruct seventeenth-century Amerindian lifeways, we can still trace the outlines, among the Algonkians of southern New England, of a fully developed nature religion.

The distinct groups whom the English Puritans first encountered were part of a related family of Indian nations. In the area framed by the Saco River, flowing southeast from present-day New Hampshire through southern Maine to the Atlantic, and the Quinnipiac River, flowing southward through central Connecticut to New Haven Harbor, Algonkian populations probably reached from seventy-two thousand to twice that number by the early seventeenth century. (By a century later the English population had only reached ninety-three thousand.)[20] But from 1616 to 1618 and again from 1633 to 1634 epidemics swept through the tribes, decimating native populations by as much as ninety percent.[21] No doubt caused by microbes from Europe brought first by transAtlantic traders, disease ravaged peoples who had no previous immunity and cultures that had no earlier preparation. Thus, the religions that Puritan observers would write about without comprehension were religions confounded by a double crisis—the jolt of foreign invasion and the catastrophe of a biological scourge worse in its relative effects than the Black Death of fourteenth-century Europe.

The four major Amerindian nations in the area—the Narragansett (of present-day Rhode Island), the Massachusett (of Massachusetts Bay), the Pokanoket, or Wampanoag (of Plymouth Colony), and the Pequot (of present-day Connecticut)—spoke related languages of the Eastern Algonkian family. They were united, too, by similar subsistence patterns and governance structures. In a mixed economy, they farmed the land, raising maize, beans, squash, and some tobacco, even as they gathered wild plants and also fished and hunted. With the coming of the English, they engaged in the fur trade. Dwelling in villages, with easy mobility to accommodate seasonal changes in the food supply (at least until the 1630s), these southern New Englanders were governed by sachems, political leaders whose power varied with each unit. On the whole, though, sachems ruled through prestige and moral authority, using generosity and persuasion more than outright coercion to gain their way.[22]

Although the personal initiative of Algonkian Indian peoples has been cited, more striking still was their strong sense of community with one another and with nature.[23] Their small-group life emphasized bonds of kinship. Their collective understanding of land tenure and their equation of ownership with use obviated European notions of private property that fostered individualism. Algonkian labor was often cooperative, as Roger Williams noticed among the Narragansetts: "When a field is to be broken up, they have a very loving sociable speedy way to dispatch it: All the neighbours men and Women forty, fifty, a hundred &c, joyne, and come in to help freely."[24] Still more, the rich ceremonial life of these Amerindians reinforced their sense of mutuality and community.[25]

Living closely as they did, Indian bands practiced an ethic of harmony within their communities. Roger Williams remarked on the lack of crime and violence among them, and William Wood—another seventeenth-century observer and probably not a Puritan—commented on their hospitality to strangers and their helpfulness. "Nothing is more hateful to them than a churlish disposition," he wrote, going on to discuss their equanimity, cheerfulness, and calm.[26] Perhaps a sociologically conditioned survival tactic, the harmony ethic was also—if we can take later Amerindian experience as an indicator—an expression of their nature religion. A "connected" view of the environment would foster the connection of community.

Connection, however, did not mean amorphousness. The southern New England Algonkians, even read through fragmentary evidence, elaborated a systematic cosmology in which the world and human life were carefully named and ordered. Keeping themselves and their world in balance, which the harmony ethic enjoined, meant an intricate network of exchanges and interactions. And such a network had to be predicated on precise and detailed knowledge of parts of the larger whole. Hence, the unfamiliarity of a concept such as nature and the familiarity of nature persons made considerable sense in the Eastern Algonkian schema. Indeed, Neal Salisbury has rightly argued that the ethos of reciprocity was paramount, and he has noticed, too, the social, natural, and—as he termed it, somewhat problematically—"supernatural" worlds that needed to be maintained in equilibrium.[27]

The equilibrium began, as in other Amerindian societies, with birth out of nature. Roger Williams told how the Narragansetts had heard from their fathers "that *Kautántowwit* made one man and woman of a stone, which disliking, he broke them in pieces, and made another man and woman of a Tree, which were the Fountaines of all mankind." "They say themselves, that they have *sprung* and *growne* up in that very place, like the very *trees* of the *Wildernesse*," he noted, just as tellingly, elsewhere. Further north, the missionary Daniel Gookin related the origin myth regarding two young squaws who swam or waded in the waters. "The froth or foam of the water touched their bodies, from whence they became with child; and one of them brought forth a male; and the other, a female child. . . . So their son and daughter were their [the people's] first progenitors." [28]

If the people were themselves the gift of nature, so, too, were their foodstuffs, especially their corn. Stories of the sacred origins of corn run through numerous Amerindian cultures, many of them southwestern and southeastern. And in southern New England, even in an area near the northern boundary of corn cultivation, the mythology of corn throve with the growing crop. Williams explained the gingerly fashion in which the Narragansetts kept the birds away from the standing corn, citing the tradition "that the Crow brought them at first an *Indian* Graine of Corne in one Eare, and an *Indian* or *French* Beane in another, from the Great God *Kautántouwits* field in the Southwest from whence they hold came all their Corne and Beanes." [29] Corn ritual, too, figured prominently in the ceremonial life of the tribe.

Williams's references to Cautantowwit (the modern spelling) point to the preeminence of this figure (or Ketan, as he was known to the Narragansetts' neighbors) among the sacred beings who favored the Indians. Cautantowwit's home in the southwest was associated with the warm and nurturing wind that encouraged the growth of the corn. His home was also the place to which the people returned at death, and so he was linked to the life force itself, which originated from his house and again returned to it. "Ketan," wrote William Wood, "is their good god, to whom they sacrifice (as the ancient heathen did to Ceres) after their garners be full with a good crop; upon this god likewise they invoke for fair weather, for rain in time of drought, and for the recovery of their sick." [30] Worship of Cautantowwit, in short, was invocation of a nature deity.

Less distinct but more pervasive than the worship of Cautantowwit was the southern New England orientation toward manitou. In
a perception shared with other Algonkians, the word *manitou* carried meanings of wonder and extraordinary power, of a godliness
inhering in numerous objects and persons. Williams remarked that
at "any Excellency in Men, Women, Birds, Beasts, Fish, &c.,"
the Narragansetts would "cry out *Manittóo*, that is, it is a God."
Gookin, linking the manitou belief to Cautantowwit, spoke of acknowledgment of "one great supreme doer of good; . . . Woonand,
or Mannitt." Other colonial New Englanders, such as Thomas
Mayhew on Martha's Vineyard, noted the use of the term. What is
clear from the references is that, if Cautantowwit possessed manitou or was manitou or a manitou, the manitou essence could also be
found in other nature beings, in humans, and even in marvelous
(for the Indians) technological objects such as English ships and
great buildings. "The most common experience seems to be that
of being overwhelmed by an all-encompassing presence," wrote
William Jones in his classic essay on the subject. Referring to a
property (adjectival) as well as referring to an object (substantive),
manitou was closely linked to "the essential character of Algonkin
religion . . . a pure, naive worship of nature." [31]

Among the beings who possessed manitou were those whom
Williams identified as deities of the sun, moon, fire, water, snow,
earth, deer, and bear, some thirty-seven or thirty-eight in all. There
were deities of the four directions, and a woman's god, a children's
god, and a house god as well. On Martha's Vineyard, Thomas Mayhew likewise found knowledge of thirty-seven deities and noted
their relation to "things in Heaven, Earth, and Sea: And there they
had their Men-gods, Women-gods, and Children-gods, their Com-
panies, and Fellowships of gods, or Divine Powers, guiding things
amongst men, besides innumerable more feigned gods belonging to
many Creatures, to their Corn, and every Colour of it." Daniel
Gookin's testimony, if less extensive, was similar. [32]

Moreover, it was clear, as Neal Salisbury has succinctly remarked, that the Indians were not "crypto-monotheists," conferring on Cautantowwit the role of creator of other gods. [33] Indeed,
the entire language of monotheism, god, and supernatural is forced
and strained when made to fit Amerindian thinking. More to the

mark, nature *manifested* sacred powers and revealed other-than-human persons of mysterious and numinous capacities. Instead of the opposition between divinity and creature or between super-natural and natural, there was—as already has been noted—a continuity between extraordinary and ordinary. While dualisms—such as body and spirit, for instance—existed, they were inserted into a different frame and bore a different, more intimate meaning than they did for Europeans.

If this observation be kept in mind, then the regard that south-ern New England Algonkians showed for animals assumes new and heightened significance. When the Narragansetts refused to kill crows or other birds that ate their crops, their behavior was consistent with other Indian practices. Thus, the English writer John Josselyn described the spiritual etiquette that attended the killing of a moose in the New England region: its heart, tongue, left rear foot, and sinews were ritually removed before the flesh was used, accomplishing the "gesture of reciprocity" that was the Amerindian response to beneficent power. Williams, in describing trapping practices for deer, cited the divine power the Indians saw in the animal to explain why the Narragansetts were "very tender of their Traps." Wood noticed that native peoples adorned them-selves with earrings in the forms of birds, beasts, and fishes, and he also remarked on the depictions of animals and birds incised into their checks. And John Eliot, the New England missionary, placed first in his list of religious questions his would-be converts asked, *"Why have not beasts a soul as man hath, seeing they have love, anger, &c. as man hath?"*[34]

The ceremonial forms of southern New England Algonkians ex-pressed regard for animals and their power and, beyond that, regard and gratitude for vegetable life. Successful hunts and har-vests were both marked by ritual (as were numerous other occa-sions in Indian life). Ceremonies accompanied spring fish runs and made supplication for rain in time of drought. The Narragansetts held a midwinter festival, according to Williams, and the feast may have been related to the time of solstice. Meanwhile, Williams also recorded the giveaways, in which people outdid one another in distributing their goods, imitating, perhaps, the bounty that ani-mals and plants had shown to them. At various ceremonial times, dances were led by shamans or powwows, who garbed themselves in skins in order to imitate bears, wolves, and other animals, howling as they danced no doubt for the same purpose.[35]

With all but one of their lunar months named for the planting cycle, Algonkian Indians expressed the significance of agriculture in their lives. But the ceremonial time of the community was supplemented by a round of other rituals, linked to hunting cultures, that focused more on individuals. Like the hunting cultures to the north and west, these Algonkians sought special guardian spirits in ritualized vision quests, and accounts tell of asceticisms and hardships incorporated into the practice. Thus, in one remarkable narrative, Williams wrote of a dying Narragansett's call to Muckquachuckquand, who had come to him many years before, bidding the Indian to seek him in time of distress. Likewise, southern New England Algonkians honored the menstrual hut used in hunting cultures.[36] At the time of her menses, the fertility power of the woman was thought so strong that it could conflict with the other, male form of power needed in the hunt. Sequestered with her during her time in the hut, the woman's power did not endanger others.

The chief religious specialist among the New England tribes was the shaman or powwow, and much of the English commentary on native life was preoccupied, invariably negatively, with this figure. The shaman's tutelary deity and the power through whom he acted was Hobbamock (Abbomacho), who was also identified with Chepi, the shaman's helper. A terrestrial spirit believed to be involved in the onset of disease and suffering, Hobbamock roamed abroad at night, commanding fear. He signaled the negative powers of the sacred, the dangers it embodied, and the need for special knowledge and prowess to deal with it securely. In similar vein, Chepi's name was linked to terms for death, the departed, and the cold northeast wind. The English called Hobbamock the devil; and, in the language of their own dualistic understanding of good and evil, they were not completely wrong. Converted natives accepted the equation. It was true, too, that when Puritans first encountered the New England Indians the cult of Hobbamock seemed to be waxing and that of Cautantowwit declining—supporting the judgment that witchcraft beliefs are strategies for control that thrive in communal crises.[37]

Shamans, as we noted, presided at the nature ceremonies of southern New England Algonkians. Such shamans entered their true estate when they became entranced, possessed and taken over by Hobbamock and the powers of manitou. On Martha's Vineyard, Thomas Mayhew related striking accounts of shamanic possession. He spoke of "Imps," whom the shamans called their "Preservers" and "treasured up in their bodies." One narrative suggested that inanimate substances, too, were alive, for the shaman Tequanonim claimed he had been "possessed from the crowne of the head to the soal of the foot with *Pawwawnomas,* not onely in the shape of living Creatures, as Fowls, Fishes, and creeping things, but Brasse, Iron, and Stone." Another shaman on the island told of his initiation through "Diabolical Dreams, wherein he saw the Devill in the likenesse of four living Creatures; one was like a man which he saw in the Ayre, . . . and this he said had its residence over his whole body. Another was like a Crow, . . . and had its residence in his head. The third was like to a Pidgeon, and had its place his breast. . . . The fourth was like a Serpent." [38]

Healers of their people, the powwows employed herbal medicines and shamanic sucking cures in ritual fashion. Their identification, in the healing ceremony, with animals was suggested by William Wood's description of one such rite. Here the powwow proceeded "in his invocations, sometimes roaring like a bear, other times groaning like a dying horse, foaming at the mouth like a chased boar, smiting on his naked breast and thighs with such violence as if he were mad." Shamans also aided their people by their divinatory powers. In one anecdote remembered after King Philip's War, it was the shaman's vision of a bear—a ravenous animal and so a bad omen—that convinced the Indians they should retreat from Bridgewater, Massachusetts. Rainmaking was also the shaman's province. And, less benignly, the shaman could, on occasion and with preterhuman aid, inflict evil on another. Thomas Mayhew reported how, at the behest of the powwow, "the Devil doth abuse the real body of a Serpent, which comes directly towards the man in the house or in the field, . . . and do shoot a bone (as they say) into the Indians Body." [39]

Significantly, even the southern New England Algonkian understanding of the afterlife expressed an Amerindian immersion in nature religion. We have already pointed to the connection between Cautantowwit's house for the dead and the warmth and life-bestowing properties of the southwest and its wind. Archeological evidence from New England burials supports the association, for not only were the dead aligned to the southwest but, in Narragansett burials, the dead were placed in fetal posture, suggesting the idea of rebirth. Similarly, red paint discovered in the graves suggests the blood and placenta that came with childbirth. And William Scranton Simmons has argued that the positioning of the skull to the southwest was related to the departure of the soul or souls in that direction.[40]

Just as striking as evidence for a nature religion associated with death are the brief literary references of English contemporaries. Roger Williams likened Indian death hopes to the Turkish expectation of "carnall Joyes." William Wood, in words that bear full repetition, was more specific.

They hold the immortality of the never-dying soul that it shall pass to the southwest Elysium, concerning which their Indian faith jumps much with the Turkish Alcoran [Quran], holding it to be a kind of paradise wherein they shall everlastingly abide, solacing themselves in odoriferous gardens, fruitful corn fields, green meadows, bathing their tawny hides in the cool streams of pleasant rivers, and shelter themselves from heat and cold in the sumptuous palaces framed by the skill of nature's curious contrivement; concluding that neither care nor pain shall molest them but that nature's bounty will administer all things with a voluntary contribution from the overflowing storehouse of their Elysian Hospital.[41]

Nature religion, in sum, formed and framed native North American life from birth until death—and, in the Amerindian view, beyond. Nature religion shaped mentality; it lay behind behavior in symbolic and ordinary settings; it worked to achieve a harmony that was also an attempt to control the powers that impinged on life as native peoples knew it.

"We are well as we are," John Eliot had an Indian kinswoman say in his *Indian Dialogues*. The words have an ironic cogency when matched against the religion of nature that characterized Indian peoples in southern New England. That William Wood found Amerindians "little edified in religion" by their encounter with the English and that Daniel Gookin, before 1674, had heard of no one in the Rhode Island colony "instrumental to convert any of those Indians" are observations less than surprising. The Puritans failed to claim the majority of the Indians for Christianity for a series of complex reasons. An English sense of cultural superiority, the growing commercial orientation of the colonists, beliefs regarding predestination, sectarian preoccupation with the already saved community, even the practice of congregational calling before ordination to the ministry—these and other factors undercut a wholehearted mission effort.[42]

Yet, basic to the Puritan failure—and what concerns us here—was the different meaning and value accorded to the symbol of nature by each culture. If Amerindians lived a nature religion without possessing the abstract and universalized European concept of nature, Puritans understood nature in overarching and universal terms but never found the centeredness in nature characteristic of native peoples. Both cultures, in the contact situation, acknowledged the existence of sacred powers and, more, saw a holy presence in the world and in daily life. And both cultures valued community and lived according to "tribal" norms. But with the absolute claims of their religious commitment, the Puritans could not find common ground in nature with southern New England Algonkians.

What place, then, did the Puritans accord to nature? And how are we to include these inward-turning sectarians, haunted by questions of supernaturalism and salvation, in any account of nature religion? To do so is possible only if we recognize the clear priority of Jehovah in the Puritan vision. For these English colonists, nature could function only as part of a sacred geography in which the *super*natural essence of the divine realm was strongly marked and in which sacred persons lived above and apart from nature. However, if we accept these limits and still continue to look for the religious place of nature in Puritan culture, the results are richer than at first we might suppose. Nature did function as a significant religious symbol for Puritans, and it was against and in interaction with nature that they made sense of their spiritual—and material—venture in the New World.

When William Bradford wrote of the Pilgrim landing at Plymouth harbor, he recalled the terror of "a hidious & desolate wilderness, full of wild beasts & willd men."[43] The language is indicative, for it underscores one strong element in a complex Puritan relationship with nature. As Roderick Nash has told in his now-classic *Wilderness and the American Mind,* for European culture in general, nature in the wilderness was manifestly different from nature in a garden.[44] The wilderness was a dangerous place, beyond human control and threatening in both physical and metaphysical ways. Outside the pale of established society and away from the culture of citied traditions, Puritans could revert to the savagery they found around them. Wilderness was, literally, the place of wild beasts: the fear was that, in the primitive forests with the beasts, one would become confused, be*wildered,* losing a sense of self and society that was essential to civilized life and to salvation thereafter. Hence, the absence of European humanity in the wilderness made it an alien and alienating landscape.

Yet both the Greco-Roman and the central and northern European cultures had found a sacred, if often negative, dimension in the wild country. For Greeks and Romans, the wilderness was home to a series of lesser gods and demonic beings—to pans and satyrs, nymphs and centaurs alike. For central and northern Europeans, wood sprites and trolls as well as other preterhuman beings inhabited the forests. Motifs of fertility, power, and danger were intertwined in this pagan heritage of Europe. With the heritage appropriated by Christian peoples as Europe was converted, moral valences were emphasized, and the ambiguous nature of forest beings was clarified. They still carried sacred import, to be sure; but, in keeping with the dualism of Christian teaching, now the spiritual force that lurked in the wilderness was purely negative. The wilderness was the territory of the devil and the powers of evil. Wild beasts and wild men who dwelled there could only be his emissaries and servants.

Hence, when Puritans regarded Amerindians in the New World for the first time, they did so wearing lenses that had been ground by centuries. Epitome of the spiritual degradation of the wilderness condition, native peoples showed the Puritans, as Daniel Gookin said, "as in a mirror, or looking glass, the woful, miserable, and deplorable estate, that sin hath reduced mankind unto naturally, and especially such as live without means of cultivating and civilizing." Except for their "rational souls," he thought, Indians were "like unto the wild ass's colt, and not many degrees above beasts in matters of fact."[45] New World nature, for Puritans, was a kingdom under Satan, and, preeminently, southern New England Algonkians were his assistants. In short, as Neal Salisbury has said, the colonists saw Indians as "the complete inversion of the world they sought for themselves."[46]

In this context, Puritan identification of Hobbamock with Satan achieves new explanatory power, and the war Puritans waged against Algonkian powwows becomes a crusade, not simply against a false religion but against elemental evil. Powwows, although they might be native herbal physicians, were also—and more significantly—"partly wizards and witches, holding familiarity with Satan," as Gookin said.[47] Prohibited under penalty by the General Court of Massachusetts, powwows no doubt seemed to most white New Englanders the embodiment of the spiritual dread the wilderness brought.[48]

Yet, in other moments, at least some Puritans linked Indians to biblical history, needing to find a place for them in the divine plan of salvation that began with the fall of Adam and Eve in the Garden of Eden. The Indians, these Puritans speculated, had descended from the ten lost tribes of Israel. "Surely it is not impossible," Gookin wrote, "and perhaps not so improbable as many learned men think." Another gospel minister sought various points of religious resemblance, noting Indian acknowledgment of a creator and of his providential relationship to the world and finding in Algonkian gestures of grief or gratitude toward a higher power evidence for the Israelite connection.[49] What makes these speculations important here is that, as a common Puritan view, they signal an ambivalence toward the wilderness and its inhabitants that gainsays the demonic dread.[50]

Thus, even as nature stood for the kingdom of evil in the Puritan myth, the resources of the Judeo-Christian tradition made of the wilderness a place with provisionally positive spiritual meaning. True, the shift from negative to positive meant the demotion of wild nature as a sacred power: not simply the embodiment of Satanic power, it became the backdrop for the action of a God above and beyond it. Still, demotion became an appropriate price to pay for change, and change led to later forms of American nature religion.

The Jewish heritage of Christianity included the origin myth of the Exodus, which explained the common ancestry of the Jews and their preparation by God for a shared destiny as the people of his choice. At the center of the story, the Hebrews who followed Moses fled the fleshpots of Egypt, experienced divine deliverance as they crossed the Red Sea, and then wandered in the deserts of Sinai for forty years. Here they endured trial and desolation, beset by temptation in the emptiness of the desert. Yet it was precisely in Sinai, with its harsh testing, that Yahweh revealed himself, giving the people an abiding pledge of his steadfastness in the commandments of the Law.[51]

As heirs to the Exodus account and the entire Jewish legacy, Christians, too, understood the wild places of the desert as sites for spiritual testing and the visitation of God. Jesus had fasted for forty days and forty nights in the (desert) wilderness, and there the devil came to tempt him and the angels came to minister to him. Accounts of fourth-century monks who fled cities for the Egyptian desert stress the solitude of these anchorites, the temptations and spiritual graces they experienced, and their communion with nature. Thus it was in the desert that the celebrated Antony of Egypt fought off the onslaughts of demons as he dwelled within a tomb, the symbol of his death to the civilized luxury of the cities and the self-indulgence they encouraged. "Monks lose their strength in towns," he was once reported to have said. The tamer of wild beasts and the tiller of a garden, when he set off to visit the hermit Paul of Thebes, according to one account Antony encountered a centaur, a satyr, and a she-wolf, all of whom proved beneficent. As Paul and Antony talked, a crow flew down from a nearby tree and deposited a loaf of bread to feed them, and when, in aftertimes, Antony returned to the cave to find the corpse of Paul, two lions came flying toward him to dig the grave of the saint.[52]

Tales such as these seem a far cry from the New World experience of the small band of English Puritans, especially in light of their Calvinist repudiation of monks and monkish superstition. Yet, within the continuity of Christian culture, something of the attitude of the fourth-century monks and their admirers had descended to these latter-day children of the Reformation. The wilderness was still a place of testing, the backdrop for a spiritual purification in which the corruption of old England might be permanently purged. As a proving ground for the saints, the wilderness might also protect them from worldly evil and even invigorate them. Indeed, it might become God's chosen place for conferring religious insight. New Englanders such as Peter Bulkeley, John

Norton, Samuel Danforth, John Cotton, and Increase Mather all saw the connection between the wilderness and divine blessing.[53]

Beyond that, although the theme would become more prominent by the time of the American Revolution, Puritans directly appropriated the Hebrew heritage of Christianity, viewing themselves and their enterprise in terms of the Exodus myth. From this perspective, the Atlantic Ocean became an extended and formidable Red Sea, an initiatory obstacle that would fit the Puritans for entry into the Canaan of New England. It was no chance metaphor when John Winthrop wrote of "the streights of the redd sea" in one of his final letters before sailing from England.[54] Fear of the ocean crossing was widespread, and events at sea were interpreted in terms of the providences of God in a wilderness testing. On board the *Mayflower,* William Bradford recounted, "a proud & very profane yonge man" had mocked the illnesses of others, telling them "that he hoped to help to cast halfe of them over board before they came to their jurneys end." Yet he himself was stricken "with a greeveous disease." "He dyed in a desperate maner, and so was him selfe ye first yt was throwne overbord," while the others "noted it to be ye just hand of God upon him." Another "lustie yonge man" was luckier—or more blessed. In the midst of a storm he was thrown overboard, "but it pleased God yt he caught hould of ye top-saile halliards," until his fellows could rescue him.[55]

Even so, as Peter Carroll tells us, the trans-Atlantic passengers "were intensely interested in the wonders of the deep which they encountered for the first time." The "concern for marine novelty," wrote Carroll, reflected "an enhanced sensitivity toward natural history among men throughout Europe," their legacy from the Renaissance. The same John Winthrop who had looked on the impending voyage as a Red Sea crossing took note of pieces of driftwood, seafowl, and whales. Exposed to the exotic realities of the Atlantic in the middle passage, it was as if, in a temporary enchantment with nature, some Puritans saw without biblical spectacles. They were filled with wonder at the vastness and novelty around them. They were also, as Carroll has argued, "conditioned" to that novelty. The conditioning would prove useful for the ocean voyagers as they settled in the "wild" country of New England.[56]

Promotional literature designed to encourage people to emigrate had, of course, stressed the bounty of the new land. William Wood, who numbered among the promoters, wrote not only of Amerindian peoples but also of the choice ground and "sweetest climate" where the settlers dwelled. The soil was "a warm kind of earth"; the marshes were "rich ground" that would "bring plenty of hay." Meanwhile, wild herbs "for meat and medicine" grew abundantly. There were "likewise strawberries in abundance, very large ones, some being two inches about," and one might "gather half a bushel in a forenoon." For other seasons, there were "gooseberries, bilberries, raspberries, treackleberries, hurtleberries, currants," the last, when sundried, being "little inferior" to what English grocers sold. For people who often endured polluted water, Wood noted that "every family or every two families" had "a spring of sweet waters betwixt them." He added that it was "thought there can be no better water in the world" and that "those that drink it be as healthful, fresh, and lusty as they that drink beer." [57] But Wood's perspective was nonsacral as he described the New World riches; and, to be sure, there was a commodity orientation in the way he eyed the gifts that nature gave.

For others, however, more imbued with a Puritan spirit, New England as the promised land of Canaan offered sanctuary and a place of spiritual nurture. In a metaphor borrowed from English Puritanism, it was surrounded by the "hedge" of God's grace, thereby becoming, presumably, an inward-blooming garden. [58] Although New England society existed in the tension between churchmen, who would maintain the protective hedge for the garden, and many members of their congregations and the settlements, who sought new plantations in the wilderness, in both cases nature mediated the experience of the New World. [59] Land, animal life, teeming vegetation, and the solitude of the heavens above impinged on these New England immigrants, so that the place where God had planted them took on sacred qualities.

Even the Indians, so frequently named as minions of the devil, could participate in the divine promise of the land, as Joseph Caryl wrote: "O let old *England* rejoyce in this, that our brethren who with extream difficulties and expences have Planted themselves in the *Indian Wildernesses,* have also laboured night and day with prayers and tears and Exhortations to Plant the *Indians as a spirituall Garden,* into which Christ might come and eat his pleasant fruits." [60] There was a mystical sweetness in the image, an evocation, perhaps, of the woman of Revelation 12:6 who fled into the wilderness to be fed in a place prepared by God. Indeed, as Cecelia Tichi has written, "the extension of man's dominion on earth was, from the Puritan perspective, the enlargement of Christ's kingdom pointing toward the Apocalypse."[61]

Conrad Cherry rightly observed that Puritan New Englanders lived in the ambiguity inherent in their perception of the land as a "place of promise and of threat."[62] A negative sacred ground in the province of Satan, it could—in the language of their myth—metamorphize into the place of God's testing and final benediction. Far removed from the relational bonds with nature persons that characterized the religion of their Algonkian neighbors, Puritans still found themselves awed by the land they had entered. In the end, they understood that the best wild country was subdued wild country, and they transformed the former Algonkian habitations from a sacred to an ordinary condition. And from the beginning their commodity orientation assured the trajectory of merchant, business, and mechanical success. Yet, on the way, they had absorbed something of the power of the Amerindian spirits who haunted the land. As Francis Jennings has argued, that land had been "widowed" by the ravages of European diseases and the dispiritment caused by Puritan displacement of the survivors.[63] But, as if the ghosts of times past (native and biblical) would make their claims on the future, the Puritans and their descendants could never experience the matter-of-fact relationship with nature that characterized their ancestors. Nature, in the America that was just over the horizon, would become a central religious symbol for many inhabitants of the land: seventeenth-century Puritans had been John the Baptists for distinctively American nature religion.

Already, by the early eighteenth century, philosophical thinking was reflecting the new experience of the Puritans. In one significant example, Cotton Mather, well-known minister in Boston, was pondering themes of nature and divinity in ways that foreshadowed the American Enlightenment and the nature religion of the revolutionary era. Heavily dependent on English authors, Mather still appropriated their material to make it his own. In *The Christian Philosopher* (1721), writing both as amateur scientist and religious poet, he added to the book of biblical revelation a second volume of revelation in nature. Mather cited the Christian saint John Chrysostom for warrant and invited readers to walk in the *"Publick Library"* of nature. *"Reader,* walk with me into it, and see what we shall find so legible there, *that he that runs may read it."* In language that adumbrated the Freemasonry on American shores a decade later, Mather admired the world as a *"Temple* of GOD, *built and fitted* by that Almighty *Architect."* [64] He wrote in praise of the stars and planets, of the earth and attendant phenomena such as magnetism. And he underscored the wonders of God in the mineral, vegetable, and animal kingdoms.

Thus, in a long discourse on the lodestone, Mather rehearsed the scientific orthodoxy of the day but, following the pattern employed throughout his book, moved on to exhort philosophers to "glorify the infinite Creator of this, and of all things, as *imcomprehensible.* You must acknowledge that *Human Reason* is too feeble, too narrow a thing to comprehend the *infinite* God." Careful not to "fall down before a *Stone,* and say, *Thou art a God,"* Mather could eschew idolatry but pay "a very agreeable and acceptable *Homage* unto the Glorious GOD" by seeing "much of Him in such a wonderful *Stone* as the MAGNET." Then, in a move prepared by the Platonism of older Puritans, he shifted from magnet to creator, from lodestone, as he said, to *"Lead-stone." "Magnetism* is in this like to *Gravity,* that it leads us to GOD, and brings us very near to Him." In a theological peroration, Mather ended with an extended discourse on the ways in which the lodestone was a "notable Adumbration" of the Savior. [65]

As he commented on the world of microorganic wonder visible with the aid of Antony van Leeuwenhoek's microscope, Mather wrote enthusiastically of the seed, the "small Particle no bigger than a Sand" that could "contain the *Plant,* and all belonging to it," and he extolled its "astonishing Elegancy." After hailing the "peculiar Care which the great God of Nature has taken for the Safety of the *Seed* and *Fruit,"* he shifted, significantly, from Nature's God to a personified Nature. "What various ways has Nature for the *scattering* and the *sowing* of the *Seed!"* And, "How nice the provision of Nature for their Support in *standing* and *growing,* that they may keep their Heads above ground, and administer to our Intentions!"[66] The slip was important: although, again and again throughout his *Christian Philosopher* Mather counseled readers to contemplate nature and go on to praise its creator, he had opened a door that would lead, in a later era, to the contemplation of nature itself.

Likewise, Mather's meditations on the physical world pointed to the analogical relationship between nature and human life in ways that linked the Puritan past to the New England Transcendentalist future. For the plants, the correspondence was simple enough, for the "*Revival* of the *Plants* in the *Spring*" signaled the Christian doctrine of the resurrection of the dead. But in a concluding contemplation Mather made the shift that linked the fate of the world to the spiritual condition of humankind. If humans would but believe and adore God and serve one another in community, then "the World would be soon revived into a desirable *Garden of God,* and Mankind would be fetch'd up into very comfortable Circumstances; till *then* the World continues in a wretched Condition, *full of doleful Creatures,* with *wild Beasts crying in its desolate Houses, Dragons* in its most *pleasant Palaces.*"[67] Mather's coda on the glory of Christ and the Trinity could not undo the changed focus of his work. Once opened, the book of nature was not easily closed, and for many Americans it began to supplant the book of scripture.

Even so, the nature that Mather wrote about was nature at what Clyde A. Holbrook would call "second hand."[68] Mather's work represented a second-order reflection on nature, not a primary report on the experience of nature itself. When Mather published his *Christian Philosopher,* the great Puritan divine Jonathan Edwards was still a student at Yale College. Presumably, though, he had already had the experiences of nature at "first hand" that would appear in his later "Personal Narrative." Edwards and his childhood friends had built a "booth" for prayer in a "very retired" place in a swamp, and Edwards had other secret haunts in the woods where he would go for prayer.[69]

In one incident that he recalled years later, Edwards told of an experience of God in nature that approximated the "cosmic consciousness" of a later day. "As I was walking there, and looking up on the sky and clouds," confessed Edwards, "there came into my mind so sweet a sense of the glorious *majesty* and *grace* of God, that I know not how to express."

After this my sense of divine things gradually increased, and became more and more lively, and had more of that inward sweetness. . . . God's excellency, his wisdom, his purity and love, seemed to appear in every thing; in the sun, moon, and stars; in the clouds, and blue sky; in the grass, flowers, trees; in the water, and all nature; which used greatly to fix my mind.[70]

The nature that Edwards had directly experienced became the prologue to philosophical (and scientific) reflection on the world around. Expressing Puritan philosophical thinking, which favored Platonism, Edwards saw that world in terms of analogies, things below that shadowed the ideal order above. His seventeenth-century forebears had read the scripture traditionally in terms of type and antitype. And they had seen spiritual signs and analogies in events as dramatic as the drowned man on Bradford's *Mayflower* and as inconsequential as a child hiding behind a sofa in a Puritan parlor. Moreover, with their preference for the Platonic logical system of Petrus Ramus as taught at Harvard College, the Puritans had placed beside their biblical typological thinking something of the ancient Greek philosopher's notion of the present world as a copy of the divine model or idea.[71]

It was these understandings from the Puritan past that informed the second-order writing on nature that Edwards undertook. In his unpublished manuscript "The Images of Divine Things," Edwards went considerably beyond his predecessor Cotton Mather to find throughout nature the truth that could be gained in sense experience. Mather's added book became a coeval book: nature, as Perry Miller argued, became authoritative even as scripture was.[72] If Mather pointed to analogy and type and sometimes employed them, Edwards embraced his own form of type-antitype thinking as encompassing framework for reading nature. Instead of mostly using nature to corroborate biblical truth, he habitually quoted biblical text to fix nature the more firmly. "The book of Scripture," Edwards declared, "is the interpreter of the book of nature." Edwards's work, wrote Miller, was "nothing less than an assertion of the absolute validity of the sensuous."[73]

"The things of the world are ordered [and] designed to shadow forth spiritual things," Edwards affirmed. Scripture confirmed the fact, and it was "apparent and allowed" that there was "a great and remarkeable analogy in God's works." In a doctrine of correspondence that, even more clearly than Mather's, pointed toward the Transcendentalists, Edwards told of the "wonderfull resemblance in the effects which God produces, and consentaneity in His manner of working in one thing and another throughout all nature." "It is very observable in the visible world," he continued; "therefore it is allowed that God does purposely make and order one thing to be in agreeableness and harmony with another."[74]

Still more, if natural things reflected one another, they imaged the divine. "The sun's so perpetually, for so many ages, sending forth his rays in such vast profusion, without any diminution of his light and heat, is a bright image of the all-sufficiency and everlastingness of God's bounty and goodness." In a reading more specifically Christian, the silkworm was "a remarkeable type of Christ, which when it dies yields us that of which we make such glorious clothing. Christ became a worm for our sakes, and by his death kindled that righteousness with which believers are clothed, and thereby procured that we should be clothed with robes of glory." And "as a type of love or charity in the spiritual world," the universe was "preserved by gravity or attraction, or the mutual tendency of all bodies to each other." Nor was nature unambiguously positive in its truth. "This world is all over dirty," Edwards wrote. "Everywhere it is covered with that which tends to defile the feet of the traveller," a clear intimation that "the world is full of that which tends to defile the soul." And nature as human physicality likewise taught its negative lessons. "The inside of the body of man is full of filthiness, contains his bowels that are full of dung, which represents the corruption and filthiness that the heart of man is naturally full of."[75]

Even with its negative truths, nature was altogether revelation, as Edwards testified. "If we look on these shadows of divine things as the voice of God purposely by them teaching us these and those spiritual and divine things, to show of what excellent advantage it will be, how agreeably and clearly it will tend to convey instruction to our minds, and to impress things on the mind and to affect the mind, by that we may, as it were, have God speaking to us." The God who spoke in nature guaranteed, then, a *continuing* revelation. Earth and sky were not simply neutral or even nurturing.

Instead they announced the active presence of God, and the active presence of God signaled the millennium at hand. The longed-for Christian future was already becoming present; and, as Mason I. Lowance and Sacvan Bercovitch have underlined, the God who heralded it promised an *American* millennium.[76] It was in the New World, in the landscape of New England, that the eschatological future would become present. It was in this specific setting that natural things would figure forth the divine.

But there was even more, for the future, in the natural shadows that whispered. There was, indeed, as Perry Miller argued and as we shall see in a later chapter, a line between Edwards and the Transcendentalist Ralph Waldo Emerson.[77] But the line was drawn from a biblically enriched Platonism even as it was expressed in mysticism. If nature was sensuous presence, it was also—in a paradox that hinted the later dilemma of Emerson, Henry David Thoreau, and assorted other Americans—material absence. By themselves, material bodies—and so the natural world—did not exist as substances. Rather, they were made real, imbued with meaning, through human perception and divine power and knowledge. Challenging both the philosophical dualism of René Descartes and that of Isaac Newton and his followers, Edwards could find no independent existence, as substance, in a natural body. The world was "therefore an ideal one; and the law of creating, and the succession of these ideas" was "constant and regular." "Nothing that is matter can possibly be God," Edwards wrote, and "no matter is, in the most proper sense, matter."[78]

Edwards was clearly teaching idealism, and he was also implying, in some sense, the divinity of nature. Just as much, he was implying the power of humans to confer meaning—and existence—by their thought. Analogical philosophy provided the logical ground for the mystical mind. The earthly copy could unite with the original divine form or idea; and, in transformed condition, Puritan analogy would become the Transcendentalist correspondence between nature and spirit.

Less mystically conceived but nonetheless significantly spoken, another word for nature came when, four years before the promulgation of the Declaration of Independence, the work of Cotton Mather's contemporary John Wise was republished. In his *Vindica-*

tion of the Government of New-England Churches (1717), Wise had written in opposition to the *Proposals* of 1705, signed by Mather, for changes in the church government of eastern Massachusetts. But, ironically, on the importance of nature the two men agreed. In fact, Wise succeeded before Mather or Edwards—and more than either of them—in advancing one form of the Enlightenment view of nature. For nature, in Wise's reading, became a fundamental principle and *law.*

Significantly, Wise placed his argument from nature first, before his argument from scripture, in the *Vindication*'s text. The churches of New England, he argued, like the primitive Christian churches, were "founded peculiarly in the Light of Nature." "It seems to me," Wise wrote, "as though Wise and Provident Nature by the Dictates of Right Reason excited by the moving Suggestions of Humanity; and awed with the just demands of Natural Libertie, Equity, Equality, and Principles of Self-Preservation, Originally drew up the Scheme [of New England church polity], and then obtained the Royal [God's] Approbation." [79]

For Wise, the "Light of Nature" or "Light of Reason" was a "Law and Rule of Right" and an "Effect of Christ's goodness, care and creating Power, as well as of Revelation; though Revelation is Natures Law in a fairer and brighter Edition." Indeed, as Wise saw it, "That which is to be drawn from Mans Reason, flowing from the true Current of that Faculty, when unperverted, may be said to be the Law of Nature; on which account, the Holy Scriptures declare it written on Mens hearts." In more concrete terms, there was "an Original Liberty Instampt upon his [man's] Rational Nature," and any who intruded on this liberty violated "the Law of Nature." And there was a natural equality, so that it followed "as a Command of the Law of Nature, that every Man Esteem and treat another as one who is naturally his Equal, or who is a Man as well as he." The power to form governments, therefore, issued from the people and returned to them again. [80] The language—and religion—of nature was ready to unfold in the "Nature and Nature's God" of the American Revolution.

2 / Republican Nature ❧ FROM THE REVOLUTION THAT WAS LAWFUL TO THE DESTINY THAT WAS MANIFEST

In July of 1776, not long after the signing of the Declaration of Independence, Royall Tyler was graduated from Harvard College. Several months later Yale accorded him an honorary baccalaureate, and by the end of the year he had joined the patriot army. He did not see much active service, though, and was already reading law during the Revolution. With a master of arts degree conferred by Harvard in 1779 and admittance to the Massachusetts bar in 1780, the young man began his career as a lawyer, a career punctuated most notably by a short-lived romance with Abigail ("Nabby") Adams, daughter of John and Abigail. Then, in March 1787, on a political mission to New York for Massachusetts Governor James Bowdoin, Tyler spurned New England rule and attended the theater. In little more than a month, his own play *The Contrast* was being staged at the John Street Theatre in New York City.[1]

It was the earliest American comedy to be presented by a group of professional actors. And, although after 1787 Tyler continued to join letters to his legal calling, his first effort became his best-known work. Produced, significantly, in the month before the beginning of the Constitutional Convention, *The Contrast* at once expressed and encouraged a new national pride. The first American play staged more than once, in New York alone, it drew audiences five times in 1787, with a return engagement at the time of George Washington's inauguration two years later. Before the close of the century *The Contrast* had played probably fifteen times outside New York City, including performances in Baltimore, Philadelphia, Boston (where it was dubbed a "Moral Lecture"), and Charleston. One contemporary reviewer called the work the "effusions of an honest patriotic heart," while, in our own century, Allan Gates Halline hailed it as "a spiritual Declaration of Independence."[2]

What was it that this young man—a Harvard graduate in the shadow of the Declaration—had done to stir the enthusiasm of his

47

compatriots and even later audiences? Why, while other American plays had been produced only once, did this one appear again and again? When one reads *The Contrast* today, it seems decidedly wooden, a stilted eighteenth-century farce, which, we learn, relied at least in part on a British model.[3] But closer scrutiny shows that Tyler turned his model upside down, imitating it to say something Americans found new. More than that, the newness Tyler spoke on their behalf was an ideology of republican nature in the wake of the Revolution.

Through the characters and action of his play, Tyler gave his citizen audiences nature as a roughhewn quality of revolutionary innocence and simplicity, a sacred estate to be cherished and favorably contrasted to the artifice of England. In the person of Colonel Henry Manly, the patriot soldier who emerged as postwar protagonist, the old Puritan motif of wilderness trial was evoked and expanded to the limits of a changed society. Striding across the stage of nature's nation in his plain, unfashionable regimental coat, Manly preached in word and deed that American nationhood was a moral category demanding personal commitment. "Luxury" was "surely the bane of the nation," he said, and it was clear he thought natural simplicity its high blessing.[4] In such a context, Manly's symbolic use of natural themes to express his political faith signaled the oblique appropriation of a religious heritage, even as it was rapidly achieving new form.

The "contrast" of the play was clear in the names and demeanors of male and female characters. Foppish Dimple, who was engaged to the virtuous and quietly heroic Maria Van Rough, in every respect countered the Manly creed. He was, as he bragged, "a gentleman who has read Chesterfield and received the polish of Europe"; and he demonstrated how well he had learned his lessons by simultaneously maintaining his engagement to Maria and courting Charlotte Manly (sister of the colonel) and her friend Letitia. Meanwhile, Charlotte's embrace of European etiquette seemed complete, as she boasted to her visiting brother of the "faces of the beaux," which were "of such a lily-white hue! None of that horrid robustness of constitution, that vulgar cornfed glow of health." Maria, on the other hand, sat home and endured her engagement to Dimple, dutifully obeying her father's wishes. While Dimple was away in England, she had schooled herself on the ideal of the

Christian gentleman by reading Samuel Richardson's *Sir Charles Grandison.* More tellingly, one day disconsolate in her room she sang the death song of the Indian, the son of Alknomook, praising "the manly virtue of courage" it bespoke for her.[5]

> Remember the wood where in ambush we lay,
> And the scalps which we bore from your nation away:
> Now the flame rises fast, you exult in my pain;
> But the son of Alknomook can never complain.[6]

Maria lamented that she must "marry a depraved wretch, whose only virtue is a polished exterior," but in the end she was spared the sacrifice. A chance meeting with Colonel Manly meant love at first sight for both. Then, in the farcical denouement of the plot, Dimple's machinations were uncovered, and the senior Van Rough, restored to his republican senses, blessed a Manly–Van Rough connection. The shamed Dimple departed abruptly, presumably taking his dapper servant Jessamy, who once had told his master that Colonel Manly looked "the most unpolished animal your honour ever disgraced your eyes by looking upon." No doubt, too, the innocent young natural Jonathan, who had pointedly told Jessamy he was no servant to Colonel Manly but his waiter, accompanied the happy couple.[7]

In the midst of the laughter, Tyler's politicized use of nature was revealing. If *The Contrast* expressed the civil religion of the Revolution, it read the faith in decidedly New World ways. Gone was Jehovah God of battles and gone the city on the hill that lit the world's path to Israel redivivus.[8] Here, instead, was the plain country virtue of those who dwelt in the free air of nature. And here, in Alknomook's son, was the haunting dark of the forest that nourished with its wilderness energies. Indeed, the initial success of Tyler's play, at the end of the revolutionary era, signaled the prestige of nature during at least the previous two decades. All unaware, the comic drama fostered a species of nature religion, mirroring the values of a culture that found political will in the strength that nature provided.

Yet, for all its achievements, *The Contrast* was only one sign, and it expressed only one public form of the symbol. It was but one instance of the power of the media—and of the patriot leaders who simultaneously shaped and were shaped by the public rhetoric. To be sure, for many nature never did attain symbolic stature, and its capacity for nonsacral ordinariness should not be overlooked. To be sure, too, the explicit fear of wild country expressed by seventeenth-century Puritans continued, and in sermons during the revolutionary era a new Exodus drama was played out in the ambiguity of the New World wilderness. By the revolutionary age the fear and ambiguity were shared by recent immigrants such as, in the most well-known example, J. Hector St. John Crèvecoeur. The Frenchman thought that living in proximity to woods and forests brought an echoing wildness to humans, with "lawless profligacy" and an "eating of wild meat" that tended "to alter their temper." He argued that the chase rendered hunters "ferocious, gloomy, and unsociable," reducing life to a state of degeneration.[9]

Here, however, we need to direct our gaze elsewhere—to the collective symbolism that was linking nature to the life and destiny of the republic. For all the fear of wilderness, there was also patriotic fascination and even veneration for it, as the song of the son of Alknomook suggests. And for all the "secular" response to nature by those who struggled with and against it in order to survive, there was also exaltation of it in the public ideology that was the legacy of the Revolution. Thus, it is instructive to search for the religious appropriation of nature within the republican venture.

When we do, we find that, in the main, nature functioned in republican religion in three related ways. First, as in Tyler's *Contrast*, nature meant New World innocence and vigor, the purity and wholesomeness of clean country living on the edge of an empowering wilderness. Second, in an American appropriation of Enlightenment religion, nature meant the transcendent reality of heavenly bodies, which moved according to unfailing law, and—corresponding to it—the universal law that grounded human rights and duties within the body politic. Third, fusing with an aesthetic tradition of landscape veneration, nature meant the quality of the sublime as it was discovered in republican terrain.

Each evocation of nature built on the other, together adding to the enormous weight accorded the symbol and, so, to its accretion of spiritual power. Unlike signs, which are distinguished by their straightforwardness, symbols are multivalent and multidimensional. What they point toward can never categorically be articulated in rational language, and their very mysteriousness leads to an amassing of energy that translates as extraordinary. So the symbol of nature acquired a life of its own as it commanded the imaginations of the patriots. Collective passion displaced onto the symbol was transformed into the wholly Other, and, as emblem of more-than-human power, nature also *became* that power. Nature, in short, became religious center and sacred force.[10]

We do not have to look far to find instances, during the Revolution and thereafter, of the first meaning of nature—that of the politicized rhetoric of nature that permeated Royall Tyler's play. If we want to underline the side of the rhetoric that proclaimed natural wholesomeness, we can turn to the ritual wearing of homespun before and during the war. It was true, certainly, that the intertwining of politics and economy overtly prompted the move. Why should protesting Americans, angered by the Townshend Acts of 1767, support the British economy by their purchase and use of imported manufactures? The nonimportation movement tightened the screws on Britain with an economic boycott that was widely successful in 1768 and 1769, and its effectiveness could be measured by the repeal, in 1770, of all the Townshend duties except the one on tea.

Yet, significantly, the constitutional protest that gave voice to colonial objections to the Townshend Acts came from the pen of the Philadelphia lawyer John Dickinson, who published his installments in the *Pennsylvania Chronicle* as "Letters from a *Farmer* in Pennsylvania to Inhabitants of the British Colonies." And, as the sanction movement spread, the negative act of economic refusal assumed positive form and function. "There began a vogue for spinning bees, wearing clothes of home-woven cloth, and brewing raspberry-leaf or Labrador tea," wrote Samuel Eliot Morison. "A freshman in the College of New Jersey who later became the fourth President of the United States, wrote to his father that every one of the 115 Princeton students was wearing homespun. The Harvard Corporation voted to let commencers wear homespun gray or brown instead of imported black broadcloth."[11] When the Continental Congress mandated nonimportation in 1774, the stage was set for a wearing of homespun that would join the symbolic counters of patriotism, rural wholeness, and uncorrupted virtue.

That the ethos lived on long after the war is suggested by Colonel Manly's regimental coat, evoking in its plainness and simplicity its American homespun virtue.

If, on the other hand, we want to underline the side of the politicized rhetoric of nature that stressed its wilderness edge, we can point to the Liberty Tree and its meaning in prerevolutionary America. The tree rose, first, at the boundary of the citied world of Boston. Protesting against the Stamp Act of 1765,

a few gentlemen hung out, early in the morning on the limb of a large tree, *towards the entrance of Boston,* two effigies, one designed for the stamp master, the other for a jack boot, with a head and horns peeping out at the top. Great numbers both from town and country came to see them. A spirit of enthusiasm was diffused among the spectators. In the evening the whole [of the effigies] was cut down, and carried in procession by the populace, shouting "liberty and property forever, no stamps." [12]

As use of the Liberty Tree spread, demonstrating its practical assets as a place from which to regard symbols of American estrangement from British power, the choice of the tree told more. It spoke of patriot involvement in a process of religious symbol making that was at once universal and distinctively American. The tree expressed themes of centering, evoking ancient myths of trees that were the axis of the world. It made implicit statements about fertility and the continuance of life—recalling the maypoles of European and, especially, English country life—now joined to the quest for liberty. And it disclosed intuitions of the requirement of blood and violence for abundant life (in the effigy deaths on the tree)—as in sacred origin myths from many cultures. [13]

But, in the end more important here, the tree marked the place where the negotiated life of the polis, the city, touched the wilderness spontaneity of natural power. In the ceremonial performances of the Sons of Liberty under the huge elm tree in Boston or under other trees in other parts of the colonies, strength was communicated through the medium of the land itself. In the background lay the language of the dissolution of government into a "state of nature," a philosophical metaphor that distinctly captured the universal mythic sense of chaos and formlessness as the source of new societal form. [14] In the foreground was the understanding that, in America, nature already modeled its forms, providing a blueprint for the kind of society that was truest and best. When, later, frontiersmen in the patriot army adopted hunting shirts as their uniform they not only succeeded in frightening the British and accommodating the shortfall in the congressional treasury. They also proclaimed a warrior mentality that only made sense in the shadow of the Liberty Tree.

The warrior mentality was reflected in Tyler's Colonel Manly, fallen in love with the maiden who approvingly sang the song of Alknomook's son and his ambush. It would be reflected in the next century, as we shall see, by another (fictional) denizen of the forest, who outperformed the Indians in his frontier neighborhood to make Colonel Davy Crockett a household name. Yet, curiously, these graphic features took their power from a second understanding of nature, one that moved the symbol from native ground to starry sky. In the Enlightenment language that shaped the revolutionary generation's public, political grasp of nature, concreteness evaporated in a quest for the universal. Impressed by the machinery of the heavens and their ceaseless motion according to canons of universal law, the sons and daughters of the Revolution learned to speak a lofty, abstract dialect. If, as Marjorie Hope Nicolson has argued, "what men see in Nature is a result of what they have been taught," then the patriots, as heirs to European (and Puritan) intellectual life, saw what their mentors pointed toward and spoke their seeing in absolute terms.[15]

Beginning in the seventeenth century, English writers had conceived of space as the infinite realm of divinity. Likewise, in a parallel intellectual move, a doctrine of absolute time was articulated, finding eventual fruition in the work of Isaac Newton, among others.[16] With the order and regularity of the Newtonian universe, the harmony of the spheres moved from ancient Greek philosophy to modern scientific law. Meanwhile, the absoluteness of nature set a new standard for estimating the significance of any human endeavor. When Colonel Manly praised American virtue, his compliment corroborated an absolute law that, following the classical dictum "As above, so below," moved from heaven to earth and back again in concepts of reason and the reasonable life. Universal law existed in the motion of the sun and other stars, and it existed in the human species with its natural perception of the requirements of morality. Among the heirs of the Revolution lay the possibility for the reasoned gathering of humans in society and for the reasoned life through moral law.

Before and through the years of their Revolution, educated upper- and middle-class patriots had been exposed to the natural religion of British worthies whose books appeared in New World libraries. Some had learned with Joseph Butler to contemplate "the conduct of Nature with respect to intelligent creatures," comparing "the known constitution and course of things . . . with what [the Christian] religion teaches us to believe and expect." Or they had understood with William Wollaston that the religion of nature was equivalent to morality, with its great law *"that every intelligent, active, and free being should so behave himself, as by no act to contradict truth."* Or, if they had read Samuel Clarke, the close friend of Isaac Newton, they had been taught that originally the natural consequence of eternal rule was happiness. Subjecting their appetites and passions to reason, they would find the most direct way "to preserve the *Health and Strength of the Body,"* while intemperance naturally brought *"Weakness, Pains, and Sicknesses* into the *Body."* [17]

The clear bow to pragmatic gain in Clarke's reference to health and disease was implicit in the philosophic language of universal natural law. If nature meant revelation through the regular working of natural law, and if natural law equaled natural morality and, so, religion, then the presence of all three would guarantee the right working of society. Nature religion implied abundance and plenty. The pursuit of life, liberty, and property could flourish under the benediction of universal nature, and the grasp of metaphysical principle could prove, in the republic, a very tangible business.

Familiarized with Enlightenment ideas of nature through English writers and through American Puritans, such as John Wise, whom we met in the last chapter, the American patriots learned their lesson well. When, during the debates of the Continental Congress in 1774, they sought a rationale for their resistance to the British government, they decided to pursue their claims by taking their cue from Richard Henry Lee of Virginia. Lee wondered out loud "why we should not lay our rights upon the broadest bottom, the ground of nature. Our ancestors found here no government." Others argued for the British constitution and their rights as Englishmen, but in the end the universalist sentiments of Lee prevailed.[18] He had conveniently transposed the abstract law of the starry heavens to an earthy bottom; and, in doing so, he had inadvertently revealed the uses of idealism to further specific class and ethnic aims in the American republic.

Still, ethnic idealism needed sociological embodiment in a community and ceremonial expression in public settings. So the lawful revolution sent its leaders to Freemasonic institutions, where the symbol of Enlightenment nature could be appropriately expressed. Freemasonry mediated the scientific culture of the Newtonian world, and, with it, a religion of nature that in America provided a model for the new democratic impulse within the body politic. Linked together in a fraternal web, the American Masonic brothers formed an intercolonial network that facilitated the flow of news and the shaping of opinion. Like the Great Awakening, which had spread a sense of unity of ideal and purpose in the colonies, the Masonic brotherhoods worked, in their own way, to achieve that end. One student of the phenomenon, Bernard Faÿ, argued that the Sons of Liberty (to whom we owe the Liberty Tree), as well as the revolutionary committees of correspondence, were Freemasonic "puppet" groups. Another Masonic scholar has stated that, with the exception of Benedict Arnold, all of the American generals during the war were Masons. Certainly, the majority of members of the Continental Congress were, and so, too, were perhaps fifty-two of the fifty-six men who signed the Declaration of Independence. And we know that after the war Masonic membership swelled, with war heroes and prominent public figures known to be Masons attracting the membership of other Americans.[19]

One need not lose sight of the obvious social reasons men joined the lodges in order to inquire what they were learning and what they were doing within these bastions of religious secrecy. How was Masonry shaping its initiates, and what kinds of ritual performances expressed and reinforced their affirmations? When, in 1783, Captain George Smith's *Use and Abuse of Free-masonry* appeared in London, it explained proudly that the Masonic craft "supereminently excels all other arts, by the bright rays of truth which it sheds on the minds of its faithful votaries, illuminating their understandings with the beams of a more resplendent light than is to be derived from the assemblage of all other arts whatsoever." [20] Smith had offered a classic sun-reason-truth analogy and, in the process, had pointed toward that chief star in the heavens on which Masonic ceremony turned. If Enlightenment nature, on the Newtonian model, eschewed particularity of place and landscape, then Enlightenment ritual in Freemasonry appropriately moved beyond the provincial to the universal sun.

Smith, and Thomas Paine who followed him, asserted Masonry's derivation from the religion of the ancient Druids who were priests of the sun. But we need not accept their historiography to take their cue regarding symbolism within the eighteenth-century lodges. "When the lodge is revealed to an entering mason," wrote Smith, "it discovers to him a representation of the world, in which, from the wonders of nature, we are led to contemplate her great original, and worship him from his mighty works." By the "great original," Smith meant God, the great Architect and Creator; but in the ambiguity that was characteristic of Freemasonry, it was the sun, that "emblem of God's power, his goodness, omnipresence, and eternity," that figured prominently in the lodge.[21] One gazed at the sun in order to understand the deity—and in the sacramental life of symbols, as we know, the emblem in some sense *becomes* what lies behind it, invested with a power that moves beyond the representation.

Paine noted that the orientation of the lodges, along an east-west axis, conformed to the sun's apparent motion through the heavens. "The master's place," he added significantly, "is always in the East." In a formal ritual that stressed the symbolic geography of sacred space, Entered Apprentices (first-degree initiates) were questioned by the master in regard to the lodge's orientation. Meanwhile, apprentices wore leather aprons, white in color—and, so, filled with Christian meanings related to baptismal purity but also, for Smith and Paine, reminiscent of the garb of Druids and of Egyptian and Grecian priests. The floor of the lodge seen by the apprentices told the story of creation, while overhead the roof displayed the great sign of the sun. Finally, with space, officiant, and objects proclaiming the solar cult, Masonic time, too, promoted the religion of the sun. For in the Christian feasts of the two Johns—Saint John the Baptist, on June 24, and Saint John the Evangelist, on December 27—Masons discovered a convenient pretext for celebrating summer and winter solstices.[22]

In fact, the prestige of the sun in the lodge was shared with architectural symbols of the great Temple of Solomon in Jerusalem, and there was visible evocation of biblical themes in Masonic rites. One could, of course, go further and point to the gnostic and metaphysical readings of biblical lore favored in certain Masonic texts. However, it is clear that the religion of the sun was intertwined with still other themes in the lodges. Indeed, with its symbols of square and compass—emblems of the operative mason's craft— and with use of these and related objects to construct a mythic model for moral development, the quest for the ideal disclosed an ethnic edge.[23]

To be sure, the Masonic ethic symbolized in the stylized construction tools spoke a language as universal as the Enlightenment could make it. With Captain Smith, Masons understood their work—or "art"—as "coeval with creation; when the sovereign Architect raised, on masonic principles, the beauteous globe, and commanded that master science, geometry, to lay the planetary world, and to regulate by its laws the whole stupendous system in just, unerring proportion rolling round the central sun." However, the triumphalism of the universal was also hardly subtle. If God had been English for early colonists, he was Mason for a key segment of their revolutionary descendants. With Smith, they contemplated their "virtuous deeds," assuming "the figures of the sun and moon, as emblematical of the great light and truth discovered to the first man; and thereby implying that, as true masons, we stand redeemed from darkness, and are become the sons of light." [24]

This Easter glory of the brotherhood at once exalted and masked the content of the moral life required of initiates. Counseled by their speculative and metaphysical Masonry, they fostered regard for active virtue—fairness and honesty in dealing with one's fellows (being "square" and "on the square"); charity and concern for brother Masons and their families; equality in community among members of the lodge; respect for secrecy and strength in maintaining silence, along with the bond these brought; love of country and willingness to sacrifice, and even die, for it. In short, American Masons were encouraged to the full panoply of Anglo-Saxon virtue, to the proverbial Protestant ethic that was linked, as Max Weber later contended, to capitalism and to the thriving mercantile classes.[25]

If the list seems unremarkable enough, we need to notice at least part of what was *not* there, what was not apparently written into the universal, natural law. In the paradox that was central to Freemasonry, universal virtue was predicated on elitist organization. Women, by definition, were excluded from a male society, but—as privileged men of their times—neither did the Masons accord equality in the brotherhood to blacks, or to the poor, or to other groups who did not "belong." Masonic virtue, in fine, was clubby, and so was the religion of nature it preached. The law of the starry skies and its human equivalent in the moral life, it turned out, were the concomitants of a recently nationalizing and ethnic class consciousness.

That consciousness, as we have already seen, was regularly drawn from heaven to its earthy foundation. Hence, nature held a third meaning for the revolutionary generation, a third meaning that lay in the landscape they had begun to glimpse in North America. Once again, Europe had given its gift to its New World relatives by shaping and cultivating patriotic sensibility, so that Americans would know what to see as they looked at nature. By the late eighteenth century, what some of them saw was the sublimity of a wilderness terrain. Taught to recognize the quality of the sublime, they lifted mind and emotion to higher realities, infusing landscape with mingled awe and admiration and even with astonishment that verged on terror. Still more, in a peculiarly republican aesthetic that separated them from Old World vision, these Americans learned to understand the sublimity of what they saw as a sign of the stature and destiny of the new nation. Even nature had smiled her beneficence on the grand political experiment the patriots had begun. She had prepared the choicest portions of the planet—indeed, the most mammoth and stupendous portions—as the space for republican government.

Like other Englishmen, the patriots had been schooled to recognize the sublime by a generation of "sublime" writers, but probably most clearly by Edmund Burke. In his *Philosophical Enquiry into the Origin of Our Ideas of the Sublime and Beautiful* (1757), Burke had distinguished between the two. He discovered the source of the sublime in whatever operated "in a manner analogous to terror" and linked the sublime to "the strongest emotion which the mind is capable of feeling." Burke explained to readers that the great and sublime in nature caused astonishment, "that state of the soul, in which all its motions are suspended, with some degree of horror." He went on to tell them of the "inferior effects" of the sublime in "admiration, reverence and respect." There was "nothing sublime" that was not "some modification of power," said Burke; and, likewise, he connected the sublime to qualities such as vastness, infinity, and magnificence.[26]

It would be almost two centuries before another European, Rudolf Otto, would dissect the experience of the Holy to find in it elements of awe, overpoweringness, and urgency, as well as a perception of total Otherness and a mysterious fascination.[27] Yet it is not far from the mark to read into Burke's description of the emotion of the sublime much of what Otto was trying to chart in *Das Heilige.* The patriots would behold the American landscape, at certain privileged moments, with a quality akin to universal religious awe. At the same time, they would never forget that, in the idealism of their vision, it was the *American* landscape they were seeing and that, with America as a moral category, the land itself shared in political virtue.

When Jedidiah Morse published his *American Geography* in 1789, his admiring description of the natural features of the new United States, in fact, could not qualify as sublime. But the book loudly proclaimed the virtue of American republicanism, as Morse followed his geographic account with a discussion of the patriot government, a reprinting of the recently adopted Constitution, a series of convention resolutions, and—after consideration of economic and military matters—a history focusing on events beginning with the Revolution. Still, some of the patriots did look to the sublimity of wild land to feast their republican sentiments. "In at least one respect Americans sensed that their country was different," wrote Roderick Nash. "Wilderness had no counterpart in the Old World." "In the early nineteenth century," he noted, "American nationalists began to understand that it was in the *wildness* of its nature that their country was unmatched." The wilderness was nature in its most unsullied form; and, for deists, it was the place par excellence where God could manifest himself.[28]

Even in the city of Philadelphia in 1786, there were adumbrations of the meaning of wild country in Charles Willson Peale's natural history museum. By the 1790s, Peale's welcoming sign at the museum's front door announced "the great school of nature" within. At the south entrance, another sign invited citizens: "the book of Nature open," to "explore the wond'rous world. / A solemn Institute of laws eternal." Peale aimed to retain natural form and attitude and—if practicable—a sense of habitat in the exhibits, and so he kept a live menagerie attached to his museum. When creatures died, they were preserved and mounted; and the specimen collection grew to include an assortment of animals, birds, and even insects from throughout the world. Meanwhile, scriptural quotations inscribed in oval frames on the walls pointedly told of the Creator's power. In its heyday in the early nineteenth century, with the bones of at least one American mastodon and a stuffed buffalo part of the collection, the museum's visitors could contemplate in imagination the grandeur of the continent that had become their domain.[29] They could travel in mind to the wilderness boundary from which not only law but also a profusion of life forms hinted the spiritual power nature gave Americans.

Not merely in mind, one native Philadelphian, William Bartram, had traveled personally through the South, partly while the Revolution was being fought. From 1773 to 1777, the naturalist absorbed messages from the wilderness more than early rumors and later reports of war. He thought the magnolia groves along the Alatamaha River, "on whose fruitful banks the generous and true sons of liberty securely dwell," rose "sublimely" to greet his view. Elsewhere in his journey he owned that he found some of his "chief happiness" "in tracing and admiring the infinite power, majesty and perfection of the great Almighty Creator." On the top of Occonne Mountain, Bartram called the view "inexpressibly magnificent and comprehensive," the landscape "infinitely varied, and without bound"; and at the summit of Jore Mountain, he "beheld with rapture and astonishment, a sublimely awful scene of power and magnificence, a world of mountains piled upon mountains." With instincts that George Smith and Thomas Paine would no doubt have endorsed, Bartram watched the sun rise near a Seminole camp. "Behold how gracious and beneficent smiles the roseate morn! now the sun arises and fills the plains with light, his glories appear on the forests, encompassing the meadows, and gild the top of the terebinthine Pine and exalted Palms, now gently rustling by the pressure of the waking breezes. . . . All nature awakes to life and activity."[30]

The Quaker naturalist had learned his love of nature from his botanist father, who, according to the "American farmer" Crèvecoeur, had placed an inscription over his greenhouse door: "Slave to no sect, who takes no private road, / But looks through nature, up to nature's God!"[31] If so, the son had transformed his father's Enlightenment republican nature to a more romantic sublime that celebrated American landscape.

Meanwhile, the younger Bartram's contemporary, the more self-consciously republican Philip Freneau, mused in the words of his "Philosopher of the Forest" on the divinity once present in the American "woods and solitudes." There, he said, "the mind still finds itself in the best humour to contemplate, in silent admiration, the great and inexhaustible source of all things." Poet that he was, Freneau in patriotic vein could behold the Hudson River "On whose tall banks tremendous rocks I spy, / Dread nature in primaeval majesty." Or he could recall the awe he felt on the hills of "Neversink":

> These heights, for solitude design'd,
> This rude, resounding shore—
> These vales impervious to the wind,
> Tall oaks, that to the tempest bend,
> Half Druid, I adore.[32]

Freneau had joined to his sense of the American sublime a developed understanding of the revolutionary era's first and second meanings of nature. Not only did he speak through his journalistic Philosopher of the Forest, but he also found an Indian voice through the papers of the fictionalized Creek Tomo Cheeki. Using the pages of the *Jersey Chronicle* and, later, *The Time Piece, and Literary Companion,* Tomo Cheeki spoke of the wilderness vigor that would infuse American virtue. Likewise, Freneau's poems echoed the language of the Enlightenment by idealist references to nature's God who was the guarantor of the liberty of the American republic.[33]

In his merging of the various meanings of nature, the poet Freneau was joined by other elite patriots, such as Timothy Dwight and Joel Barlow. No deist, Dwight—most notably in "Greenfield Hill"—waxed eloquent on the wholesome rural virtue of American country life, which was not also without its grandeur and, more, its millennial promise: "Profusely scattered o'er these regions, lo! / What scenes of grandeur, and of beauty, glow." Barlow, more comfortable with the Enlightenment God of Freneau, in a series of ambitious poems culminating in "The Columbiad" (1825) but already in "The Vision of Columbus" (1787), had pulled all stops, celebrating nature in a millennial vision of the republican future. "For here great nature, more exalted show'd / The last ascending footsteps of her God."

> What lonely walks, what wonderous wilds are these?
> What branching vales run smiling to their seas?
> The peaceful seats, reserved by Heaven to grace,
> The virtuous toils of some illustrious race.[34]

Roderick Nash has noted some of these connections, linking concepts of the sublime and the picturesque to deism in order to explain developing American attitudes toward the wilderness.[35] Here, however, we need to remember that republican nature meant more than wilderness, and we need to immerse ourselves fully in the ambiguity of the symbol. Wholesome country virtue and wilderness vigor, stars in planetary motion according to unchanging law, reason's rule and its expression in human moral life, American landscape sublimity—all were evoked in the nuanced life of nature among the patriots. Still more, all of the meanings, whether they were aligned along a horizontal (earthbound) or a vertical (heavenly) axis, disclosed in nature the conceptual expression of a spiritual ideal. And yet—and this was the rub and the distinctively American paradox—all used the ideal as a means to feather material nests and, at the same time, to refuse to see what others might have termed the real state of affairs. For nature provided the theological frame on which to hang a civil religion of the American republic, and it also provided a grand principle of obfuscation for patriots in the decades, even centuries, that followed.

None of the meanings of nature came to grips with what we might call a "secular" version of the events of the revolutionary era, with the pragmatic struggle of a prosperous group of colonists to free themselves from an empire they no longer required. Liberated from the older power, the former colonists could begin to fashion an empire of their own, exercising the self-determination that would enable them to conquer a continent. They could be universal when they chose (and avoid the specificities of blacks, Indians, immigrants, and even their female counterparts). Or they could be particular when expansionist stirrings so dictated, amassing vast reaches of territory for the civilizing mission of the republic. In short, the patriots, with nature as their banner, could have things any way at all and, mostly, any way they chose.

Yet, this reading of the symbol of republican nature should not deny the bright and hopeful dreams it mediated. Idealism still was idealism, and, as nature religion fused with civil religion in the person of the patriot leaders, we catch a glimpse of the grandly seductive vision they beheld. We can look at Thomas Jefferson as one representative man among them, for in his words and deeds he articulated the conceptually and morally ambiguous meanings of nature that informed the emerging republican mentality.

Chosen to the subcommittee to draft the Declaration of Independence, Jefferson had quite literally stumbled into formal authorship. A brusque John Adams decided that the younger man should do the actual writing, and so it was the Virginian who composed the political statement that became a national creed. Jefferson's document gave classical utterance to the Enlightenment view of nature and also, in its lofty universalism, justified a specific revolution. Predicated on a contract theory of government, the Declaration assumed that a people had the power and right "to dissolve the political bands which have connected them with another." It announced forthrightly that "the laws of nature and of nature's god" entitled them to a "separate and equal station" "among the powers of the earth" and went on to list their endowments from the Creator God. In the list of grievances against the British monarch that followed, Jefferson, in draft form, attacked the king for his role in the slave trade, accusing him of waging "cruel war against human nature itself, violating it's most sacred rights of life & liberty in the persons of a distant people." Jefferson's earlier, more general statement had already proclaimed "life, liberty, and the pursuit of happiness" as being among the inherent rights of humanity and had understood government as security for these rights.[36]

The Declaration, in effect, offered a brief for nature as an ideal and metaphysical principle. Far removed from the flora and fauna of a Virginia landscape, nature had become a fixed source of right and order in the world; and so, like the inactive creator deities of many small, noncitied societies, nature could explain without involvement and legitimate without interference. The claims of the past had been nullified, and the new order of ages could emerge unparented out of universal nature.[37]

At the same time, the Freemason Jefferson was no abstract philosopher, and his empiricism as firmly brought nature back to earth. Natural rights were "inherent" rights; they could be found not floating in ideal realms but constituent in human beings. They were akin to the voice of nature speaking through the moral sense that informed each individual life. Writing more than a decade later to his nephew Peter Carr, Jefferson told him that "the moral sense, or conscience, is as much a part of man as his leg or arm." This sense of right and wrong was "as much a part of his [man's] nature as the sense of hearing, seeing, feeling."[38]

Conscience was, in fact, the individual version of universal moral law, and Jefferson could tie it to Christianity in the person of Jesus of Nazareth, whose teachings embodied the law of nature. In the two compilations of New Testament extracts that Jefferson carefully constructed, he excised miraculous and divinizing materials to present Jesus as the quintessential natural man of the Enlightenment. What Jesus taught was universal ethical doctrine; and Jefferson's view of moral law, as Charles Sanford has suggested, seemed "similar to the law of gravity." Even so, Jefferson had taken great pains to historicize the universal teaching by discovering it in the words of the founder of Christianity: his ideology of nature was in the end pragmatic and concrete.[39]

And Jefferson's materialism was thoroughgoing. He had learned from Joseph Priestley, buttressing with the Englishman's arguments his own convictions that spirit was matter. Writing late in life to John Adams, Jefferson succinctly stated his position, explaining to Adams that he considered thought "an action of a particular organisation of matter, formed for that purpose by it's creator." Still more, after drawing an analogy between the power of thinking in matter and, tellingly, the power of attraction in the "Sun . . . which reins the planets," he launched into full confession. "To talk of *immaterial* existences is to talk of *nothings*. To say that the human soul, angels, god, are immaterial, is to say they are *nothings*, or that there is no god, no angels, no soul." [40]

Jefferson's brief for the material spirit was radical doctrine among the patriots, but he had only uttered explicitly what they were already absorbing in more intuitive terms. In Jefferson's version, Jonathan Edwards's denial of material substance was surely nowhere to be seen, but a monism akin to Edwards there was. The ideal of nature became real in the public, political life of the republic: functionally, spirit had no existence apart from matter—and more, if the whole truth would be told—matter on the American continent. Later in the century, as we shall see, there would be other Americans who would push the implications of materialism further still. In fact, it might be said that if any genuinely *new* popular religion arose in New World America, it was a nature religion of radical empiricism, with the aim of that religion to conflate spirit with matter and, in the process, turn human beings into gods.

In Jefferson's case, as Daniel Boorstin reminds us, "his materialism was no appendage to the rest of his thought, but an assumption—or rather a predisposition—which colored all his ideas." And if the materialism was no appendage, it might properly be said to have sprung from Virginia soil. Whatever else they may be, religions are human constructions, expressions of human labor to effect definite ends and goals. Jefferson's first understanding of work was the farmer's, and Adrienne Koch was surely right in saying that "he never quite lost the farmer's sense that the products of the orchard, the garden, and the fields are born of arduous labor." [41] Hence, we are brought squarely to Jefferson's involvement in agrarian life and, within it, his appropriation of a second understanding of nature: that rural country wholesomeness that strode across the New York stage in the person of Royall Tyler's Colonel Manly.

Before Colonel Manly ever graced the John Street Theatre, Jefferson was writing from Paris to John Banister, Jr., warning of the dangers of a European education. Away from home, one acquired "a fondness for European luxury and dissipation and a contempt for the simplicity of his own country." Jefferson found the consequences "alarming," for in Europe an American lost "in his knowledge, in his morals, in his health, in his habits, and in his happiness." By contrast, as his *Notes on the State of Virginia* explained, "corruption of morals in the mass of cultivators is a phenomenon of which no age nor nation has furnished an example." As for the individual, so for the body politic. "The proportion which the aggregate of the other classes of citizens bears in any State to that of its husbandmen, is the proportion of its unsound to its healthy parts, and is a good enough barometer whereby to measure its degree of corruption." [42]

Yet, beyond his fears of corruption—whether from European immorality or, as detailed in his *Notes,* from excessive manufactures—Jefferson held a positive religious vision of life in tune with the land. "Those who labor in the earth are the chosen people of God, if ever He had a chosen people, whose breasts He has made His peculiar deposit for substantial and genuine virtue. It is the focus in which he keeps alive that sacred fire, which otherwise might escape from the face of the earth." [43] Jefferson's language evoked Puritan notions of special destiny in the New World, linking to them the high moral ground that had inspired the old Puritan ethic of righteousness. Still, in his evocation of the past, Jefferson had advanced it for another day. The idyllic nature religion of the soil was, if examined from a different perspective, a charter for expansion—not unlike the vision of those earlier Puritans who, dissenting from New England church leaders, had sought wilderness plantations. Now, though, in the new nation manufactures would require concentration of resources into smaller, more efficient units. They would foster geographical compression and citied living. Agriculture, on the other hand, demanded wide, open spaces; and so it demanded the acquisition of territory—and, implicitly, an encounter with wilderness—to support the multiplying American generations.

When, in 1802, Jefferson, as president, learned that Spain had ceded the Louisiana territory to France, a concatenation of American anxieties and European events led to the huge sale of French real estate that annexed perhaps 828,000 square miles to the national domain. The new Constitution had been silent about the acquisition of territory, but by the end of 1803 the United States Senate had confirmed the Jefferson purchase. The sage of Monticello could dream of the agrarian future he had negotiated for the nation. For whatever the immediate circumstances of the land transfer, the Louisiana Purchase was, as Boorstin wrote, "an authentic expression of the Jeffersonian spirit." Now Americans could flourish, as Jefferson had proclaimed in his First Inaugural, "kindly separated by nature and a wide ocean from the exterminating havoc of one quarter of the globe; too high-minded to endure the degradations of the others; possessing a chosen country, with room enough for our descendants to the hundredth and thousandth generation."[44]

Surely, there was an irony in the Manly wholesomeness that Jefferson had inadvertently embraced. As Boorstin incisively remarked, the Jeffersonian's "professed belief, deeply rooted in his cosmology, that no piece of the universe was more important than another, that man's task everywhere had to emerge from his local condition, was overshadowed by the magnificence of the American destiny." And, indeed, "expansiveness and boundlessness seemed themselves a kind of destiny and definition."[45] Jefferson dreamed on, thinking of Canada and Cuba as part of the American empire. Thus it is in light of the dream of empire that we need to view his appropriation of the third understanding of nature, when Jefferson beheld the national landscape as American sublime.

Writing to Maria Cosway, with whom he had formed a romantic attachment, Jefferson in Paris pictured the scene that Cosway, a landscape artist, might paint at Monticello:

Where has nature spread so rich a mantle under the eye? mountains, forests, rocks, rivers. With what majesty do we there ride above the storms! How sublime to look down into the workhouse of nature, to see her clouds, hail, snow, rain, thunder, all fabricated at our feet! And the glorious Sun, when rising as if out of a distant water, just gilding the tops of the mountains, and giving life to all nature![46]

If the expanse was awesome, it was also clear that Jefferson was in the high place looking down. Expansion and expansiveness gilded the sight he saw: it was the aesthetic and religious equivalent of his republican dream. "The Falling spring, the Cascade of Niagara, the Passage of the Potowmac thro the Blue mountains, the Natural bridge," Jefferson declared to Cosway. "It is worth a voiage across the Atlantic to see these objects."[47]

Nor did he keep these sentiments only for private communication. "This scene is worth a voyage across the Atlantic," he wrote in *Notes on the State of Virginia* after he had described for readers the passage of the Potomac River through the Blue Ridge Mountains. It was, "perhaps, one of the most stupendous scenes in nature."

Caleb Boyle, *Thomas Jefferson at the Natural Bridge,* ca. 1801. Oil on canvas; approximate size, 96″ × 62″. (Courtesy, Kirby Collection of Historical Paintings, Lafayette College, Easton, Pennsylvania.) Thomas Jefferson owned the Natural Bridge as real estate.

You stand on a very high point of land. On your right comes up the Shenandoah, having ranged along the foot of the mountain an hundred miles to seek a vent. On your left approaches the Potomac, in quest of a passage also. In the moment of their junction, they rush together against the mountain, rend it asunder, and pass off to the sea.[48]

Jefferson went on, in a Burkean move, to write of the "distant finishing" of the picture, of its "true contrast to the foreground . . . as placid and delightful as that is wild and tremendous."[49] However, if the sublime yielded to the beautiful for the distant gaze, we need to notice that, in the foreground, the sublime equaled wilderness equaled power. The equation had been shaped in Europe, but it was being reshaped in America under the aegis of forces that stressed magnitude as a way of being, a necessary landscape for the virtuous republic.

It was at Natural Bridge, though, that Jefferson found "the most sublime of nature's works." Although few had walked to the "parapet of fixed rocks" to look out over the "abyss," he had done so. "You involuntarily fall on your hands and feet, creep to the parapet, and peep over it," he wrote. "Looking down from this height about a minute, gave me a violent head-ache." The view from the bridge had been "painful and intolerable," but that from below was "delightful in an equal extreme." Jefferson was enthusiastic: "It is impossible for the emotions arising from the sublime to be felt beyond what they are here," he affirmed. "So beautiful an arch, so elevated, so light, and springing as it were up to heaven! the rapture of the spectator is really indescribable!"[50]

Yet, if Jefferson had conformed his memory to Burkean categories, he had also confused them, finding sublimity both in the view from below that gave him delight and in the (painful) view from above. Moreover, as Garry Wills has shown for Jefferson's delight, he had altered his evidence. Immediately following his account of the spectator's rapturous pleasure below, Jefferson described the scene as the mountains were cleft by the fissure. Significantly, he told of what could only be viewed from the high place. "The fissure continuing narrow, deep, and straight, for a considerable distance above and below the bridge, opens a short but very pleasing view of the North mountain on one side and the Blue Ridge on the other, at the distance each of them of about five miles."[51] Jefferson had been caught in the act, so to speak. It was an *American* sublime that he had experienced; and, in American sublime, rather than being terrified, one liked and enjoyed being on top. That Jefferson was the legal owner of Natural Bridge as real estate only underlined the connection: American sublime hinted of empire and dominion.

Beyond that, the Americanness of American sublime mediated a certain danger. What was stupendous bore the risk of becoming merely stupefying in dimension, as if magnitude in size could serve as equivalent for moral magnitude. Already, in his *Notes,* Jefferson was expressing the American mentality that would flourish into the nineteenth century and beyond. He boasted of the "tusks, grinders, and skeletons of unparalleled magnitude" found in large numbers on the Ohio River and elsewhere. And he waxed, for the benefit of the French naturalist the Count de Buffon and others, on the putative mammoth whose remains had been recently discovered on American soil. Its skeleton told of "an animal of five or six times the cubic volume of the elephant," and it was certain the mammoth was "the largest of all terrestrial beings." With one animal—even such as this—not sufficient, Jefferson painstakingly assembled and elaborated a chart that compared the body weights of the "Quadrupeds of Europe and of America." He would establish to his and his countrymen's satisfaction the superiority of American specimens.[52]

The patriotism of Jefferson's polemic was evident. But what is important here is how patriotism, for Jefferson and his countrymen, was—for all the starry skies of Enlightenment law—mingled inextricably with an "earthy bottom." The land and its products must correspond in their stature to the perceived stature of the young republic. Nature must stand beside liberty; and if true liberty broke down Old World bonds and limits, nature, too, must defy Old World categories in its expanse. In the surroundings of the continent's seemingly unending space, the American translation for value was becoming size and magnitude. Nature religion meant communion with forces that enlarged the public life of the nation. And with Jefferson and other American patriots always on top, it meant conquest to insure that nature's forces would flow as the lifeblood of the body politic.

The logic and energy of the symbol were real: it contained power and mediated power, acting as mythic broker for an evolving American mentality. Meaning piled on meaning even for the revolutionary generation, with nature and its religion moving in a kaleidoscope. And, as we shall see in succeeding chapters, the lens of the Revolution, turned by new times, could lend surprising and even contrary linc and form to an American nature religion. It is in the context of this symbolic pluralism that we need to pursue the Jeffersonian vision into a new age, keeping sight of the light and dark of the dream.

We gain one view of how the lens turned for the nineteenth-century future by glancing at a popular republican near midcentury. Already fictionalized in the midst of public life, this man—a southerner like Jefferson—expressed and exploited the nature religion that the revolutionary generation had bequeathed. In his person, the symbolic counter of nature manifested its wilderness power, its political wit, and its moral problem in an age of manifest destiny. The figure is Davy Crockett, and the life that he lived embodied the political world of the American Congress and the "savage" realm of the Tennessee frontier.

David Crockett, the historical figure, had moved from two terms in the Tennessee legislature (1821–24) to two terms in the United States Congress beginning in 1827.[53] As representative from the state of Tennessee, he early broke with Andrew Jackson, the democratic hero of the state who became president. Fighting with Jackson's forces over the Tennessee Vacant Land Bill and, later, the Indian Removal Bill, Crockett championed poor Indians in his home district by introducing legislation for their aid. After two terms in Congress, he sat out the years from 1831 to 1833 but was subsequently reelected for a final congressional term. A year later he was dead at the Alamo.

It was during his last term in Congress when, probably combining financial need with political ambition, Crockett with some assistance produced his *Narrative of the Life of David Crockett* (1834).[54] Cast in frontier style and idiom, the work celebrated life in the woods and the hunter hero's exploits, culminating in his slaughter of 105 bears within the space of a year. Yet, throughout the autobiography with its tall tales and its heroic caricatures, Crockett talked politics in explicit and unmistakable terms. The *Narrative* was a running polemic against Andrew Jackson and his "kitchen cabinet," and it hinted, as well, that Crockett might soon become president of the United States. Whether as campaign biog-

Vol. 2.] "GO AHEAD!!" [No. 3.

THE CROCKETT ALMANAC
1841.

MANNING DEL.

HARTWELL SC.

Tussel with a Bear. See page 9.

Containing **Adventures**, **Exploits**, **Sprees** & **Scrapes** in the **West**, & Life and **Manners** in the **Backwoods**.

Nashville, Tennessee. Published by Ben Harding.

"Likeness of Crockett When Eight Years Old." From *Crockett's Almanac, 1851,* published in Philadelphia, New York, and Boston by Fisher & Brother, (unnumbered page) 14. (Courtesy, American Antiquarian Society.) Even in childhood, Davy Crockett dominates the land, suggesting a kind of mystical engulfment.

Opposite: Front cover, *The Crockett Almanac, 1841.* (Courtesy, American Antiquarian Society.) This Nashville almanac, purportedly published by the seafaring captain Ben Harding, graphically proclaims the embrace of nature that Davy Crockett boasted.

raphy or as literary entertainment, the work was enormously successful, exhausting seven editions (including a London edition) within the year.

Although even before the autobiography there had been mythicizing productions to make the congressman from Tennessee a legend, it was in 1834, again, that a work was published that completed the transformation of David into *Davy* Crockett. That year, in Nashville, there appeared the first edition of an almanac—*Davy Crockett's Almanack of Wild Sports of the West, and Life in the Backwoods*—which would continue in one form or another until 1856. Produced mostly, if not entirely, in Eastern cities, the Crockett almanacs suggested their own success by internal evidence and external circumstance. Like other almanacs of the era, they added

to standard almanac information pages of anecdotes—here concerning Crockett and his intimate friends and foes. In doing so,
they recounted, quite clearly, exorbitant fictions; and in the pages
of the almanacs David Crockett the man became Davy Crockett
the myth.

Examining the myth of Crockett as it appears in the almanacs
means looking into the republican kaleidoscope with the affirmations of the revolutionary generation turned and twisted. To
view Crockett is to encounter an American isomorphism between
farmer and hunter, between hunter and warrior, and between
warrior and politician.[55] To see him is to see transformation in
republican nature under the strains of a romanticizing age. The
Tennessee folk hero moves through the pages of these almanac episodes as a gargantuan figure, deliberately and distortedly larger
than life. Crockett required a twelve-foot cradle made of snapping
turtle and varnished with rattlesnake oil to rock him in infancy;
and by age eight, with his shoes off and feet clean, he weighed
two hundred pounds and fourteen ounces. Meanwhile, he had
been weaned on whiskey and always made it a practice to take a
pint with mustard before breakfast. As almanac tales made clear,
Crockett could outsavage any savage in hunt or fight. Indeed, at
least subliminally aware of Enlightenment law and science, he and
his foes still acted like animals as they fought. Consider, for example, this rather typical account from an almanac of 1850:

I stood up and spit in his face. He pulled up his breeches, and crowed
three times. I felt my flesh crawl over, and my toe-nails moved out of
place. I moved my elbow in scientific order, and got ready to take a twist in
his hair. When he seed that, he squealed and ran around me three times. I
jumped up, and planted my heels in his bowels. . . . he caught me 'round
the thigh and war goin' to throw me down: but I stopped over and cotched
him by the seat of his trowsers and held him up in the air, when he
squirmed like an eel, and tried to shoot me with his pistol. I twisted him
over, and took his knee-pan in my mouth and bit clear through to the bone.[56]

The animal sounds and behavior and the veiled cannibalism of
the Crockett who "bit clear through to the bone" contrasted sharply
with the "scientific order" of the Tennessean's elbow. So, too, on
another occasion, did his address to Congress stand in juxtaposition
to the conventions of that body. The mythic Crockett, like his historical prototype, was a congressman; but he was congressman-

qua-animal as, in almanac fashion, he accosted the speaker and the House. "Who—Who—Whoop—Bow—Wow—Wow—Yough," he began, in a speech in which he declared himself a "screamer" and a "*horse.*" "I can walk like an ox, swim like an eel, yell like an Indian, fight like a devil, and spout like an earthquake, make love like a mad bull, and swallow a nigger whole without choking if you butter his head and pin his ears back." [57] With a cannibalism that was now not merely innuendo and with a racism that was blatant and unapologetic, Crockett identified himself with the denizens of the forest even as he sat in the halls of Congress.

That the fictional Crockett took his congressional charge seriously was evident in the political preoccupation that haunted the pages of the almanacs as surely as it had run through the *Narrative.* The "savage eucharist," as Richard Slotkin has called it, meant a fusion of self with wilderness forces, a fusion that culminated in the act of cannibalism, the ritual feeding that guaranteed the prowess of the enemy would be absorbed into oneself. [58] The ultimate act of conquest, it was also the ultimate form of nature mysticism, an eating in which external foe and victim became internal sustenance. Yet, in the symbolic ambiguity that invested the figure of Crockett, the war and hunting cannibalism of the forest became the collective political cannibalism of empire.

Championing the manifest destiny of his age, Crockett was certain that Texas, Oregon, and California all belonged to the territorial domain of the United States. He could show Americans, he said, "the chap fit to send to Congress, and one that knows how to talk about Oregon, annex Texas, flog Mexico, swallow a Frenchman whole, and lick John Bull clar out of his breeches!" Communion with nature through conquest signaled the eucharist of cannibalism and the eucharist of imperial absorption. As early as 1836, the almanac Crockett had delivered his "squatter speech" to the Congress, arguing that Americans "shall squat the face of this tarnal 'arth, from the *Hatlantic* ocean to the *Specific!!!*" And, in an allusion to his historical role in fighting under Andrew Jackson in the Creek (Indian) War, he later boasted that "some of the fokes talked of putting me up for President bekase I had showed myself a military hero." [59]

"You see, feller citizens," Crockett declared without equivocation in an 1845 almanac, "I go in for Texas and the Oregon, clar

"Crockett's Patent Gouging; Or, Using Up Two Indian Chiefs," *Crockett Almanac, 1849*, published in Boston by James Fisher, (unnumbered page) 9. (Courtesy, American Antiquarian Society.) The graphic accompanies the almanacs' one completely explicit account of Davy Crockett's cannibalism.

up to the very gravel stone; for they both belong to Uncle Sam's plantation, jist as naturally as a cabbage leaf belongs to a cabbage stalk." The agrarian metaphor was not without significance, for— as the Jeffersonian dream reminds—it was the demands of agriculture that supplied the rationale for empire—and, indeed, in that other dark side of American life—for slavery. The historical Crockett had farmed the land before he occupied himself in politics, and the mythic Crockett was likewise unafraid to admit his livelihood as a farmer. Once, when he caught a party of Indians stealing his horse fodder, he mowed them down with his twelve-foot scythe, until "the red nigger's sap both watered an manured my field, till it war as red an striped, as Uncle Sam's flag." "Thar's a stack o' thar bones standing in the medow to this very day," he confided, "an from the large majority o' thar blood that watered it all over, I have had a treble crop o' the tallest injun grass every summer."[60] If Crockett had inadvertently admitted that, in the pornography of violence, blacks and Indians were of a piece, he had also told that their wildness could fertilize the fields of empire under blood-red stripes of the American flag.

It is against such a backdrop that we can better understand the Crockett who, stalking out one January morning for a hunt, found the earth frozen fast on its axes and the sun jammed between two cakes of ice. Crockett rescued the cosmos by unloading a bear from his back, beating the hot oil out of it, and squeezing it over the axes of the earth until they were thawed. After that, it seemed an easy affair for the colonel to squeeze "about a ton on it [bear grease] over the sun's face" and "give the airth's cog-wheel one kick backward." "In about fifteen seconds the airth gin a grunt, and begun movin'—the sun walked up beautiful—saluten me with sich a wind o' gratitude, that it made sneeze." Crockett nonchalantly "walked home . . . with a piece of sunrise in my pocket, with which I cooked my bear steaks, an' enjoyed one o' the best breakfasts I had tasted for some time."[61] The innocence and wholesomeness of the account, its fresh country humor and implied concern for compatriots suffering from the sun's predicament, cloak the expansionist impulse. Crockett had exposed the universal natural law as subject to American manipulation. The ideal order of things did, indeed, have an earthy bottom.

Hence, to view the mythic Crockett who entertained Americans from the 1830s to the 1850s—and, in his later manifestations, beyond—is to examine one transmutation of the nature religion of the revolutionary age. Its three strands of meaning are present in the grotesquerie of the almanac episodes. The innocence of the Crockett who unfroze earth and sun exists side by side with the wild ferocity of the man whose thumbnail achieved renown for its prowess at gouging panther and human alike.[62] The "scientific order" of Crockett's fighting mimicked the eternal law of the heavens but also hinted that wilderness strength could overcome it. At the same time, the law of nature's noble primitive proved to be, in another version, the law of political manifest destiny. For construed as fundamental law discovered in the contour of the land and in the character of the American people, manifest destiny accomplished more concretely what eighteenth-century patriots had intuited all along. Finally, the American sublime of Jefferson and his Enlightenment friends was echoed, in more discordant key, in the ecstasies of the hunter hero who celebrated nature even as he ingested it through conquest. The savage eucharist was the ritual culmination of the imperial gaze of the patriot—always on top, and always looking down.

What all of this suggests is that Davy Crockett and the demands of manifest destiny represent, in fact, the underside of revolutionary idealism. The twisted vision of Crockett and the contorted figures with whom he grappled reflect the twists in a popular American mentality grown arguably overlarge. In this nineteenth-century American enactment of its themes, nature religion had become dominance over the land and, simultaneously, escape and illusion. The embrace of matter had become avoidance of matter, the celebration of a grandness that glanced off the reality of the continent and its peoples in fulfillment of the urge to empire. The other-than-human persons of the Algonkians of another age had fled into the forests; the Puritan dialectic of fear and fascination had played itself into another key; and the Enlightenment had yielded its rationalism to the powers of the irrational. Dream had come to shape destiny, as nature, turned to new American purposes, presided over the unfoldment—and terror—of history.[63]

On the other hand, it was clear that the nature religion of the revolutionary age could move in different directions. Jeffersonian materialism, conflating matter and spirit, could be used to additional purposes; and the implications of the revolutionary age could be discovered in other configurations as the nineteenth century turned the kaleidoscope of nature. Well before David Crockett put his mind to autobiography, another man—soon to be a lawyer like Royall Tyler and, like him too, a native of Massachusetts—had put his hand to paper. When his words were finally published in 1817, his readers were an elite few and his chosen genre was poetry. In his "Thanatopsis," a youthful William Cullen Bryant announced to subscribers of the North American Review a version of the religion of nature, with a romanticism profoundly different from that which would characterize Crockett.

> To him who in the love of Nature holds
> Communion with her visible forms, she speaks
> A various language; for his gayer hours
> She has a voice of gladness, and a smile
> And eloquence of beauty, and she glides
> Into his darker musings, with a mild
> And healing sympathy, that steals away
> Their sharpness, ere he is aware. . . .
> . . . .
> Go forth, under the open sky, and list
> To Nature's teachings, while from all around—
> Earth and her waters, and the depths of air—
> Comes a still voice.[64]

Bryant's words in many ways would find their parallel in 1836 when another youthful American—a restive Ralph Waldo Emerson—sounded the opening lines of his Transcendentalist gospel *Nature*. And years later, in 1864, when Bryant was seventy, Emerson would say that the celebrated poet was "always original." Reading other popular American and English poets, Emerson thought they appeared "to have gone into the art galleries and to have seen pictures of mountains." "But this man," he paid tribute, had "seen mountains." With as much admiration, Emerson went on to affirm that there was "no feature of day or night in the country" that did not "to a contemplative mind, recall the name of Bryant."[65] Hearing, like the poet of "Thanatopsis," a divine voice in the land, Emerson and other Transcendentalists would explore the legacy of nature religion left by the revolutionary generation—and, as much or more, the legacy left by the Puritans before them. But they would follow the historic line to end at a different place. Davy Crockett was not the only heir to nature's law.

3 / Wildness and the Passing Show ❧
TRANSCENDENTAL RELIGION AND ITS LEGACIES

"A foolish consistency is the hobgoblin of little minds," wrote the still-youthful Ralph Waldo Emerson.[1] If so, he had already practiced what he preached, for some five years previously Emerson's book *Nature* had announced the virtues of inconsistency by embodying them. In this, the gospel of Transcendentalism, its leader proclaimed a message that inspired with its general principles but, with the opaqueness of its rhetoric, mostly discouraged analytic scrutiny. Yet Emerson's *Nature* was to have a profound effect on many, even outside Transcendentalist circles. Still more, *Nature* was to reflect and express patterns of thinking and feeling that found flesh in two seemingly disparate nineteenth-century movements—that of wilderness preservation and that of mind cure.

In turning our attention to Emerson and other Transcendentalists, we turn to a question at the heart of mid- and later-nineteenth-century American religion. The question is this: What happens when the heirs of Puritanism, Platonism, the Enlightenment, and the Revolution seek answers to religious questions in a world in which traditional faith is unraveling? What do they discover, and what can they hold fast? How do they theologize, and how do they build meaningful religious worlds in a new era? In what ways do they enact their consciously constructed faiths, and—most important here—in what ways are these enactments expressions of nature religion or nature religions?

To answer these questions we need to move beyond Transcendentalism, to confront a broad popular mentality that could be found in key segments of American society. The mentality was compounded of a lingering Calvinism, with its deep sense of evil and sin; an idealist tradition that molded Platonism and Neoplatonism to modern times and purposes; a romanticism that turned to nature no longer contained (in the Enlightenment and early revolutionary mode) but more expansive to accompany the liberation of self and society; and an emerging "scientific" view in which mesmerism and Swedenborgianism became guiding intellectual lights.

To answer these questions, though, we turn, first, to the Transcendentalist gospel that reflected and, in some measure, shaped the popular mentality. Standing at the intersection of elite and popular worlds, Transcendentalists such as Ralph Waldo Emerson and Henry David Thoreau at once absorbed and created religious insight, giving ideas compelling shape and extended currency through their language. Emerson, especially, in his lectures to lyceum audiences faithfully proclaimed his new views, and dutiful newspaper reporters summarized for those unable to attend lyceum gatherings. "In the decade of 1850–1860," Perry Miller wrote, "he achieved a kind of apotheosis," [2]—an apotheosis, we may add, that continued to endure. Thoreau, the "sleeper," did not engage in lyceum activity to nearly the degree that Emerson did. But in his writings he became a prophet to a later generation of seekers. Together the two and their disciples handed on an ambiguous heritage, bringing the Emersonian inconsistency into service to obscure a crack in the religious cosmos. Together they enabled variant forms of nature religion to discover their commonality.

When Ralph Waldo Emerson published *Nature* in 1836, he had constructed it from two previous and now loosely joined essays. As early as 1832, Emerson had stood entranced before the exhibits at the Parisian Garden of Plants, and, as he wrote about them for a lecture audience, he outlined the shape of things to come in the early chapters of *Nature*. In the way that Emerson conceived his work, an essay on "Nature" was to be followed by one on "Spirit," the two together to make a "decent volume." [3] In fact, as Ralph L. Rusk tells us, "Spirit" became the seventh chapter in *Nature;* but, before it could join the first five chapters of the essay, there was, as Emerson said, probably in reference to the problem, "one crack in it not easy to be soldered or welded." The sixth chapter, on "Idealism," evidently provided the weld, and—if James Elliot Cabot was right in the nineteenth century and Robert E. Spiller in our own—the sixth chapter brought together two essays that Emerson had turned into one. [4]

All of this might be dismissed as arcane textual history were it not for the far-reaching implications of the Emersonian patch. The importance of Emerson's essay for the Transcendentalist movement can hardly be overstated, and its importance for understanding a wider American culture is also primary. Thus, the problems of *Nature* in making a coherent statement suggest the dilemmas of later religious answers. For Emerson's rhetoric masked and revealed theological substance—and the substance of what Emerson said was rich in ambiguity. Textual history, therefore, provides clues for textual criticism, for insight into the confusion that followed Transcendentalists and other and later Americans. If, as Gail Thain Parker has acknowledged, popular faiths may have helped because they were "muddle-headed,"[5] Emerson and his friends had done their share to contribute.

Put briefly, the confusion was between—on the one hand—a view of matter as "really real," the embodiment of Spirit and the garment of God, and—on the other hand—a view of matter as illusion and unreality, ultimately a trap from which one needed to escape. Nature, in other words, might be sacramental, an emblem of divine things that in some way actually *contained* the divinity to which it pointed. And nature might therefore have a quality of absoluteness about it. Or—to follow the logic to a conclusion not willingly admitted by Emerson—nature might be the subject of erroneous perception. In stronger terms, it might be an obstacle to bedevil those who would truly seek for higher things. And, at the very least, it might simply be part of the flux in the midst of which one needed to seek some sort of permanence.

As this last suggests, confused views of matter led to ambivalent programs for action. If nature was, indeed, real and sacramental, then corresponding to it became paramount. Harmony with nature became the broad highway to virtuous living and, more, to union with divinity. One discovered what was permanent and lasting precisely by identifying with the regular tides of nature's flux. If, however, nature was at best a passing show, a foil to obscure the Absolute behind and beyond it, then seeking the enduring truth of Mind became key. Mastery *over* nature through mental power became the avenue to a "salvation" that transcended, even as it managed, nature.

To understand how Emerson moved between the two conceptions of matter (or the first and a softened version of the second)—and between the two agendas that followed from them—is to explore the deftness of his rhetoric, to glance at its masking function. The Transcendentalist, like a master craftsman disguising an imperfection, glosses Nature Real with Nature Illusory, telling us it isn't so even as he tells us that it is. The success of his craft in *Nature* may be measured by the success of his essay and by the long shadow of creative confusion it has cast.

Emerson began with a hymn of praise for nature with its living presence in contrast to the desiccated rattling of the past. "Embosomed for a season in nature, whose floods of life stream around and through us, and invite us by the powers they supply, to action proportioned to nature, why should we grope among the dry bones of the past?" He told readers that "the universe is composed of Nature and the Soul," and that Nature is all that is "NOT ME." If a person wanted truly to be alone, "let him look at the stars." "One might think the atmosphere was made transparent with this design, to give man, in the heavenly bodies, the perpetual presence of the sublime. . . . If the stars should appear one night in a thousand years, how would men believe and adore; and preserve for many generations the remembrance of the city of God which had been shown!"[6]

Surely there was no lack of reverence for nature in this rhetoric of exaltation—or in the ascending climax of delight that the first chapter of *Nature* continued to mount. "The lover of nature is he whose inward and outward senses are still truly adjusted to each other," Emerson informed his readers. And, with intimations of communion feast, he stated that "intercourse with heaven and earth, becomes part of his daily food. In the presence of nature, a wild delight runs through the man." "Crossing a bare common," Emerson confessed, could bring him "a perfect exhilaration." In the woods he found "perpetual youth," and in the woods a return to "reason and faith." The culmination was a mysticism of nature in a passage often cited: "Standing on the bare ground,—my head bathed by the blithe air, and uplifted into infinite space,—all mean egotism vanishes. I become a transparent eye-ball. I am nothing. I see all. The currents of the Universal Being circulate through me; I am part or particle of God."[7]

The agenda for action was not far behind. If, as Emerson said, "the greatest delight which the fields and woods minister, is the suggestion of an occult relation between man and the vegetable," realizing and strengthening the relation became the burden of the harmonial ethic he unfolded. In succeeding chapters he developed a "higher" instrumentalism, expounding the "uses" of nature under the four headings of commodity, beauty, language, and discipline. What is important about all of them here is that they were expressions of the law of correspondence, expressions in which nature, as mother and teacher, nurtured humans and wrote large the lessons they needed to imitate. With material benefits, nature assisted life lived through the senses and flowering in the practical arts (commodity). With an attractiveness at once physical, spiritual, and intellectual, nature assuaged "a nobler want of man" (beauty), supplying an object for soul, will, and intellect. Likewise, nature pointed to the "radical correspondence between visible things and human thoughts," suggesting the words that were "signs of natural facts" and exhibiting the "particular natural facts" that were "symbols of particular spiritual facts" (language). And, finally, by its hard facticity nature trained the understanding to conform to the shape of things and taught the will to comprehend the moral law (discipline). "Every natural process is but a version of a moral sentence," Emerson declared.[8]

While there is not space here for thorough exploration of Emerson's pyramid of uses, we have seen enough to notice how embedded in the *material* of nature the spirituality of uses was. The mother and teacher could not be a trickster, for nature supplied the "fit" for every human loose end. The mother and teacher could not vend illusion and unreality, for, to the contrary, nature purveyed the true and good. In fact, as Barbara Novak writes, truth and beauty did not oppose the actual but were "of a piece" with it.[9]

What, then, are we to make of Emerson's opening salvo in the sixth chapter, after the series of chapters on nature's uses? Echoing the question that had already provoked Jonathan Edwards and centuries of Platonists, Emerson began to doubt. "A noble doubt perpetually suggests itself," he uneasily acknowledged, "whether nature outwardly exists." "It is a sufficient account of that Appearance we call the World, that God will teach a human mind, and so makes it the receiver of a certain number of congruent sensations, which we call sun and moon, man and woman, house and trade." Of course, Emerson mused, natural laws were permanent and "sacredly respected." But the question was whether or not nature possessed "absolute existence."[10]

Faith in the absolute existence of nature was instinctive for "the senses and the unrenewed understanding," Emerson continued. "In their view, man and nature are indissolubly joined. Things are ultimates, and they never look beyond their sphere." There was, however, another point of view (the ideal), for "the presence of Reason mars this faith." The "despotism of the senses" was relaxed, and "causes and spirits" could be seen. "The best, the happiest moments of life, are these delicious awakenings of the higher powers, and the reverential withdrawing of nature before its God."[11]

Moreover, just as nature had its uses, so did the ideal theory. "The advantage of the ideal theory over the popular faith, is this," argued Emerson, "that it presents the world in precisely that view which is most desirable to the mind." The world was always "phenomenal" when "seen in the light of thought," and, in fact, "virtue subordinates it to the mind." Indeed, the same absorption in the present and rejection of a dead past that contemplation of nature brought (at the beginning of the essay) was also a function of idealism. "It beholds the whole circle of persons and things, of actions and events, of country and religion, not as painfully accumulated, atom after atom, act after act, in an aged creeping Past, but as one vast picture, which God paints on the instant eternity, for the contemplation of the soul."[12]

Atom for atom, though, Emerson had moved past the stuff—the matter—of the universe and its earthly incarnation in nature. And he was painfully aware of what he had done. "I own there is something ungrateful in expanding too curiously the particulars of the general proposition, that all culture tends to imbue us with idealism," he had already admitted. "I have no hostility to nature, but a child's love to it. I expand and live in the warm day like corn and melons. Let us speak her fair. I do not wish to fling stones at my beautiful mother, nor soil my gentle nest."[13] Nagged by guilt and apology, he still could not escape the logic of the idealist stance. He had tried, as it were, to modulate from key to key; but in the shift from Nature Major to Nature Minor some wrong notes had been struck. And their echo would continue.

Similarly, action for action, Emerson had moved past the harmonial program that conformity to the laws of nature enjoined. Now, taking his stand on the ideal theory, he propounded an ethic that inverted the rule of harmony in an astonishing way. He thought that, after all, "a true theory of nature and of man . . . should con-

tain somewhat progressive." The ideal theory met this requirement (in Emerson's view, it was another "use" of idealism that it
did so) because it led, precisely, to human mastery *over* matter. It
brought that control over self and environment that rendered humans divine and lordly beings. If nature was "a great shadow
pointing always to the sun behind us," it was also true that the sun
once emerged full force from the human. As Emerson said a "certain poet sang," "man" was "a god in ruins," now only "the dwarf
of himself." "Once he was permeated and dissolved by spirit. He
filled nature with his overflowing currents. Out from him sprang
the sun and moon." [14]

But the problem was that "man applies to nature but half his
force. He works on the world with his understanding alone. He
lives in it, and masters it by a penny-wisdom." It was only by re-
deeming the soul that the world could be restored to its "original
and eternal beauty." By using "ideal force," by acting on nature
with "entire force," a person could inaugurate what to ordinary
appearances seemed utterly extraordinary. Emerson supplied examples of the brief moments when Reason had momentarily grasped
"the sceptre," of "the exertions of a power which exists not in time
or space, but an instantaneous in-streaming causing power." [15]

Such examples are; the traditions of miracles in the earliest antiquity of
all nations; the history of Jesus Christ; the achievements of a principle, as
in religious and political revolutions, and in the abolition of the Slave-
trade; the miracles of enthusiasm, as those reported of Swedenborg,
Hohenlohe, and the Shakers; many obscure and yet contested facts, now
arranged under the name of Animal Magnetism; prayer; eloquence; self-
healing; and the wisdom of children. [16]

If self-healing was only penultimate in Emerson's list, he had
made his point. There would be a "correspondent revolution in
things" when life was made to conform to the "pure idea" in the
mind; and "so fast" would "disagreeable appearances, swine, spi-
ders, snakes, pests, mad-houses, prisons, enemies, vanish." In a
final affirmation of Transcendentalist and idealist faith, Emerson
closed his essay. "The kingdom of man over nature, which cometh
not with observation,—a dominion such as now is beyond his
dream of God,—he shall enter without more wonder than the
blind man feels who is gradually restored to perfect sight." [17]

Emerson had begun by gazing in ecstasy at the stars, contemplating the works of God before him and yielding to their harmonizing influence, but by the time he had welded the two pieces of his essay together he was setting the heavenly lights in their places. Harmony between microcosm (man) and macrocosm (nature) had become the mastery in which humans claimed their true dominion and revealed themselves as the gods they were. Here, already, was a blueprint for a preservationist movement to hold onto wilderness and, at the same time, for a mind-cure movement to leave lower for "higher" nature. Emerson's confusion did not cause America's confusion, but it became America's confusion and, to some degree as well, the confusion of that second-generation Transcendentalist, Henry David Thoreau.

The author of *Walden* has sometimes been praised for his naturalism, for his attachment to the grainy particularities of the world of nature. Thoreau, in this reading, left behind the idealism of Emerson in an unchastened embrace of matter.[18] In short, Thoreau was a reconstructed heathen, one for whom, as Philip F. Gura has written, "man did not have to get anywhere; he was there already."[19]

There is, indeed, much to be said for this view of Thoreau: his commitment to the specificity of things separated him decisively from his mentor, if mentor Emerson was. Where Emerson saw corn and melons (or simply the landscape of parts blurring into parts), Thoreau saw a textured world filled with innumerable and distinguishable species, for many of which he could supply botanical names. Better able to name, Thoreau was better able to grasp the essential reality of what he saw, to experience the wilderness eucharist that brought him into sacramental relationship with the world.

In *Walden,* in one expression of the eucharist, Thoreau confessed how, as he returned from fishing after dark, he "caught a glimpse of a woodchuck" and then "felt a strange thrill of savage delight, and was strongly tempted to seize and devour him raw." "Not that I was hungry then," he added, "except for that wildness which he represented." And in milder vein, in the semicompleted "Huckleberries" Thoreau spoke of the fields and hills as "a table constantly spread." The berries invited to "a pic-nic with Nature." "We pluck and eat in remembrance of her," Thoreau said. "It is a sort of sacrament—a communion—the *not* forbidden fruits, which

Walden Pond in May. Photograph by Herbert Wendell Gleason (1855–1937), ca. 1905. (Courtesy, Concord Free Public Library.) The photo captures some of the delicate sensuousness of the pond.

no serpent tempts us to eat." [20] Here, surely, was an example of what Cecelia Tichi meant when she wrote that Thoreau's wildness was held in a "domestic embrace." [21] On the other hand, the domesticity should not trick us into missing the wild for the tame, the uncontaminated purity of the communion for a household feast.

Traveling in the Maine woods in 1857, Thoreau found the communion by contemplating one specific phenomenon in what Mircea Eliade would call a hierophany. When Thoreau, encamped at Moosehead Lake, awakened unexpectedly at night, he saw "a white and slumbering light." It came from phosphorescent wood; but "I was in just the frame of mind to see something wonderful," Thoreau recalled, "and this was a phenomenon adequate to my circumstances and expectation." He "exulted like 'a pagan suckled in a creed' that had never been worn at all, but was bran new, and adequate to the occasion." He "let science slide, and rejoiced in that light as if it had been a fellow-creature," believing that "the woods were not tenantless, but choke-full of honest spirits" as good as he. He stood, in fact, in "an inhabited house," in which, "for a few moments" he "enjoyed fellowship with them." The revelation of the sacred was complete, and for Thoreau it brought, as Donald Worster has noted, "a community of love." [22]

Yet, for all the eucharistic celebration, there was another side to Henry David Thoreau's life in nature. He could not escape from his inherited knowledge that there were "higher laws." The Calvinist affirmations of his Puritan forebears lingered on in him, transmuted into a quest for moral purity and purification of the senses.[23] It is in this light that Thoreau's much-vaunted, if somewhat eclectic, Hinduism needs to be seen; and it is in this light, too, that we need to place his confessions of paganism.

If we return to Thoreau mentally feasting on the raw woodchuck, we follow a trail that leads, with Thoreauvian twists, not to carnivorous eucharist but to vegetarianism. The woodchuck incident opens the chapter in *Walden* entitled "Higher Laws"; and for Thoreau higher laws were laws of ascetic separation from the food of the communion table. "I have found repeatedly, of late years," he mused, "that I cannot fish without falling a little in self-respect." He found "something essentially unclean about this diet and all flesh" and owned that he objected to "animal food" because of its "uncleanness." The fish had not fed him "essentially." "Like many of my contemporaries," Thoreau went on to admit, "I had rarely for many years used animal food, or tea, or coffee, &c.; not so much because of any ill effects which I had traced to them, as because they were not agreeable to my imagination." [24]

Thoreau had more reasons for reserve than we usually associate with imagination. All of life, he said, was "startlingly moral." In terms that seem almost Pauline (save for contiguous allusions to the Chinese philosopher Mencius and to the Indian Vedas), he declared that "we are conscious of an animal in us, which awakens in proportion as our higher nature slumbers." In the associative logic that followed, thinking about the "animal" led to thinking about chastity, "the flowering of man." "Man flows at once to God when the channel of purity is open. By turns our purity inspires and our impurity casts us down. He is blessed who is assured that the animal is dying out in him day by day, and the divine being established." [25]

All of this seems like an invitation to deliberate austerity—to a moral vegetarianism of some sort. But in the puzzling conclusion to Thoreau's meditation, the way to be chaste was not to deny the senses through self-conscious asceticism but rather to "work earnestly, though it be at cleaning a table." As if to underline the radical nature of his prescription, Thoreau recounted the cryptic fable of John Farmer, who "sat at his door one September evening, after a hard day's work, his mind still running on his labor more or less." Farmer had bathed and now wished "to recreate his intellectual man." "He had not attended to the train of his thoughts long when he heard some one playing on a flute, and that sound harmonized with his mood." The notes John Farmer heard "gently did away with the street, and the village, and the state in which he lived. A voice said to him,—Why do you stay here and live this mean moiling life, when a glorious existence is possible for you? Those same stars twinkle over other fields than these." [26]

The results of the reverie point toward a complexity that Thoreau's "startlingly moral" discussion only opaquely reveals. "But how to come out of this condition and actually migrate thither?" the fable had John Farmer query. "All that he could think of was to practise some new austerity, to let his mind descend into his body and redeem it, and treat himself with ever increasing respect." [27]

Evidently, Farmer should have worked some new field—or should have worked his own field in a radically new and dedicated way. Here, indeed, were a program—and a questioning—that went beyond Emerson. And here was a purification of the senses, not to close them off but the better to engage them. [28] Still, even as Thoreau strove to play the pagan, the nature he worshiped led beyond itself. "Man flows at once to God when the channel of purity is open," Thoreau had said. The trail to vegetarianism was also the trail to a confused, but still operative, idealism. Beyond that, it was the trail to an idealism cast in moral (and Calvinist) categories, to a control of nature as much as to a harmony with it.

"I long ago lost a hound, a bay horse, and a turtle-dove, and am still on their trail," Thoreau had written in a puzzling passage in "Economy," the first chapter of *Walden*. He had, he said, spoken to many travelers about them, "describing their tracks and what calls they answered to." But his queries brought no reclamation of his own, only the reports of "one or two who had heard the hound, and the tramp of the horse, and even seen the dove disappear behind a cloud." On the trail of the animal and the sensuous, Thoreau moved between the economic bite of loss and the other economy of quest. He could talk with a few travelers who "seemed as anxious to recover them [hound, horse, and dove] as if they had lost them themselves."[29] But—ironically, in a search for the tangibly real—Thoreau had to keep his eye on the far horizon, on the place that was high, cloudy, and ideal. And to transpose his own words about John Farmer, "all that he [Thoreau] could think of" was the need to repossess—and so to tame and control—the elusive animal power.

Nor was the Thoreau of "Higher Laws" and "Economy" anomalous. Take, for instance, his well-known essay "Walking," an emphatic witness to the religion of real earth. Thoreau reveled in the earthiness as he proclaimed the delights of the "saunterer." "In my walks," he announced, "I would fain return to my senses. What business have I in the woods, if I am thinking of something out of the woods?" This was no mere verbal formula, for there was something even scatological about Thoreau's nature religion. "When I would recreate myself," he wrote,

I seek the darkest wood, the thickest and most interminable, and, to the citizen, most dismal swamp. I enter a swamp as a sacred place,—a *sanctum sanctorum*. There is the strength, the marrow of Nature. The wildwood covers the virgin mould,—and the same soil is good for men and for trees. A man's health requires as many acres of meadow to his prospect as his farm does loads of muck.[30]

We hear echoes of John Farmer's attempt to "recreate his intellectual man," and it is clearer how and why Farmer's meditation resolution was wrong. But if "life consists with wildness," as Thoreau said, and if, as he also insisted with creedal solemnity, he believed "in the forest, and in the meadow, and in the night in which the corn grows," his mucky swamp of wildness underwent a curious transformation as the essay progressed. Wildness, it turned out, was necessary to develop higher faculties: the nourishment of the watery swamp was the nourishment for a more elevated *mist*—and an attempt to reach beyond the still earthly mist to the sun. "My desire to bathe my head in atmospheres unknown to my feet is perennial and constant," Thoreau declared. He sought "Sympathy with Intelligence," a "higher knowledge" that was "the lighting up of the mist by the sun." "With respect to knowledge," he owned, "we are all children of the mist." Indeed, "this vast, savage, howling mother of ours, Nature," was also "a personality so vast and universal that we have never seen one of her features."[31]

We can suspect a Transcendentalist leap into at least the borderland of idealism here. And Thoreau did nothing to disconfirm the suspicion as he concluded the piece. "We hug the earth,—how rarely we mount!" he exclaimed. "Methinks we might elevate ourselves a little more." Underlining the point in a narrative symbol, he told the story of the time he climbed a white pine tree tall on a hilltop. He found flowers no one else had seen: "on the ends of the topmost branches only, a few minute and delicate red cone-like blossoms, the fertile flower of the white pine looking heavenward." But to gaze at the flowers of the pine, Thoreau—in a posture that subtly recalled the earlier Thomas Jefferson—was in the high place. From this perspective the moral character of the flowers was clear. "Nature has from the first expanded the minute blossoms of the forest only toward the heavens, above men's heads and unobserved by them." We might suspect that the lost hound, horse, and dove of "Economy," always on the farther side of the horizon, silently assented. Thus it was to a metaphysical religion of nature that Thoreau pointed when, in the final lines of "Walking," with swamp and wildwood behind him, he intoned: "So we saunter toward the Holy Land, till one day the sun shall shine more brightly than ever he has done, shall perchance shine into our minds and hearts, and light up our whole lives with a great awakening light, as warm and serene and golden as on a bank-side in autumn."[32]

Thoreau had not found the world illusory, as the asceticism of "Higher Laws" and the vanished animal power of "Economy" in some ways suggested, but—in the move from swamp to mist to awakening sun—he had found it penultimate. What Donald Worster called Thoreau's "vacillation between pagan naturalism and a transcendental moral vision" was, even with its sharper emphasis on the naturalism, a muted version of the dilemma of Emerson's *Nature*.[33] Thoreau *did* move further than the older, more conservative Emerson toward the spiritual paganism of one kind of nature religion. But he never fully got there. And even John Muir, his celebrated spiritual heir in the preservationist movement, never fully got there either.

Thoreau, in fact, had already pointed toward the preservationist path that Muir would walk. "In Wildness is the preservation of the World," he had written in "Walking." And in "Huckleberries," he had made his case for preservation in terms that were practical and compelling. "Let us try to keep the new world new, and while we make a wary use of the city, preserve as far as possible the advantages of living in the country," he urged. He went on to offer practical suggestions for other citizens. "If there is any central and commanding hill-top, it should be reserved for the public use," Thoreau wrote. "If the people of Massachusetts are ready to found a professorship of Natural History—so they must see the importance of preserving some portions of nature herself unimpaired." And, he continued, "I think that each town should have a park, or rather a primitive forest, of five hundred or a thousand acres, either in one body or several—where a stick should never be cut for fuel—nor for the navy, nor to make wagons, but stand and decay for higher uses—a common possession forever, for instruction and recreation." [34]

"In God's wildness lies the hope of the world—the great fresh unblighted, unredeemed wilderness," John Muir would later write in his journal. Between the two men and before the two men, there was an environmental religion of nature that resonated with the first affirmations of Emerson's *Nature* and with the more pagan affirmations of Henry David Thoreau. It even resonated, in part, with their Puritanism, as Sacvan Bercovitch and Mason Lowance have pointed out. But, moving away from Puritanism to Thoreau's land of mists and vapors, nineteenth-century nature writers proclaimed a new gospel. Many were imbued with a romanticism that was "biocentric," seeing all of nature as alive and demanding a human moral response. Nature, as Barbara Novak has observed, became a "natural church" that fostered a sense of communion. If "from vernal woods" America could "learn more of good and evil than from learned sages," Perry Miller asked more than three decades ago, "could it not also learn from that source more conveniently than from divine revelation?"[35]

Not that the nation would formally reject the Bible. On the contrary, it could even more energetically proclaim itself Christian and cherish the churches; but it could derive its inspiration from the mountains, the lakes, the forests. There was nothing mean or niggling about these, nothing utilitarian. Thus, superficial appearances to the contrary, America is not crass, materialistic: it is Nature's nation, possessing a heart that watches and receives.[36]

It was a heart, too, that expected the millennium of things to come; and the paradise of the natural world was a sign of perfection growing in the nation. Thoreau purified his senses to make a "perfect body," and Emerson recollected that from man "sprang the sun and moon"—both men fully of a piece with much in the popular mentality.[37] Paradoxically, to turn to nature meant to share something of what was happening in the great revivals of the era, when men and women said they received new hearts and spirits, knowing themselves now perfect and without blemish. Perfectionism had become an American way to think; and, for those to whom God and nature were virtually one, preservation of the wild came to mean saving the space in which the human spirit could stretch to its limits. It came to mean, in short, the time of millennial dawn.

Moreover, even as the millennium dawned, new understandings of the sublime were at the disposal of nineteenth-century people. Now especially marking the presence of God in nature, the sublime lost some of its eighteenth-century trappings of fear and gloomy majesty, in a luminist perception of divine glory.[38] For a nation still at least partially under the spell of Calvinism and drawn continually to the evangelical message of the revival, the guilt of the embrace of matter could be assuaged in idealism. At the same time, the joy of the embrace could be celebrated in a religion of nature that reveled in field, hill, and stream. The sublime meant new revelation and, as Barbara Novak would have it, could even signal the apocalyptic moment of destruction or the more intimate moment of personal conversion. Under the aegis of romanticism, the sublime evoked distant pasts and beckoning futures, telling of freedoms in measureless space and canceling the societal present in the timeless present of nature.

In this context, the William Cullen Bryant whom we saw contemplating nature in "Thanatopsis" was harbinger of a new age of perception. It should be no surprise that throughout the nineteenth century, as Lee Clark Mitchell has shown, preservationists sounded the alarm as "witnesses to a vanishing America." As early as 1833, George Catlin had suggested the idea of a national park, predating by decades Thoreau's more modest exhortations for town and village forests. With the possession of a vast public domain to support the endeavor, it was possible for state and national governments to consider reserving land for its spectacular beauty or, later, simply because it was wilderness. Moreover, there was, as Mitchell noted, "ambivalence felt among even those who participated in the nation's triumphant conquest of the wilderness." [39]

But it was the presence of the religion of nature that gave to preservationism its vital force. And that presence was nowhere better expressed than in the life and words of John Muir, the man who, more than any other person, rallied public support and legislative votes to the preservationist cause. From 1868 to 1908, Lee Mitchell has written, Muir was "America's premier naturalist." And through it all, Michael P. Cohen has suggested, Muir was the man who "articulated for America just how important it was for men to live in and through a loving relationship to Nature." [40]

In Muir's complex response to wilderness we can find the inherited Calvinism he shared with Emerson and Thoreau (as well as so many others). And we find, expressly, the romantic Transcendentalism he learned from them, mingling idealistic and—more than they (especially, more than Emerson)—pantheistic-vitalistic strains. Certainly what distinguished Muir most from them and from other writers on the sublime in nature was that he joined a personal religion of nature to a rhetoric inspiring his readers to direct action to preserve the wilderness. [41] The rhetorical process began, however, in Muir's private religious experience. And so it is to Muir's personal life that we turn in order to understand the religious grounding of the preservationist movement he led.

Born in 1838 in Dunbar, Scotland, Muir immigrated to Wisconsin with his family when he was eleven years old. His father, Daniel, a Presbyterian turned Disciple of Christ, reared his children in what Linnie Marsh Wolfe has called "a stern heritage." [42] John Muir rebelled. After a stint at the University of Wisconsin, he spent his time wilderness walking, botanizing, and odd jobbing. Then, when an industrial accident in Indianapolis nearly blinded him, Muir left for a southern walking tour and subsequently sailed for California and the valley of the Yosemite.

When he found Yosemite, Muir found himself. From 1868, his life achieved a growing sense of purpose, culminating in the series of articles and books he wrote, first on the glaciation theory as an explanation for the formation of Yosemite Valley and then, increasingly, on the grandeur and spiritual power of the mountain environment. By 1874 he was consciously working to publicize the human value of wilderness experience in the mountains, and his public career as a preservationist was launched. Its successes in the establishment of Yosemite National Park, in the foundation of the Sierra Club, and in telling Americans of the importance of wild land are too well-known to require more than mention here.[43]

The nature religion that undergirded this public expression was hardly so simple as a bit of "transcendental" mountain joy. Rather, this religion was an intricate act, an artful working of old and new that integrated past with present without any apparent self-consciousness on Muir's part. Not to be dismissed was the lingering Calvinism that trailed him, and indeed, as for the Transcendentalists and others, Muir's idealism provided a way to accommodate a former Calvinism without acknowledging it. If the world in all its alluring beauty pointed beyond itself to spirit, then, as we have noted, it could be safe to contemplate matter without guilt or stain. And so long as one held onto the emblematic theory that nature made sense as sacramental sign of spirit, it could be safe to relish the splendor of mountain and forest.

Moreover, close beside the lingering Calvinism and intrinsic to it came a biblically steeped witness to the glory of the land. The familiar language of nature as the book of God was comfortable for Muir, and, in fact, Michael Cohen has argued that Muir's literal language of glory was cast in the mold of Old Testament usage, signifying the presence of God. As Cohen has also shown, the Yosemite experience that integrated Muir and gave direction to his life was one of religious awakening or conversion. The witness of Muir's mountaineering narratives was the record of what happened. "If there is such a thing as a 'wilderness experience,'" wrote Cohen, "these narratives attempt to say what that might be.

It is the most powerful kind of religious conversion, and is not to be seen as anything less than complete rebirth." [44]

Climbing Mount Ritter in the High Sierra, Muir gave the public something of a sense of the inner drama. Gazing at the mountain seemed to be gazing at the Holy. "I could see only the one sublime mountain, the one glacier, the one lake." Although Muir admitted that he could not expect to reach the top from the side where he was, he "moved on across the glacier as if driven by fate." He was becoming "conscious of a vague foreboding of what actually befell," when he found that he must climb a sheer cliff carved by an avalanche if he wanted to continue. "After gaining a point about half-way to the top, I was suddenly brought to a dead stop, with arms outspread, clinging close to the face of the rock, unable to move hand or foot either up or down. My doom appeared fixed. I *must* fall." [45] What happened next evoked in translation the revival rhetoric of deliverance.

When this final danger flashed upon me, I became nerve-shaken for the first time since setting foot on the mountains, and my mind seemed to fill with a stifling smoke. But this terrible eclipse lasted only a moment, when life blazed forth again with preternatural clearness. I seemed suddenly to become possessed of a new sense. The other self, bygone experiences, Instinct, or Guardian Angel,—call it what you will,—came forward and assumed control. Then my trembling muscles became firm again, every rift and flaw in the rock was seen as through a microscope, and my limbs moved with a positiveness and precision with which I seemed to have nothing at all to do. Had I been borne aloft upon wings, my deliverance could not have been more complete.

. . . I found a way without effort, and soon stood upon the topmost crag in the blessed light. [46]

Muir had been saved by his body's assertion of its oneness with nature, and rescue came through somatic forces that assumed control. They were of the earth and yet transcendental, just as Muir's religion of nature would always be both. But Muir had been saved to become what Cohen called "a fundamentalist of the wilderness." If he saw the mountains dissolved in holy light, he must spread the gospel to the nation. John of the mountains was John the Baptist: "Heaven knows that John Baptist was not more eager to get all his fellow sinners into the Jordan than I to baptize all of mine in the beauty of God's mountains." [47] Thus, it was a John-the-Baptist strategy that informed Muir's public efforts, and it was a

Portrait of John Muir at Yosemite. (Courtesy, The Bancroft Library.) The photograph (author unidentified) suggests the numinous quality of Muir's pilgrimage to the Yosemite.

John-the-Baptist passion that he embodied after his wilderness baptism. The Calvinist-tinged Christianity of Muir's childhood, like the Puritanism of Emerson and Thoreau, did not vanish but, instead, played itself out in a different key.

To say that, though, is very far from saying all. For major aspects of Muir's religion of nature carried him well beyond what Christianity taught or could endorse. And if Muir left Christianity deliberately, he did not leave it for trailing vagaries but built upon conscious plan and purpose. "If my soul could get away from this so-called prison," he wrote in 1870, "I should hover about the beauty of our own good star."

I should study Nature's laws in all their crossings and unions; I should follow magnetic streams to their source, and follow the shores of our magnetic oceans. I should go among the rays of the aurora, and follow them to their beginnings, and study their dealings and communions with other powers and expressions of matter. And I should go to the very center of our globe and read the whole splendid page from the beginning.[48]

The physical sense of unity with nature that the Mount Ritter experience signaled made the study of Nature's laws akin to a mystical path. "Now we are fairly into the mountains, and they are into us," Muir wrote, in words that echoed Henry David Thoreau's once-confessed desire, "I to be nature looking into nature." "We are part of nature now," confided Muir to his journal, "neither old or young, but immortal in a terrestrial way, neither sick or well." All the wilderness "in unity and interrelation" was "alive and familiar." Indeed, "the very stones" seemed "talkative, sympathetic, brotherly." Out of a sense of sympathy with the animals, Muir would not hunt, and he often went hungry in the wilds.[49]

And if Muir was one with all of nature, so was God. In fact, as Linnie Marsh Wolfe tells, the maturing Muir began to substitute in his manuscripts the words "Nature" or "Beauty" for "God" or "Lord." Nature was "one soul" before God; but, more, nature was divinity incarnate. Muir would "fuse in spirit skies" and "touch naked God" because "all of the individual 'things' or 'beings' into which the world is wrought are sparks of the Divine Soul variously clothed upon with flesh, leaves, or that harder tissue called rock, water, etc." "All of these varied forms, high and low," he wrote, "are simply portions of God radiated from Him as a sun, and made terrestrial by the clothes they wear, and by the modifications of a corresponding kind in the God essence itself." [50] Indeed, man was the highest, most godlike being because he contained the most of matter:

The more extensively terrestrial a being becomes, the higher it ranks among its fellows, and the most terrestrial being is the one that contains all the others, that has, indeed, flowed through all the others and borne away parts of them, building them into itself. Such a being is man, who has flowed down through other forms of being and absorbed and assimilated portions of them into himself, thus becoming a microcosm most richly Divine because most richly terrestrial. [51]

To promote things terrestrial, there were transcendental communion feasts. "Every purely natural object," declared Muir, "is a conductor of divinity." In language that evokes Thoreau's purification of the senses, he owned: "We have but to expose ourselves in a clean condition to any of these conductors, to be fed and nourished by them. Only in this way can we procure our daily spirit bread. Only thus may we be filled with the Holy Ghost." [52]

Muir had found that "the clearest way into the Universe is through a forest wilderness," and in Yosemite he rejoiced at the sequoia sacrament he tasted. In an ecstatic letter to Jeanne Carr in the fall of 1870, Muir's eucharist made Thoreau's feast on woodchuck and huckleberry seem almost anemic. "Do behold the King in his glory, King Sequoia," Muir began. What followed was utterly remarkable. "Behold! Behold! seems all I can say. Some time ago I left all for Sequoia: have been & am at his feet fasting & praying for light, for is he not the greatest light in the woods; in the world." [53]

I'm in the woods woods woods, & they are in *me-ee-ee*. The King tree & me have sworn eternal love—sworn it without swearing & I've taken the sacrament with Douglass Squirrell drank Sequoia wine, Sequoia blood, & with its rosy purple drops I am writing this woody gospel letter. I never before knew the virtue of Sequoia juice. Seen with sunbeams in it, its color is the most royal of all royal purples. No wonder the Indians instinctively drink it for they know not what. I wish I was so drunk & Sequoical that I could preach the green brown woods to all the juiceless world, descending from this divine wilderness like a John Baptist eating Douglass Squirrels & wild honey or wild anything, crying, Repent for the Kingdom of Sequoia is at hand.

There is balm in these leafy Gileads; pungent burrs & living King-juice for all defrauded civilization; for sick grangers & politicians, no need of Salt rivers sick or successful. Come Suck Sequoia & be saved.[54]

The letter continued, exuding sequoia rapture and closing with a reference to Lord Sequoia. Muir had successfully taken biblical language and inverted it to proclaim the passion of attachment, not to a supernatural world but to a natural one. To go to the mountains and the sequoia forests, for Muir, was to engage in religious worship of utter seriousness and dedication; to come down from the mountains and preach the gospel of preservation was to live out his life according to the ethic that his religion compelled. Millennialism and a sense of the sublime intertwined to praise an earthy paradise and, at the same time, to effect its salvation.

The note of rapture pervades John Muir's personal writings, and it is clear that for him nature religion meant nature *worship* as consistent theme. Wolfe tells us that Muir tried to keep the "unutterable things" out of his articles, but Christine Oravec's fine study of his language convinces that enough got past the censor to evoke something of his mood for countless other Americans.[55] But what direct connection, if any, does all of this have with Transcendentalism? Are we simply looking at a series of striking parallels, or is there any more proximate linkage? Did John Muir evolve his personal religion and spirituality in actual contact with Emerson or Thoreau or their writings? The answer is that he did and that the rhetorical echoes of Transcendentalism found in Muir's writings are more than coincidental.

In his classic study of wilderness, Roderick Nash remarked that Muir steeped himself in the writings of Emerson and Thoreau during his first winters in the Yosemite. "When the high-country trails opened again, a tattered volume of Emerson's essays, heavily glossed in Muir's hand, went along in his pack." And Wolfe has traced the lineage more thoroughly, beginning with Muir's introduction to Emerson and Thoreau through James Davie Butler, his professor at the University of Wisconsin, and, especially, through Jeanne Carr, wife of his professor Ezra Slocum Carr. Jeanne Carr knew Emerson personally, and it was she who made possible a personal meeting between Muir and the now aging Concord sage when Emerson traveled to California in 1871. Whatever the disappointments of the visit for Muir, (Emerson, "protected" by his friends, did not camp out in Yosemite despite Muir's repeated urgings), he later remembered the incident as one of "the two supreme moments of his life."[56]

Muir's own account of the visit was tinged with sadness at the decline of the Eastern sequoia giant and at the effeteness of his friends. But, more, it spoke of awe and admiration for Emerson among the Sierra trees. "During my first years in the Sierra I was ever calling on everybody within reach to admire them, but I found no one half warm enough until Emerson came. . . . He seemed as serene as a sequoia, his head in the empyrean." "Emerson was the most serene, majestic, sequoia-like soul I ever met," an undated journal entry echoes. "His smile was as sweet and calm as morning light on mountains." "He was as sincere as the trees, his eye sincere as the sun." Indeed, Emerson was one of those who urged Muir to write; and, after the personal encounter with the Transcendentalist, he began to study Emerson's essays the more seriously. He did not always agree with them, as Stephen Fox's amusing account of Muir's blunt marginal notes makes clear. But the two corresponded, and Emerson added Muir's name as the last in his short list of those he esteemed "My Men."[57]

Compared with this, Muir's relationship to Henry David Thoreau was at once cooler and closer. It was cooler because Muir never knew or met Thoreau personally (Thoreau was already dead in 1862). It was closer because there was a nearer meeting of minds between the two and a clearer rhetorical dependency on Thoreau in some of Muir's writings. Linnie Marsh Wolfe wrote that it was Thoreau, among the authors Muir best loved, "whom he came in maturity to regard as the wisest of them all." More than that, Michael Cohen supplies details of how Muir modeled his language and literary strategy on Thoreau's. Muir dubbed himself in later life "a self appointed inspector of gorges, gulches, and glaciers," echoing Thoreau's *Walden* confession.[58] Muir's narrative account *My First Summer in the Sierra* likewise followed *Walden* in compressing several summers into one. Meanwhile, his rhetoric of wildness surely owed a debt to the New Englander.

There *were* differences between the two. Cohen has noted that Muir "neither believed that Nature was making certain parts of the earth for man, nor that she could be hostile." And Thoreau's exposure to wild country, impressive as it was in the Maine woods, was mostly in the neighborhood of Concord. The "domestic embrace" of Tichi was both his gift and his limit. On the other hand, unlike Thoreau, Muir's exposure to Eastern religious classics was severely limited. He read his first Hindu book (sent to him by Jeanne Carr) at Yosemite; and it was not until 1903 and a trip around the world that he traveled to India and recorded Hindu materials in his journal.[59]

Stephen Fox has argued that "evidently Emerson and Thoreau only corroborated ideas that Muir had already worked out independently."[60] If so, they provided a powerful language for articulating these ideas. And, if we accept the force of words in evoking and elaborating thought, Emerson and Thoreau gave to Muir a profoundly important instrument for forging his own religious view. For the continuities between Muir and the older Transcendentalists were unmistakable. In fact, in spite of the missionary zeal for wilderness that fueled his life, as late as 1873 Muir, with Emerson and Thoreau, could recognize contemplation as his vocation. Muir would "stand in what all the world would call an idle manner, literally gaping with all the mouths of soul and body, demanding nothing, fearing nothing, but hoping and enjoying enormously. So-called sentimental, transcendental dreaming seems the only sensible and substantial business that one can engage in."[61]

And what are we to make of such idealist intrusions as Muir's "Rock is not light, not heavy, not transparent, not opaque, but every pore gushes, glows like a thought with immortal life"? How are we to read his reference to the *"grand show"* that was "eternal?" Or this equally transcendental utterance?

How infinitely superior to our physical senses are those of the mind! The spiritual eye sees not only rivers of water but of air. It sees the crystals of the rock in rapid sympathetic motion, giving enthusiastic obedience to the sun's rays, then sinking back to rest in the night. The whole world is in motion to the center.

. . . Imagination is usually regarded as a synonym for the unreal. Yet is true imagination healthful and real, no more likely to mislead than the coarser senses. Indeed, the power of imagination makes us infinite.[62]

But, even as Muir praised the infinity of imagination, he embraced the harmonial vision that celebrated the concrete spirituality of nature. As early as 1869, at Smoky Jack's sheep camp, he was

exclaiming on the "perfect harmony in all things here." In mountain thoughts on the Sierra, he heard the "pure and sure and universal" harmony of "the Song of God, sounding on forever." Later,
as he described the mountains of California for readers, he told of
"the arrangement of the forests in long, curving bands, braided together into lace-like patterns" and noted that the "key to this beautiful harmony" was the "ancient glaciers."[63]

That the vision was also an ethic was clear from Muir's gentle-
ness in nature, from his unwillingness to do the violence that the
life of a hunter demanded. In fact, Cohen faults him for the very
reason that the harmonial ethic in general is often faulted: for not
facing the realities of eater and eaten, of violence and vulnerable
dependency, that make of life a savage, often destructive communion. Even so, harmony was a lived experience that seemed to rise
out of deep levels of Muir's personality. There was the Mount
Ritter experience with his "other self," some greater power in nature—external or internal—that took over in him, integrating all
of his faculties in its service. And Muir told of a similar experience
in 1873 on Mount Whitney, when the other self forced him to go
back instead of trying, under perilous conditions, to scale the summit. He felt, he said, "as if Someone caught me by the shoulders
and turned me around forcibly, saying 'Go back' in an audible
voice." "Muir made no secret," observed his biographer Wolfe, "of
his faith in guidance by the not yet understood forces of nature either within or without ourselves."[64]

Muir's empirical sympathy with these forces was revealed again
in a series of telepathic incidents that followed him. He found the
missing link to his glaciation theory, the evidence that he needed
and had sought, because of a strong and overpowering intuition.
On North Dome at Yosemite, he sensed with categorical certainty
that his former professor James Davie Butler was below in the
valley. He obeyed internal promptings to travel east in time for
both his father's and his mother's death. Significantly, when asked
once how he explained such events, his answer affirmed the transcendental harmony. "Anyone who lives close to the mountains is
sensitive to these things," he said. Indeed, by the end of his life
Muir had even made his peace with spiritualism, holding for it "a
basis of truth" that was "founded on natural laws."[65]

Hence, as a latter-day Transcendentalist, Muir championed, for the most part, the side of the Transcendentalist gospel that proclaimed the spiritual power in nature. His idealism—an apology to his once-and-former Calvinism—was a muted breed, more muted even than the idealism of Henry David Thoreau. Meanwhile, his embrace of nature went beyond Emerson and Thoreau in its sensuousness, in its sheer and unqualified delight in matter. Lord Sequoia and the sequoia sacrament had made of Muir a religious radical, seeing in the stuff of the earth the ultimacy that others had placed in the starry sky and in the God beyond the stars.

Muir had been a do-it-yourself theologian and, like a Wisconsin farmer, had grown his own creed and ethic out of various seeds supplied. Moreover, the preservationist movement he led found its life and strength, as Stephen Fox has so well argued, in amateurs. By the first decade of the new century, "back to nature" was becoming, for many, a national slogan. Natural history writers such as John Burroughs, James Oliver Curwood, Jack London, and Stewart Edward White were being avidly read, while Gene Stratton Porter was writing wilderness novels that were bestsellers. The Boy Scouts appeared in 1910, followed two years later by the Girl Scouts; more and more summer camps "rescued" urban children from their plight. Meanwhile, the publication in 1906 of the collected works of Henry David Thoreau brought a new generation of readers to real or imagined Walden Ponds. National park visitors, Fox tells us, climbed from 69,000 in 1908 to 200,000 two years later and to 335,000 in 1915.[66]

Even as the visitors filed through the gates of the national parks, however, other Americans (perhaps some of the same Americans) were pledging allegiance to a different, more ostensibly religious movement. Like preservationism, this, the metaphysical movement, drank from many streams, some of them centuries old. It drew sustenance, too, from popular contemporary ideas of science, as well as from mesmeric and Swedenborgian views. But, for whatever other reasons it succeeded (and there were many), metaphysical religion succeeded in part because the Transcendentalist confusion about the relative reality of matter and mind was, arguably, paralleled in the popular mentality.

We gain something of a sense of the confusion from a brief article that appeared in *Outlook* magazine in 1903. Manifestly a review of Charles Goodrich Whiting's *Walks in New England,* the piece began by acknowledging the debt that Americans in a back-to-nature mood owed to Emerson, Thoreau, and the Transcendentalists in general. These New Englanders "early gave direction and impulse to a movement which has contributed immensely to the health, vigor, and joy in life of the American people," wrote the unnamed author of the article. *Outlook's* reviewer went on to reflect on the meaning of nature, telling readers that it was "more than birds and flowers, animals and trees." It was, instead, "a middle ground between God and man" and "the playground of the soul . . . full of marvelous analogies with the life of man."[67]

The ambiguity was already unmistakable, but what came next suggested an author with one foot in the preservationist camp and the other in a metaphysical class meeting. "There is no better approach to truth," observed the writer, "than going into the fields with the open mind and the quick imagination." "The gospel of nature that Emerson preached was the gospel of the personal relation of every man to the world about him, and through that world to God." Even so, the reviewer felt sufficiently threatened by the charge that Emerson might be "unscientific" to speak for the defense. "Emerson," he or she wrote, "was not unscientific; the view of the true poet is always scientific; for by science one means the recognition of all the facts of nature and not of a single order of facts." Weaving in dutiful references to the Whiting book, the author concluded with a lengthy quotation from its text. Significantly, the penultimate sentence hailed the valley of Paradise, out of which "flow the streams of healing for the discomforts of civilization."[68]

Outlook had provided a catalog of overlapping concerns that led, associatively, from preservationism to mind cure. Not that we can be certain that the same individuals to any great degree embraced both; but, in the mental climate that produced the Transcendentalist inconsistency, language for soothing a pervasive national trouble became available. "Mind cure, like the conservation movement which developed during the same period," Gail Thain Parker noticed insightfully, "gave thousands of Americans a way of expressing the fear that their personal resources were inadequate to the demands of the twentieth century. The All-Supply and the national park system, influx and the strenuous life—these were the dreams of people who felt crowded and pinched."[69] And, we could add, they were also the dreams of those who felt the need for greater control and mastery.

For an American culture that, even in the middle years of the nineteenth century, had "stressed Mind—Mind raised to the level of divinity,"[70] the early manifestations of metaphysical religion in what became New Thought are not surprising. What may at first appear so, however, is that the New Thought movement (and, beside it, even in part Christian Science) expressed a form of nature religion. To understand what this statement may mean beyond a tour de force of the Emersonian logic, we need a longer look at American metaphysical religion. And there is no better way to gain a sense of its presence than to turn to its embryonic stages in the life and teachings of Phineas Parkhurst Quimby. Like preservationism's John Muir, Quimby gave the metaphysical movement an identifiable leader as a do-it-yourself, amateur theologian. Not Elijah for Muir's John the Baptist, Quimby still profoundly influenced a generation of disciples. Indeed, before his death in 1866, he had been doctor and teacher to metaphysical leaders ranging from New Thought's Warren Felt Evans and Julius and Annetta Dresser to Christian Science's Mary Baker Eddy.

Quimby had been engaged in the practice of spiritual healing for the twenty-five years prior to his death. But he had begun as a clockmaker and had then become a stage performer in a demonstration of clairvoyance in healing.[71] Traveling the lyceum circuit with an inquiring and critical mind, he pondered how his healing partner, Lucius Burkmar, when mesmerized to reach a trance state, could diagnose and prescribe accurately for illness. Quimby became convinced that the real agent of both Burkmar's knowledge and each would-be patient's cure was the mental (neural) process in the individual or group involved. Burkmar read not merely the ailment but, more, people's beliefs about it. Burkmar's cures worked because of the power of suggestion. Then, in the midst of a continuing effort to test and try, Quimby discovered his own clairvoyant abilities. He parted ways with Burkmar to set up a healing practice that evolved, over the years, further and further from its mesmeric roots.

Mesmeric teaching spoke of animal magnetism and explained that an invisible fluid provided the vehicle for the "mutual influ-

ence between the Heavenly bodies, the Earth and Animate Bodies."
The fluid, permeating all living things, provided a medium for
them, so that "the properties of Matter and the Organic Body depend[ed] on this operation."[72] His power to manipulate this "magnetic" fluid explained for Quimby his success in entrancing Burkmar. But, more important, the presence of the fluid in a balanced
ebb-and-flow pattern guaranteed health and vitality, whereas in-
terruptions resulted in what we know as illness. Bathed in this
fluid (and, thus, material) atmosphere, humans were always in
touch with unseen forces that shaped their lives and destinies.
Therefore, when illness struck, the magnetic doctor acted as hero-
priest, using his or her innate animal magnetism to alter the flow
in the invisible fluid—to unblock obstruction—so that a steady
supply of the life-force could reach the ailing person.

Quimby never forgot this magnetic cosmology. Assuredly, he
moved into what should properly be called mental healing, but his
explanation of disease and cure retained something of the mesmeric model. The power of the magnetic theory as a means of
imaging the mysterious process of sickness and health continued
to persuade in new ways. Thus, in writings that bear all the marks
of their roughshod construction, Quimby hammered out a confused—but still commanding—theology of healing, forming a charter document for American metaphysical religion. Even in collated
and edited form, Quimby's writings carry the imprint of a fresh
and inquisitive mind, an American "original" constructing his
world out of bits and pieces that culture supplied.[73]

Take, for example, Quimby's sometime reflections on the "odor"
of illness. In a striking series of references, Quimby linked the invisible substance that was altered in the magnetic state to the odor
or "atmosphere" of disease. "Now where and what was this invisible something that could pass in and out of matter?" he asked of
mesmerism and clairvoyance. He thought the answer required
going back to the "First Cause," "back of language," and he found
there the primacy of the sense of smell for attracting man and
beast to food. For Quimby it was only a small jump from the sense
of smell to the power of speech. "The sense of smell," he argued,
was "the foundation of language," and "as language was introduced the sense of smell became more blunt till like other instincts
it gave way to another standard." Thinking, it followed, "came to

be as much of a sense as smelling." Hence, when Quimby confronted disease, he was able to diagnose by a process akin to smelling. When a woman brought her sick five-year-old son for him to help, Quimby observed that the boy's "feelings were as intelligent as any odor with which I am familiar."[74]

The associative links he had pointed toward, however imprecisely, were still clear. Magnetic fluid, as invisible attractive force, was like odor, which was also an invisible attractive force. And, similarly, thought, as an evolved and added human sense, was also like odor in being an invisible attractive force. "To every disease there is an odor, [mental atmosphere]," wrote Quimby, "and every one is affected by it when it comes within his consciousness. Every one knows that he can produce in himself heat or cold by excitement. So likewise he can produce the odor of any disease so that he is affected by it."[75]

Nor is this all. Elsewhere Quimby escalated more. The magnetic fluid—the life-force—must by implication be the living power of God upholding the creation. God was "the great mesmeriser or magnet," who spoke "man or the idea into existence." And odor assumed still greater meaning in its linkage with "Wisdom."

Now suppose that man calls Wisdom the First Cause, and that from this Wisdom there issues forth an essence that fills all space, like the odor of a rose. This essence, like the odor, contains the character or wisdom of its father, or author, and man's wisdom wants a name given to it, so man calls this essence God. Then you have wisdom manifest in God or the essence, then this essence would be called the Son of Wisdom. Then Wisdom said, "let us create matter or mind or man in our image," or in the likeness of this essence or God. So they formed man out of the odor called matter or dust, that rises from the grosser matter, and breathed into him the living essence, or God, and the matter took the form of man.[76]

Quimby had moved from magnetism to mind. His homespun theology had provided a muddled link between matter and spirit, achieving through the metaphor of odor a cohesion that hid as much as it revealed. Like Emerson and so many other Americans, Quimby was having things both ways and any way he liked. In fact, as he explained elsewhere, like Wisdom (or Truth) error was "an element or odor." And since, as he also said, "the minds of individuals mingle like atmospheres," it was clearly easy for error, like a noxious magnetic fluid, to spread. "Man, like the earth," was continually "throwing off a vapor," and the vapor contained "his knowledge." [77]

Quimby's ability for original synthesis did not stop with the theories of Franz Anton Mesmer. His writings also suggest his acquaintance with the teaching of the eighteenth-century visionary theologian Emanuel Swedenborg, although neither in this case nor in the case of Mesmer can we surmise that he had firsthand knowledge. But certainly, at least through his patient and student Warren Felt Evans, who had left the Methodist ministry for the Swedenborgian New Church, Quimby would have come to know major Swedenborgian themes. The doctrine of correspondence, revived and reinterpreted by Swedenborg—and promulgated by the Transcendentalists—was not lost on the American healer. In fact, correspondence was key to Quimby's understanding of illness. "I know that a belief in any disease will create a chemical change in the mind," he declared, "and that a person will create a phenomenon corresponding to the symptoms." "Every phenomenon that takes form in the human body is first conceived in the mind," observed Quimby; and, more generally, "every idea having a form visible to the world of matter, is admitted by that world as matter." [78]

Swedenborg's view of divine influx in the natural world was, in general outline, not unlike Mesmer's model of invisible fluid. Even further, in his copious reports of his visionary experience, Swedenborg had collapsed the distinction between matter and spirit in ways that could encourage a similar indistinction in the popular mentality. Swedenborg's three heavens were filled with color and odor, with houses and gardens that strikingly resembled those of the Swedish nobility of his time. On the other hand, he taught that heaven and hell were essentially internal states. Swedenborg's teaching on "conjugial marriage" told of nuptial bliss in the world beyond this one; and his doctrine of God waxed on the Divine Human and its role in making heaven human. "Heaven in its entire complex reflects a single Man," Swedenborg had written, "and corresponds to all things and each thing in man." And again, he had affirmed, spiritual or substantial things were "the beginnings of material things." [79]

It is, of course, impossible to trace these conceptions in the writings of Quimby, but they were, to borrow his language, part of his odor and atmosphere. And perhaps that odor and atmosphere were most clearly expressed in Quimby's allusions to "spiritual matter." Here, at the heart of his understanding of his healing practice, he bequeathed his followers a confusion as ripe with ambiguity as Swedenborg's—and the Transcendentalists'—had been. In his autobiographical reminiscences relating his work with Lucius Burkmar, Quimby owned that he thought of "mind" as "something that could be changed." What followed for him is somewhat startling. "I called it [mind] spiritual matter, because I found it could be condensed into a solid and receive a name called 'tumor,' and by the same power under a different direction it might be dissolved and made to disappear." [80]

Not to be identified with the First Cause, mind was matter, and so was thought. Disease, therefore, was "what follows the disturbance of the mind or spiritual matter." Or, in an inverted expression of the same view, disease came from the "spiritual body," while mind was "the spiritual earth which receives the seed of Wisdom, and also the seeds of the wisdom of this world of reason." "Disease is the fruit of the latter," he went on, explaining also that "the application of the wisdom of God or Science is the clearing away the foul rubbish that springs up in the soil or mind." These innuendos suggest that for Quimby there was something—First Cause, Wisdom, the Christ (in many of his references)—that lay beyond even spiritual matter. And so, as with Swedenborg and the Transcendentalists, matter shaded off into another realm, and the inexpressible took on the familiar contours of idealism. Quimby's New Thought editor, Horatio W. Dresser, tells us that the "true Science" or "wisdom" Quimby sought would "take into account man's real as opposed to his apparent condition" and that its basis lay, in part, in "the discovery that the human spirit possesses senses or powers which function independently of matter." [81]

In fact, if the mind was "spiritual matter," Quimby thought the body "nothing but a dense shadow, condensed into what is called matter, or ignorance of God or Wisdom." Writing to a patient from Portland, Maine, in 1860, he explained how he could affect her through absent healing. "You are as plain before my eyes as you were when I was talking to the shadow in Portland," he assured her. "For the shadow came with the substance, and that which I am talking to now is the substance." In another letter to a patient a month later, he identified eternal life with "Christ or Science," adding that "this teaches us that matter is a mere shadow of a substance which the natural man never saw nor can see, for it is never changed, is the same today and forever." "The wisdom of God," Quimby wrote again, "sees matter as a cloud or substance that has a sort of life (in the appearance)." [82]

But, tellingly, he called the substance "the essence of Wisdom" and declared it to be "in every living form." "Like a seed in the earth, it grows or develops in matter," he said. [83] There is no avoiding the ambiguity in the teaching—an ambiguity that dissolves into a total mixing of models when we confront the ethical practice that emerged from Quimby's thought. In brief, Quimby was advising, in clear and direct terms, the application of mind over matter. It was by destroying "error" in the "truth" that he would banish disease, by brushing away opinion and belief with true knowledge that, as for Emerson, "a correspondent revolution in things" would follow. Yet, when Quimby *spoke* about what he advised, without apology he identified it with laws of sympathy and harmony that evoke a different model.

Consider, for instance, Quimby's explanation of the genesis and treatment of disease. "There is a principle or inward man that governs the outward man or body, and when these are at variance or out of tune, disease is the effect, while by harmonizing them health of the body is the result. . . . This can be brought about by sympathy, and all persons who are sick are in need of this sympathy." Speaking very personally, he revealed details of his healing method. "When I am in communication with the patient, I feel all his pains and his state of mind, and I find that by bringing his spirit back to harmonize with the body he feels better." Or consider, again, this demonstration of the slipperiness of Quimby's logic:

Now as our belief or disease is made up of ideas, which are [spiritual] matter, it is necessary to know what beliefs we are in; for to cure the disease is to correct the error, and as disease is what follows the error, destroy the cause, and the effect will cease. How can this be done? By a knowledge of the law of harmony. [84]

In short, Quimby had effectively shown that there was no difference, for him, between harmonizing and being in charge. He had proclaimed the same double message of the moral life as the Transcendentalists.

Like the Transcendentalists, too, Quimby had problems with the Christianity of the churches. For him, medical doctors and denominational clergy represented a professional establishment of gloom, broadcasting error in the world. "Truth has destroyed the power of the priests," he announced. "Yet it has not enlightened the people, but transferred the idea of disease to the medical fraternity." By contrast, Jesus had explained "where the people had been deceived by the priests and doctors, and if they learned wisdom they would be cured." And again, in language that would have gladdened Emerson had he read it: "The religion that Christ opposed consisted in forms and ceremonies." [85] Yet, as Quimby's identification of Wisdom with Christ or Science already suggests, explicitly Christian teaching figured prominently in his thought. In fact, it is impossible to read more than a few pages of his writing without confronting biblical rhetoric.

Consider, for instance, Quimby's report of Jesus's answer to the Pharisees who had said that he cast out devils by the power of Beelzebub (Matt. 12:24–28; Luke 11:15–20). According to the Quimby version, Jesus rebuked the Pharisees by saying: "If I cast out devils or diseases through Beelzebub or ignorance, my kingdom or science cannot stand; but if I cast out devils or disease through a science or law, then my kingdom or law will stand, for it is not of this world." [86] Nor was this language an exception. Like Thoreau's writings, Quimby's pages were steeped in scripture. Yet, also like Thoreau's writings, it was scripture that, decidedly, had been "doctored." For, Quimby misread the biblical text in blatant and creative ways, molding it into allegory that taught exactly what he wanted to say.

In his own way a theologian of liberal Protestantism, Quimby also allegorically replicated the evangelical and general cultural millennialism of his time. Through knowledge of his "Science" he would bring "new birth" in the perfect body Thoreau had earlier celebrated; and cured by Quimby, a former patient could expect to be a new being. Even more, Quimby was surely the harbinger of a new age. "Then will arise a new heaven and a new earth to free man from disease or error, for this old world or belief shall be burned up with the fire of Science and the new heaven shall arise wherein shall not be found these old superstitions of bigotry and disease, but there will be no more death or sighing from an ache or pain which arises from the superstitions of the old world." [87]

From this perspective, Quimby's mysterious assumption of the pain of his patients assumed the formal character of a communion rite. With neither the huckleberry innocence of Thoreau nor the sequoia passion of Muir, he still enacted a eucharist that pointed toward the new order he would create. "I take upon myself all your feeling and see all your troubles," Quimby wrote, in words that adumbrated the identification he had made. He was a Christ figure for his people, and it was fitting that his communion should now be a communion in pain. But a new age was dawning, and his own understanding of his role in its inauguration was not modest. "I stand alone, as one arisen from the dead, or the old theories, having passed through all the old ideas and risen again, that I may lead you into this light that will open your eyes to the truth of Him who spake as never man spake, and who spake the truth." [88]

In sum, Quimby had managed to knit together major currents in the popular mentality, and in doing so he had shown himself strikingly similar to the Transcendentalists. To be sure, it seems inconceivable that Quimby would not have been aware of Emerson's general teachings, if only through newspaper summaries of his lectures on the lyceum circuit. Indeed, without finding references to Emerson in Quimby's writing, Charles S. Braden could assess that Quimby "was probably either consciously or unconsciously . . . affected by the religious ferment of his time represented by the Transcendentalist thinkers." And, even further, Stewart W. Holmes more than forty years ago could call Quimby "the scientist of Transcendentalism" and argue that he "demonstrated visibly, on human organisms, the operational validity of Emerson's hypotheses." The largest difference Holmes noticed between Quimby and the Emersonians was that Quimby practiced what they preached. [89]

What Holmes did not go on to notice, though (and what has here already been suggested), was that Quimby also mingled in Emerson's "odor and atmosphere" because he constructed an analogously flawed cosmology. In regard to the reality of nature, the doctor had been caught in the same conceptual ambiguity that had shadowed the Transcendentalist. Leaning hard on the idealist side of the equation, Quimby had yet managed to turn in a decidedly physical reading of metaphysical reality; and he had managed a similar confusion in his ethical model. Quimby's religion, like Transcendentalist religion, was caught in the crack: it was still a species of nature religion.

Horatio Dresser tells us that it was not until 1887, well over two decades after Quimby's death, that those who emerged as leaders in the New Thought movement turned to Emerson's writings. In his *Facts and Fictions of Mental Healing,* said Dresser, Charles M. Barrows noticed Emerson's "idealistic wisdom," which he identified with that of ancient India. Others began to follow his cue, and Emerson became prophet to a new generation of mental healers— so much so that by 1963 Charles S. Braden could write that it was "quite customary for New Thought leaders to claim Emerson as the Father of New Thought." As talk of the All-Supply increased, the doctor from Portland was all but forgotten in the embrace of more learned ancestors such as Emerson and Swedenborg.[90] By this time, however, the ambiguousness of Quimby's theology was less fashionable. New Thoughters cultivated idealism more consistently, even as they found ways to transform the material world with Truth. Still, something of Quimby's "vapor" remained—consonant with Transcendentalist vapors and fogs—and New Thought continued to live, in some measure inconsistently, in the breach.

It remained for Mary Baker Eddy, former Quimby patient and student, to achieve the greatest clarity, given the inconsistencies of the heritage. More loyally Calvinist, truer to a Puritan and Congregational ancestry than were any of the others, she pushed the idealist cosmology as far as it would go. But even Mary Baker Eddy could not totally escape the allure of nature. Once, in a poem that evoked Philip Freneau and William Cullen Bryant, she had solemnly addressed an oak on a mountaintop:

> Oh, mountain monarch, at whose feet I stand,—
> Clouds to adorn thy brow, skies clasp thy hand,—
> Nature divine, in harmony profound,
> With peaceful presence hath begirt thee round.

In the first edition of her textbook *Science and Health* (1875), Eddy could own her belief that "man epitomizes the universe, and is the body of God." And she could repudiate "mortal man" as "a very *unnatural* image and likeness of God, immortality," while meta-phors of harmonizing and governing chased each other in her pages. A decade later she could still tell her followers that Jesus "was a natural and divine scientist."[91]

Even at the pinnacle of Eddy's authorial career, as she taught that matter was a false belief and the error of "mortal mind," the final, authoritative edition of *Science and Health* separated nature from matter and found ways to speak admiringly of what Emerson had called his "beautiful mother." "The legitimate and only pos-sible action of Truth is the production of harmony," Eddy wrote. "Laws of nature are laws of Spirit."[92] However inconclusively, Eddy had shown that nature religion could be inverted to coexist with the denial of matter. Idealism did not do away with nature: it simply killed nature's body. Wildness had been outlawed and the passing show had been declared an error, but nature still remained.

Yet, while some Americans joined Mary Baker Eddy in the slaughter, more were content to cherish matter, living in the crack between Nature Illusory and Nature Real. In fact, for decades before Eddy came to Christian Science, other healers and their followers were preaching a nature religion that was decidedly physical. Not only present in the mountains and forests, the em-bodied deity of their version lived nearer still. The God of nature, they proclaimed, was the tenured inhabitant of the human body.

4 / Physical Religion ❧ NATURAL SIN AND HEALING GRACE IN THE NINETEENTH CENTURY

In April 1843 a curious testimonial appeared in the *Health Journal and Independent Magazine*. One William A. Ghaskins, a committed follower of the health reformer Sylvester Graham, there confessed:

> I knew nothing at all, then, of the principle that you, Mr. Graham and some others, are laboring to disseminate; yet, there was a something within me,—"a still small voice"—that incessantly whispered to my conscience, in accents too plain to be misunderstood, that I was in "the broad beaten path." About this time, I obtained some extracts from the Graham Journal, or the Health Journal, respecting the laws of life and health. As I had partaken very fully of "the tree of the knowledge of good and evil," my eyes were opened immediately, and I forthwith began to work out my own salvation. . . . I subsisted on a quantity of coarse bread, so small that it was barely sufficient to sustain life. I at the same time paid particular attention to bathing, exercise, &c. I had not proceeded far, before I became as "a little child." . . . My mind underwent a most surprising change, and a flood of light was poured in upon it. It appeared to me that I could see into almost every thing, and I was constantly led to trace effects to their causes. I was able to see into the real nature and moral bearing of the various institutions of Society, and the domestic and religious habits and practices of the busy world around me. . . . I took great delight in reading the Bible, and nearly every passage appeared to unfold some new physiological truth.
>
> I had not long persevered in my new way of living, before my bodily health and social character improved greatly. . . . I was a new creature, physically, morally, and spiritually.[1]

The language of the "broad beaten path" and the "still small voice," of the tree of knowledge and opened eyes, of working out one's salvation and the millennial new creation—all of this, of course, recalls the pervasive evangelical culture of nineteenth-century America. By the early part of the century, the great collective revivals that had transformed Puritanism had swept the land at least twice, and the new evangelical religion of the times had put its premium on the direct experience of individuals as the test of true religion.[2] Now it was not enough to be told or to "believe" in an abstract sense: one had to know the truth by feeling and by doing. The awakening of the early nineteenth century was surely, as Donald Mathews has told us, an "organizing process,"[3] but the basic human material to be organized proved remarkably self-focused.

William Ghaskins had obviously absorbed the message. And when he changed his life radically to heed the injunctions of Grahamism, he understood his decision in evangelical terms. But what also needs to be underlined in this conversion account of sin and grace (and others like it at the time) is that the gospel good news concerned *natural* sin and *natural* grace. This would-be convert had sinned against—not God or Jesus directly but, instead—physiological nature. Violation of nature's immutable laws had brought its stern and debilitating judgment of disease. In like manner, health, when it came, was a work of harmony with the same immutable laws. Healing grace arose in the nature of things when one cooperated with the decrees written into one's physical frame. Hence, the evangelical message had not stifled the Enlightenment: it had only recast it in new form.

The eighteenth century, we recall, had already shown Americans the social utility of Enlightenment thought. Nature had manifested itself for new American patriots as *republican* nature, the fit and perfect concomitant to their political enterprise. Now, in the nineteenth century, for many it was the republic, and not nature, that acted as backdrop.

In the late eighteenth century, nature had been a great machine that moved according to intrinsic laws. Created by God, it had received, in his grand design, an autonomy and absoluteness that meant for order, predictability, and power. Patriots measured political and social realities by how well they corresponded to nature. But patriots *could* also move "naturally" to measure their individual status and worth by how well they corresponded to the natural world.

In the logic that unraveled the connection between body politic and body sole, American democracy became the starting point. It was natural for the community to govern itself, because it had been constituted by social contract, as anyone who had read or heard of John Locke knew.[4] Unlike Europe with its centuries of feudal hierarchy and authority, the new United States was a nation built on the middle class, on farmers who were swiftly turning industrialists. In *this* body politic, all the parts were, at least theoretically, equal and equally needed. Hence, the democratic community already, in its inception, could give way to individualism. It was as though, on the model of the federal system that had transformed the former colonies into states, each autonomous person was a separate planet revolving around the sun. Or, to use another metaphor, each person was an atom spinning in concert with neighboring atoms to form molecules.

Already at the beginning, then, the *idea* of the republic concealed a tension between community and individual. It was assumed that every atom would "naturally" work in harmony with every other, that democracy would be the smooth and oiled running of the great political machine that conformed to nature. In practice, however, the results were often less than satisfactory, and later, in the nineteenth century, the body social would grow too unwieldy for many, lumbering out of shape and out of control. In the new republic, the body perfect would reveal its hidden gaps and its hidden sources of decay and disease. For there were jolting changes.

Indeed, by the 1830s the nation was experiencing progressive and unsettling times. The industrial revolution was sweeping the eastern seaboard, and urbanization was proceeding apace. A transportation revolution was insuring the miles of track that meant transition from stage coach to railroad. Many were heading west; many others—foreigners with alien customs and values—were heading for the cities. New techniques in printing guaranteed an accompanying communications revolution, and a rising mass popular culture demanded access to reading material shaped to its mentality. In this climate, evangelicalism and Enlightenment were swiftly going to Romantic seed. A softness crept around the edges of the old ideas; and privatization—already implicit in the individualism of the legacy—grew.

As the social body was pulled at the joints and felt wear and tear from its inordinate stretching, individual Americans felt the deficiency as loss of mastery. Even in the heyday of the birth of the republic, the community in which Americans participated had been a creature of the moment and its necessity. That Americans had to "ground" their political community in the starry heavens, with immutable natural laws, was already a clue that the bonds of history, of common experience and identity, were insufficiently strong. Thus, in a reversal that was not surprising, when the plural communities of the colonies became the pluralistic states of the nineteenth century, the individual body, for many, became the ground for complaint or celebration. Here was a place that, conceivably, could be mastered and made perfect. Here was a terrain and landscape in which, perhaps, deficiency could be overcome and the beauty of pure form and function could emerge.

But, in the physical religion that was evident, for the most part complaint ruled the day. Americans were voicing numerous individual grievances regarding not the state of the republic but the state of their own bodies. Medical historians tell us that dyspepsia, or indigestion, was a national ill, and the record contains a host of caricatures of Americans, with gargantuan appetites, gulping down plates of greasy animal food and alcohol. Besides these, the popular literature of the era paints pictures of wasting consumptives whose disease was evidently every bit as rampant in their century as cancer is in our own. And by the post-Civil-War era, George Beard was introducing his fellow-citizens to the concept of "American nervousness" to describe the ills that beset many of them.[5]

As William Ghaskins penned his confession to Sylvester Graham, it is unlikely that he was reflecting on historical themes or contemporary sociology. But it is not hard to see him as a man shaped by many of the historical and sociological forces of the times. Certainly in the case of the revival and the Enlightenment, his rhetoric itself affords the primary clue. Although, as we have already done, we can look past Ghaskins to the end of his century, when Mary Baker Eddy would lose nature's body, now—in the Ghaskins moment—a different view ruled. For Ghaskins and others the "ghostly" spirit qualities of sin and grace had acquired physiological form. Nature lost flesh with Eddy; spirit snatched it up beforehand, not only in the musings of Thomas Jefferson (as we have seen) but also in the evangelical form of nature religion. Without turning to metaphysical religion, some Americans had found their way to the "spiritual matter" that, later in the century, Phineas Parkhurst Quimby would identify. Theologically speaking, American materialism was alive and well.

Always, though, beneath the individual body graced hid a collective body politic with its federalized form and functions. Nature's law, in the republic, was a clue to the constitutional nature of reality for the individual. In physical religion, republican nature was transposed to atomic status, even as it fused with Puritanism-turned-evangelicalism to produce a new, Romantic religion of nature.

There are, of course, a number of ways to construe the relationship between religion and healing. What may come to mind initially is the competition and even hostility between certain religious attitudes, on the one hand, and scientific medicine, on the other. Or, in a second, less dramatic relationship, preacher and doctor may go their separate, but peaceful ways, with the doctor's growing in importance as modernity advances. In still a third relationship, the paths of preacher and doctor begin to converge again, as religion and medicine come to look on each other as allies concerned with aiding a patient.

But, finally, there is a fourth relationship between religion and medicine, and this is the one that concerns us here. In this model, medicine itself becomes a spiritual process with religious claims and powers. Healing works as sacred manifestation, and healers work as religious officiants. In America this could mean that, as in ancient times, the priest (or religious leader) was the fittest dispenser of healing, that he or she was the Euro-American version of an Indian medicine person. Or, conversely, it could mean that "secular" healers absorbed religious functions and came to make religious claims about their curing arts. It is this fourth relationship between religion and medicine that physical religion illustrates, especially in its "secular" manifestation.

Generally, before they turned to physical religion, sickly Americans had used the "heroic" medicine that provided the standard health care of the times. This medicine was heroic because it so challenged a body that it stimulated all of the patient's recuperative powers to get well. The "heroic" sick were bled and blistered. As the Hutchinson Family Singers have already told us, they were fed mercury compounds and other poisonous substances. They sometimes got well, and they sometimes died. But the testimony was nearly universal that the regimen of cure in the standard way was excruciating and exhausting, not less for pocketbook than for person.[6]

Hence, it is not remarkable that Americans should try something else. What is remarkable, though, is that so many of them should look to what were essentially methods of religious healing.

And what is noteworthy, too, is that nature became the great healing symbol in the religious regimes they embraced. Perhaps the growing myth of individualism made an appeal to a more social kind of symbol unattractive. And surely the difficulties of making community in the fast-paced, industrializing, and plural society of the times encouraged the turn to nature as a way to achieve place and control. Perhaps, again, the ideology of republican nature had taken hold so tenaciously that, even amidst the triumph of evangelical times, authentic religion, authentic healing, had somehow to be "natural."

In any case, as we have already noticed, Americans were learning more and more from new intellectual movements of European provenance. As Robert C. Fuller has traced its progress, animal magnetism was capturing media attention and, with it, the popular mentality.[7] Mesmerists were lecturing widely in the cities and small towns of the nation, giving demonstrations to confirm the validity of their teachings. Entrancement and healing on stage were becoming spectacles that many in the rising middle class observed. Others, still more numerous, read in local or national newspapers accounts of mesmeric events.[8] In part mesmerism attracted because it evoked the Enlightenment heritage with which Americans were familiar. But its genius was to add to the Enlightenment the occult tradition of the West, so that nature, the motif of the republic, began to be played out in another key.

Meanwhile, the flux of the magnetic tides easily blended in the popular mentality with another overflow. The Swedenborgian "influx" of the divine, its corresponding spheres, its conflation of spirit and matter, were, as we have seen, persuasive metaphors. While many of Swedenborg's followers came together as the Church of the New Jerusalem, other Americans knew his ideas more informally. Swedenborg's numerous writings concerning his heavenly visits were early translated into English and published on the American side of the Atlantic as well as abroad. Even further, the interest of an elite group of Boston Unitarians helped to disseminate his teachings, and so did nineteenth-century Swedenborgian periodicals such as the *New Jerusalem Magazine* and the *New Jerusalem Messenger*. Individuals such as the fabled Johnny Appleseed spread Swedenborgian literature and ideas with evangelical zeal; and so, in their own way, did intellectuals like Ralph Waldo Emerson.[9] Thus, Swedenborgianism found its way, inobtrusively but pervasively, into the American mix. In doing so, Swedenborgianism worked hand and glove with mesmerism to provide a religious and metaphysical buttress for physical religion.

How, more precisely, can this physical religion be described? As suggested earlier, it was, above all, *healing* religion—religion in which acts of caring and curing constituted the central ritual enterprise for believers. And since any religion is an action system as much as it is a thought system, physical religion systematically linked beliefs about nature and grace to behavior that incarnated them. Moreover, physical religion found expression not only in specific, highly constellated symbols, i.e., individual acts of healing that were performed. It also found expression in the life-style injunctions and admonitions that, in effect, formed an ethical system for everyday life—to walk the path of "prevention" that, at least theoretically, led to fewer and fewer celebrations of the ritual of cure. Like the evangelical conversion that, ideally, happened only once in a person's life, curing could be a potent sacrament even in disuse.

In what follows, we look specifically at two forms of physical religion in the lives of some nineteenth-century Americans. First, following an explicitly evangelical model, we explore the "Christian physiology" movement of the time, perhaps best typified by individuals such as Sylvester Graham (of Graham-cracker repute) and William Andrus Alcott (the cousin of Transcendentalist Bronson Alcott, who fathered Louisa May).[10] Second and more extensively, in a more diffuse setting we view a series of medical sectarians who operated on the perimeters of the orthodox medicine of the era. In all of the cases, we find at least traces of conflation of evangelism and Enlightenment, and we find the traces mostly expressed in a distinctly Romantic form. If, as we saw in the last chapter, Americans were confusing the physicality of nature with metaphysical idealism and if they were equating harmony with control, they were also merging the gospel of grace and the Goddess of Reason.

It was especially in the Christian physiology movement that, as James C. Whorton tells us, health reformers were able "to transform individual hygiene into a moral-social crusade."[11] Indeed,

Christian physiology was a fusion of the books of nature and of revelation, a fusion that was also a marriage of the Enlightenment and the revival. And, like the double heritage, the Christian physiology movement sharpened the emphasis on individual perfection at the same time as, with social zeal, it created communities of the enlightened or saved. Throughout, Christian physiology signaled the millennium at hand, the future to be made present—and present perfect—in a golden dawn of health.[12]

True, intellectual precision demands that we distinguish between health reformers, who sought to change the way people lived in order to prevent disease, and alternative healers, who tried to cure sick people by methods other than the "heroic" remedies of the times. In practice, though, the two are not separable. Health reformers, Graham and Alcott among them, had often been converted to their new physiological regimes by the experience of serious illness. *They* saw their path as a healing one, and so did the numerous individuals who followed them. In fact, Graham even articulated a disease theory that transmuted his preventative regimen into a cure. Disease, for him, was not the result of invasion but, as John B. Blake has noted, "a derangement of the vital functions" through the failures in a person's way of living.[13]

However, it is the explicitly religious quality of the work of the health reformers that is especially important here. In fact, in his *Crusaders for Fitness,* James Whorton begins by describing their "hygienic ideologies." These ideologies, he tells us, are "idea systems that identify correct personal hygiene as the necessary foundation for most, even all, human progress, and that invite acceptance by incorporating both certain universal feelings about man and nature, as well as the popular aspirations and anxieties peculiar to distinct eras." Even further, Whorton speaks of the "levels of devotion, asceticism, and zeal" that have so often attended hygienic ideologies and concludes that "they must ultimately be described as hygienic religion."[14]

Calling the health reform movements "physiologies of perfection" and "religions of physical purification," Whorton rightly points to their apotheosis of nature and nature's laws at the same time as he notices their "physical Arminianism."[15] In this as in other ways, the Enlightenment and the revival were intertwined, for if nature was the gift of the Enlightenment, the revival spread an Arminian mentality among Christian believers. Like the Dutchman Jacobus Arminius for whom the new theology was named, revivalists and health reformers alike preached a can-do religion, in which grace became the divine blessing on human effort.

Significantly, Sylvester Graham's grandfather and father had both been ministers, and both had supported the revival. And Sylvester Graham himself, before he had begun to preach health reform, had been ordained to preach from a Presbyterian pulpit.[16] Nor had William Alcott's career as a teacher afforded fewer opportunities to moralize. With scriptural echoes in its title, his autobiographical *Forty Years in the Wilderness of Pills and Powders* hailed "Physical Education" (to natural hygiene) and acclaimed "the mighty work for this fallen world" that education had "yet to achieve; especially Physical Education!"[17]

If the leaders of the Christian physiology movement echoed revival and gospel, so did the followers. "The truths of physiology, like all other truth, belong to the Lord," wrote one contributor to the *Health Journal*. Another, commenting on Graham's widely hailed *Lectures on the Science of Human Life,* announced: "It is our solemn and deliberate conviction, after faithfully studying the book, much of the past year that, next to the Bible, Graham's Lectures on the Science of Human Life should be read and studied by every family and especially every minister and medical man." "He that would have salvation must present his body as well as his soul 'a living sacrifice' to the truth—harmonize with every law of his being," urged still another. In fact, revival leader Charles Grandison Finney himself had become a physiological follower. Finney, so the report went, regarded it "a settled and unalterable truth, that until the physiological and dietetic habits of men are corrected, spiritual declensions and backslidings are inevitable. The laws of the physical system are the laws of God."[18]

Thus, even as they preached an evangelical revival through physical religion, over and over again Christian physiologists pronounced the truth of nature's laws and the crime of their infraction. As the *Health Journal* in similar verbal formulas repeatedly told:

The natural appetites of man—and through them all the higher faculties—having become perverted from their original simplicity, by an improper indulgence, and his liberty and happiness thus sacrificed by a departure from the plain and obvious laws of his nature, he can only regain his lost paradise, by voluntarily yielding to the simple truth, and freely conforming to the laws established in his constitution by his Creator.[19]

Nor is the "constitutionalism" of the declaration incidental. What Stephen Nissenbaum has noticed insightfully about Sylvester Graham can be applied to his followers. And Nissenbaum's words are worth quoting:

Inverting the process by which traditional political theorists had used "organic" language to describe the social order, Graham applied the rhetoric of late eighteenth-century republican social philosophy to the individual human organism. The human body, he claimed, had its own proper form of "government," based on a natural "constitution" which in turn provided for "constitutionally established laws." This physiological government was "endowed" with certain specific "powers," and when these powers were misused or undermined, the inevitable consequence was a state of "anarchical depravity" or "despotism."[20]

The revision of traditional Christian theology that such constitutional thinking entailed was significant. No longer was disease the result of God's punishment or a test by God to help sanctify the virtuous further still. Rather, it was one's own decision; and saving grace, likewise, would come as the inevitable result of one's initiative. Consider this typical expression of Christian constitutionalism, which editor Joseph S. Wall contributed to the *Health Journal*. "What may be justly termed a heaven and a hell, in the common acceptation of these terms," Wall wrote,

is *constitutionally established in man's nature,* to one of which he may elevate himself, and plunge himself into the other at his own pleasure. If man ever attains a heaven of happiness he must do it by yielding obedience to the laws of his being, and coming into harmony with himself and with the universe around him. If he does not do this, he will inevitably plunge himself into what may be justly called a hell of torment and misery.[21]

Wall's Christian constitutionalism, with its emphasis on the heaven and hell that were self-created, had a Swedenborgian ring. But beyond Wall's heaven and hell, the grace that was nature and the salvation that was self betokened the appearance of a new heaven and a new earth. In a merger that brought constitutionalism to the threshold of the Christian future, physiological saving grace was a sign of the millennium at hand, a giant step in its inauguration.

The cult of progress among Christian physiologists already suggested the millennial theme. Rallying his readers around the cause of physical education, William Alcott could own that "moral or spiritual advancement has been the chief end to which our eye has been directed." And he could also eye the future, proclaiming that "if it is something to raise him [man] from the condition and capacity of a brute, and make him a 'man,' it is still more to make him, as the poet Young expresses it, a 'god.'"[22] More to the messianic point, Sylvester Graham announced his John-the-Baptist status for readers of the *Health Journal:*

To bring in the fulness of the reign of God, as revealed in Jesus Christ, hath God raised me up. Not to teach men that they shall live by bread alone, but by every law of God in their nature and relations—by *every* law, physical, physiological, intellectual, moral, spiritual . . . that they may enjoy through true godliness "the life that now is and that which is to come."[23]

If the language of becoming a god was not explicit enough, the *Health Journal* hastened to print next to its letter from Graham a feature titled "Grahamism *alias* Millennialism." The unsigned editorial excerpted generously from the *Botanico-Medical Recorder,* proposing to readers that "instead of Grahamism, we have Millennialism—and for Grahamites, we substitute Millennarians [*sic*]; for, of a truth, our views carried fully into practice, by strictly observing the physical, moral, and intellectual laws of our being—sinless in every respect—would constitute the Millennium."[24]

Indeed, the millenarian vocation of Grahamites was clear even in matters such as increasing the circulation of the journal. Seeking a dedicated subscription agent "in every city, town, village, and district in our land," the editor's rhetoric was revealing:

Is there not *one* person to be found in each of these upon whose countenance the light of truth has dawned, like the Sun of righteousness, with healing in its beams, and into whose family it has introduced health and happiness? If there is, then will they not use their exertions to let the same ameliorating light shine into the mansions and upon the *minds* of their friends and neighbors, that they, too, may rejoice in the visitations of the harbinger of mercy, which, in dispelling suffering and disease, will have the effect, as it were, to make glad the barren and desolate place of the earth?[25]

Although the message seems oversize to twentieth-century eyes (the "cause" was, after all, a simple matter of drumming up business), editor and readers were convinced of the importance of the future that was dawning. One convert, a former Thomsonian (herbal) physician, recanted the Thomsonian heresy for Grahamism, to discover that he simultaneously felt that he was "'born again,' and that the day of my 'millennium' had arrived." Erstwhile, the journal had published an excerpt from the *Botanic Ledger* with which it seemed to agree. "The dawn of a new era has broke upon the world," announced the piece sententiously.

Physiology and Phrenology have opened up the fountains of his [man's] understanding, and have already taught those who will listen to the solemn warning, that of all the works of Nature, it is most requisite for man to obey the laws of his being. . . . When this light shall have been universally spread, and obeyed, the earth shall present a scene worthy to be looked upon.[26]

The millennium to come bespoke a paradise, and physiological millennialism pointed, especially, toward its character. For this paradise was an *earthly* paradise, and it was also a paradise that was almost deja vu. Myths of the end are, as the introduction to this book has noted, inverted replicas of myths of the beginning: the former Thomsonian who was both born again and transported into the millennial future was on the mark.[27] Thus, in emphasizing the heaven that would dawn in America, Christian physiologists expressed a terrestrial Edenic theme within their religion of nature. Their millennium resembled, on closer scrutiny, a once-perfect past, when earth had been a garden and when no illness had appeared. And their pursuit of American innocence cloaked a bid for personal dominance in the time of what Fred Somkin has called the "unquiet eagle."[28] Like the untainted wilderness at the city's edge in Royall Tyler's *Contrast,* their heaven on earth signaled a refusal to grow into history. Whether as deists or as Christians, Americans had shown themselves, if anachronism be pardoned, as so many Peter Pans.

In bringing Eden to their religion of nature, Christian physiologists were only saying again what had already, in the eighteenth century, been said. If their millennialism had grown less republican and more private, it was still responding, in tune with the times, to an inherited message. But others who were linking religion and medicine found their own ways to join past to present. Physical religion extended beyond the Christian physiologists, health reformers of the Graham and Alcott variety, to encompass a series of alternative healers in sectarian medical movements. Together, these make up the second important group of nineteenth-century healers who looked to physical religion.

What distinguished these individuals from the health reformers was their willingness to move beyond the preventive, proper-life-style approach to sickness by actively promoting more-strenuous therapies. And as the medical sectarians or "irregulars" did so, like the Christian physiologists but often less explicitly, they linked evangelism to their championship of a romanticized, popularized Enlightenment. Like the Christian physiologists, too, they harbored millennial expectations; but, even beyond the postmillennialism of the physiologists, medical sectarians expected the dawning of the new age in general and diffuse "secular" terms. More than the Christian physiologists, they were captured by distinctly mesmeric metaphors; and, as ever, the Swedenborgian doctrine of correspondence hovered in the wings. The message of sin and grace was still there, and it featured prominently, for example, in the water-cure movement. But the overlay of other motifs was also strong.

Who were these medical sectarians? It would be impossible to name them all here, but chiefly they were Thomsonians (followers of the herbalist Samuel Thomson), homeopaths, hydropaths (water curers), osteopaths, and chiropractors. They appeared on the scene in the order in which they are here listed, with Thomsonianism coalescing into a significant movement by the 1820s and with chiropractic not appearing until 1895. The language of religion that these medical sectarians created from the material supplied by their culture deserves further exploration.

Take, for example, Samuel Thomson and his followers. In his book *The Healers,* John Duffy calls their movement "religious, political, and cultural." Thomson himself, Duffy points out, had a "fundamentalist religious background," and his chief agent Elias Smith also, notes Duffy, was a "fundamentalist."[29] While we may quarrel with Duffy's anachronistic use of the label (fundamentalism is a product of a later time), it is clear that he intends the evangelical fervor of both men. For Thomson's organizing talent led to the creation of Friendly Botanic Societies, in which, with the purchase of his *New Guide to Health; or Botanic Family Physi-*

cian, members earned the ability to treat the sick within their families. Acclaiming the efficacies of lobelia and cayenne, Thomson's book went through thirteen editions, and by 1839 he boasted that one hundred thousand "family-right" purchases had been made.[30]

Nor did evangelism stop with Samuel Thomson and Elias Smith. Thomsonian journals were, if anything, bolder still in their estimate of the allegiance of Americans to their system. As early as 1834 in Columbus, Ohio, the *Thomsonian Recorder* intimated that "more than two millions of the American People" were Thomsonians. By 1840 the *Boston True Thomsonian* was editorializing that "Thomsonism" numbered "among its converts, at least, *one fourth* part of the inhabitants of America." And less than two years later, Aaron Douglass could tell the *Boston Thomsonian Manual* that "three years ago Thomsonians were nearly as scarce as white crows, but now we can number one-third at least of our whole population converted to common sense." Such growth was evidently a sign of the advancing millennial age. "Light is beginning to dawn upon the minds of the people in various quarters of the Union, and they are embracing the truth in every quarter," one correspondent to the *Recorder* affirmed. "I anticipate the time is near at hand when every man will be his own physician."[31]

Meanwhile, Thomsonians preached the same message of natural sin and self-initiated grace that, more expressly, had inspired Christian physiologists. An article from the *Boston Thomsonian Manual* in 1842, for instance, could inveigh against humans by comparing them to animals: "Alas! the beast that roams the forest in pursuit of his prey, unaided by the light of reason, ungoverned by the dictates of a moral nature, claiming no higher destiny than that of a brief existence in his native wilds, may boast of greater consistency, of a more implicit obedience to the laws of Nature, and Nature's God, than proud Man!"[32]

Nature was everywhere the norm, and disease was rebellion against it, a "consequence resulting from a violation of Nature's laws." By contrast, "those who live[d] the nearest to a state of nature, [would] also approach the nearest to a state of perfect health." Natural food for humans was vegetable or "frugivorous" food, as one could tell from a study of the teeth (with only four canines among the thirty-two). And, in a judgment that often made temperance men out of medical sectarians, natural drink was "pure, cold water." Even death, when it came, should be natural—the perfect term to a harmonial life and not the result of disease.[33]

The harmonial teaching of Thomsonians, moreover, found easy company with magnetic themes. Thomson's herbal remedies would clear away the obstruction of disease, restoring the free flow that the laws of vitality governed. Thus, Thomsonian editors Benjamin Colby and Stephen Webster announced as part of the motto for their journal: "NO POISONING, BLEEDING, BLISTERING OR PHYSICING—NO SECRET NOSTRUMS—THE UNITY OF DISEASE, IT BEING AN OBSTRUCTION TO THE FREE OPERATION OF THE LAWS OF VITALITY—THE USE OF THOSE REMEDIES ONLY, THAT ACT IN HARMONY WITH NATURE'S LAWS." Indeed, Thomsonians generally hailed the virtues of "electric" energy in new magnetic models.[34]

What needs to be stressed here, however, is that Thomsonians more strongly hailed the latent virtues of the people. At the apex of the harmonial life was Samuel Thomson himself, whom followers linked to Isaac Newton and to Benjamin Franklin. Thomson's "medical directions," an ardent admirer said, were "founded upon the immutable laws of nature." Yet, in a more radical sense, Thomson was only the first among equals. In a virtual plethora of periodicals, the Thomsonians proclaimed—and loudly—the democratic message of potential power for the masses. "O America! Highly favored America!" admonished one correspondent to the *Thomsonian Scout*. "Boasted land of light and liberty! When will the day dawn that shall evince to our land and world, that we are a people capable of thinking and acting for ourselves, of knowing good from evil, of discriminating between medicine and poison!"[35]

"Truth is mighty, and will prevail," read the masthead of the *Thomsonian Advertiser,* in an unsubtle echo of John Locke. And prevail it must against the doctors, latter-day versions of the British redcoats of old. Evoking the term "regular," used for physicians of the day who practiced in the standard, heroic mode, the *Thomsonian Scout* linked the regulars of the British army to "the college learned doctors . . . called regulars." In turn, the *Boston True Thomsonian* announced that "Regularism and Paganism are of almost equally ancient date." And it prayed for the day "that the *people* will assert their rights, exercise the grand prerogative of reason on this subject, and fortify themselves against the snares of crafty and evil doers." [36]

Thus, if Thomsonism could free the people to be their own democratic masters, it did so to help subject them to laws of Christian virtue. Such conflation of Enlightenment and gospel meant sometimes the coming of the apocalypse. "'Regular' Murder" indicated to the *Boston Thomsonian Manual* that "the time draws nigh when the curtain must be drawn, and unfold the horrors of the beast. Behold! the cloven hoofs are already visible. Truth is our weapon, and with it the beast is destined to be conquered." Indeed, the Thomsonian army had been equipped for battle, with officers at the south, east, and west. For Thomsonianism had "seemingly marched through North America with gigantic strides, carrying all antagonistic impediments before it, like a light floating upon the surface of the swift-gliding current of a mighty river." [37]

At other times, the conflation of Enlightenment and gospel meant the more idyllic new creation when, as the *Thomsonian Recorder* would have it, readers would go "to the fruitful fields, green pastures, and flowery banks of sweetly-gliding streams and grassy fountain sides, to gather roots, and leaves, and blossoms, barks and fruits, for the healing of the nations." "We can now gaze upon the effulgent gleams of Thomsonism," proclaimed one advocate in the *Thomsonian Scout,* "once a small taper, that has steadily burned amid the gloom of time's dark night, until its beams have shone far and wide, and suffering humanity now behold a healing balm, to which they can resort and find relief." "Soon," the writer thought, the "sun of 'regular quackery'" would "set in endless night, and the lucid beams of Thomsonism" would "gild" the "happy land." More simply, the *Thomsonian Recorder* cited one "Minister of the Gospel . . . of eminence" who claimed he had "no doubt but that this system is the beginning of the millennium." [38]

Thomsonians were not alone in their hopes for the millennium, as the discussion of the future that Christian physiologists envisioned already shows. But Thomsonians were joined later by homeopaths and hydropaths, among other proponents of alternative healing. These newer medical sectarians shared most of the sentiments Thomsonians had expressed, the largest difference being the method that each group advocated when there was need for cure. In keeping with the theological rubric of physical religion, each healing movement considered its method simple and "natural." Others might or might not agree, as, for example, when Thomsonians criticized homeopaths for drugging the sick only somewhat less than did orthodox physicians. The point here, though, is not so much the objective reality of the "medicine" but rather the perception that accompanied it. And the perception was religious, an expression, once again, of a theology of nature religion.

Healing grace, for homeopaths, came from following the law of similars and the law of infinitesimals. The law of similars was, in fact, a physiological version of the law of correspondence. For the German Samuel Hahnemann, who founded homeopathy, and for his American followers from the 1830s, a substance that produced the symptoms of a specific disease in a well person became the remedy for that disease in one who was sick. Like, in other words, healed like; a secret harmony inhabited the natural world, and its discovery could bring the end to illness. Likewise, in the law of infinitesimals Hahnemann and his followers experimented with greater and greater dilutions or "potentizations" of the healing substance, so that only its traces (up to one-thirtieth times one-millionth) of the remedy eventually remained.[39] And if the law of similars resembled the doctrine of correspondence that was in the air, the law of infinitesimals in its own way echoed the mesmeric theory of fluids. Invisible energies were at work in homeopathic remedies. Matter had been transmuted into spirit, and nature's patterns spiritualized possessed the greater strength.

Indeed, so spiritualized did the infinitesimals become that they stood at the doorway of Quimby's world of mental energy. Homeopathic correspondence, coupled with potentizations to seeming infinity, spirited the practitioner into the world of mind. Physical religion, as ritualized in the dilution of the remedy, looked less and less somatic. Thus, in 1851 the physician O. A. Woodbury could write in Keene, New Hampshire's *Homoeopathic Advocate and Guide to Health* to celebrate the German founder. Hahnemann's mind, Woodbury told readers, "became impressed with the great truth, that diseases, instead of being produced by a material morbid principle, were 'purely dynamic aberrations, which our spiritual existence undergoes in its mode of feeling and acting.'" But Hahnemann, perforce, had been a practical man, and now the time had come to ground his practice in theory. The "laws of life and vitality," or "the laws of our being," supported Hahnemann's system; and, argued Woodbury, *the doctrines of Homoeopathy arise spontaneously out of them.*[40]

What were these laws, as Woodbury understood them? The answer, for one devoted to the physical analysis at the base of homeopathic healing, was at first glance astonishing.

The *mind* is the power which produces, in the human body, not only the *intellectual* and *moral* but also the vital phenomana [*sic*]. As the almighty mind produces all the wondrous and mysterious workings throughout the material universe, from the insensible growth of vegetation to the earthquake's shock, and thence onward to the revolution of distant worlds, . . . all in accordance with its own inherent impressions of love, mercy, justice, goodness, wisdom and truth, so does the human mind produce in its own little universe, the body, all its varied phenomena, from the lowest action of vitality to the most powerful physical motions, and thence upward to the highest grade of intellectual and moral phenomena.[41]

The "as above, so below" of Emanuel Swedenborg, Ralph Waldo Emerson, and a host of others found new advocacy in Woodbury's argument. Nature's law was a law about how the mind shaped the body, a brief for how metaphysic gave birth to physic. And yet, in the physical world, sin and grace pervaded the analysis as thoroughly as they had governed the explanations of Christian physiologists and Thomsonians.

Thus, the *Homoeopathic Advocate* explained that a sick person "through ignorance . . . has violated some law of nature, and pain and sickness is the inevitable result." "Pain is but the result of violated Nature," the journal reiterated, "hence it is of vast importance that we should all understand those laws which govern our own constitutions, and how to obey them in order to enjoy all the blessings designed by nature to flow from their obedience, as well as to escape the penalties attached to their infraction." Alternately, in a discussion of spinal curvature, the *Advocate* thought the deformity came from "a want of balance, in the intellectual and physical departments of the system." The means to restore the equilibrium were simple, "founded on God's immutable laws." All the sick had to concern themselves with was "undoing" what they had done, "ceasing to disobey the laws of our being, and learning to obey."[42]

In fact, though, the sin of the individual was abetted by the collective sin of false healers. The "filthy touch of Allopathy" had defiled the land. As "a part of the kingdom of *sin* and *Satan*," it was "now in the ascendant." Reversing the Thomsonian estimate, homeopaths contended that Thomsonians were mired in wrong. But their sin and the sin of the regulars were linked to the sin of the people at large. "So long as the people desire to take calomel and opium and other deleterious poisons by grains, or lobelia and cayenne pepper by the drachm, there will always be found enough ready to gratify them, regardless of consequences." Still, in the familiar pattern, if evil reigned now, good would eventually triumph. "The time is soon coming when the light of God's truth will sweep away the last vestige of [Allopathy] . . . from the earth." [43]

The *Advocate,* moreover, was not loath to predict the apocalyptic future that awaited regular physicians. "Then will those who *now* boast of *their* wisdom and skill, and look down with scorn and contempt, from the pinnacle of heathen superstition upon which they are perched, call on the rocks to fall on them and hide *them* and their *shame,* which the light of truth will then reveal." All the same, an address by Charles Neidhard could view millennial events in more-positive terms. "In the distant horizon, I see a light arise, which is becoming gradually brighter and brighter; it is our own divine science of homeopathy, whose rays will entirely dissipate the darkness created by the ancient method." [44]

Even as the rays dissipated the darkness, the heralds of the dawning day were Samuel Hahnemann and other homeopathic physicians. Homeopaths could savor the messianic identification, for they had been persecuted by allopathy just as Jesus and the early Christians had been persecuted by the Jews: "It is the destiny of Homoeopathy, like all other innovations since the son of man overthrew the jewish ceremonials, to receive the most bitter opposition." And, writing from Illinois, one medical student preached his own version of the homeopathic healing of the nations: "In the hands of the true follower of the immortal Hahnemann," he declared, "Homoeopathy is destined to become the only system for healing the nations." Indeed, Hahnemann was compared to Fulton, Harvey, Galileo, Columbus, Newton, Locke, and Jenner: "The time will ere long arrive, when the united world will rank him by the side of those great men." [45]

By 1855 the centenary of Hahnemann's birth was prompting still more effusive messianic identifications. The *Homoeopathic News,* for example, printed the program for the Philadelphia celebration featuring choruses from Haydn's *Creation* ("Chaos," "And there was light," and "The Heavens are telling the glory of God") and Handel's *Messiah* ("He shall feed his Flock," "His yoke is easy," and "For unto us a Child is born"). That the messiahs had not forgotten the republic was clear as well. The Cincinnati celebration of the Hahnemann centenary included toasts to "*Homoeopathy in America—The child of Hahnemann thrives well in the cradle of liberty*" and to "*The laws of health, and the health of the laws—May the one be established, and the other maintained.*" [46]

Homeopathic salvation, however, was joined by another midcentury means to grace. For hydropaths, the virtues of pure water occupied the space that herbs and remedies occupied for Thomsonians and homeopaths. Following the Silesian Vincent Priessnitz, whose cold-water cure in Grafenberg (Silesia) used ordinary (not mineral) water, they saw in "pure" water the primary healing agent for illness of whatever sort. So it was that water-cure establishments sprang up in the East and the Midwest to accommodate a generation of refugees from the heroic medicine of the era. There, drinking tumbler after tumbler of cold water, the sick were packed or rubbed in wet sheets; they took head baths, leg baths, sitting (pelvic) baths, washtub baths, half (body) baths, and plunge baths. In nineteenth-century style they experienced douche, cataract, and hose baths that were variants on shower baths also offered. Meanwhile, as they became inured to the waters, they assiduously observed a regimen of diet and exercise to continue harmonizing their systems.[47]

However, whether the sick were institutionalized for water therapy or, less dramatically and more commonly, were doctoring at home, healing came neither from medical advice nor from institutional assistance. Rather, water-cure journals were vociferous in announcing the message: healing came from nature and from the rightly ordered person who had learned to follow its laws. Sin, it was declared over and over again, was nature's violation. In a striking example, the *Water-Cure World* of Brattleboro, Vermont, asserted emphatically in its first (1860) issue:

We regard Man, in his primitive and natural condition as the most perfect work of God, and consider his present degenerated physical state as only the natural and inevitable result of thousands of years of debauchery and excess, of constant and wilful perversions of his better nature, and the simple penalty of outraged physical law, which is as just and more severe than any other.[48]

The implications of the proclamation were unpacked for readers in subsequent issues. One physician, W. T. Vail, for instance, in an argument that was familiar to many, questioned whether God was the "author of Disease." The theory that in some mysterious fashion disease was willed by God and the theory that the sin of Adam and Eve brought disease into the world crumbled before Vail's linguistic thrusts. Death was meant to be the natural end of life; it was not the result of disease but the necessary disorganization of form at life's term. "The idea indulged by some good people that disease grows out of a transgression of the *moral* laws is false," wrote Vail. And yet, disease *was* the result of transgression. "It is impious to attribute our diseases to the will of the Almighty when it is obvious that we ourselves are the sole cause of them in the various transgressions of which we have been guilty," Vail continued. "If we eat poisons, and drink poisons, and breathe poisons, and medicate with poisons, God will have to remodel the order of his universe or we must have disease; there can be no help for us." "Let us therefore," he urged, "abandon Satan's system of poisoning, based as it is upon a lie, and working as it does the most disastrous results for our race, and adopt God's system, based on truth—on the harmonies and congenialities of nature."[49]

"Wash, and be healed," proclaimed the water-cure gospel, and a Christian physiology surely pervaded the analysis.[50] Moreover, gospel good news meant evangelical action. Mary Gove Nichols envisioned students who would "go out a band of apostles, ready for good words and good works." "They will teach the life-giving knowledge of the laws of health, thus giving the people God's regenerating truth," she prophesied. "And they will apply Water-Cure with skill, discrimination, and unremitting care, to heal their patients of the diseases consequent upon hereditary taint, or in other words 'original sin' and the 'actual transgression' in their own lives." Meanwhile, readers of the *Water-Cure Journal* also heard the call.

DOUCHE BATH.

SHOWER BATH.

CATARACT BATH.

HOSE BATH.

RUBBING WET SHEET.

PLUNGE BATH.

HEAD BATH.

WET SHEET PACK.

LEG BATH.

SITTING BATH.

WASH TUB BATH.   THE HALF BATH.

Line drawings depicting forms of water cure. From front papers of Joel Shew's *The Hydropathic Family Physician* (New York: Fowler & Wells, 1854). (Courtesy, Cornell University Library.)

"We solicit and entreat all Men and Women," urged the journal, "to join in this work of physical redemption, and 'lift up' sick and suffering humanity upon a higher and a happier plain" [*sic*].[51]

It was clear that the link to nature still augured the evangelical world of new birth and millennial hope. The water-cure physician James C. Jackson proclaimed himself "an enthusiast" and witnessed, "I have felt the power of the Water-Cure in my own person." "How gloriously and sublimely is the Water Cure *reformation* advancing!" he exclaimed. "Twenty years from this time it will be acknowledged to have been the greatest and best blessing to the human race man has ever known." For his part, Russell T. Trall urged readers of the *Water-Cure Journal* to "sow broadcast" everywhere the "seeds of a new epoch, a brighter era, a better humanity, a higher destiny—an age of *true glory*." And one J. Berry hymned his own celebration to the future destiny of water, predicting that "like the silent dewy shower which is now falling on the physical world, water will descend on the moral world, dispersing its fogs of gloom, refreshing the landscape of society, revealing the sun of temperance, and reviving the withering flowers of humanity."[52]

Like Hahnemann for the homeopathic movement, Vincent Priessnitz acquired a stature larger than life as inaugurator of the new age. Priessnitz had burst the "shackles imposed by the medical profession" and "then freed his fellowmen, and led them back to nature." Such action, indeed, illustrated the fact that "when his [man's] spiritual condition demands a new impulse—an awakening of the divine element of his character, a reformer noble and true to his divine instincts comes into active being, and stamps the impress of his character upon that age." More succinctly, for H. C. Foote, Priessnitz had done for medicine what Martin Luther had done for Christianity.[53]

Beyond that, in the familiar transmutation of Enlightenment and revival, water cure just as strongly told the good news of correspondence. Russell T. Trall, one of the leaders of the movement, summarized:

When the people are as intelligent as we hope they soon will be, it will be deemed actually discreditable to be diseased in body. It implies transgression—sinning against the laws of being. Think you God's physical laws are less dear to him, or less holy in themselves, than his moral laws? If His

laws which govern life and health are, like Himself, just, true, and immutable, can we infringe them without guilt?[54]

The answer was obviously no; and Trall, on another occasion,
made it clear that he considered sin against physiological laws to
be the gospel sin against the Holy Ghost. On the other hand, the
gospel truth that the God of nature proclaimed was water. With an
essay appearing in the *Water-Cure Journal,* the Christian physiologist William Alcott himself could announce the message: "The
God of nature has never yet made—at least for the globe we inhabit—any other drink but water." Even "milk, which some drink,
is four-fifths water." Tea and coffee, by contrast, were unnatural
drinks, as the journal elsewhere indicated: "As a permanent law of
the constitution, written by the finger of God himself, both these
substances . . . *are always positively injurious to both bodily and mental health.*[55]

The familiar constitutional language hinted a republican flavor,
as the Fourth of July meditations of Russell Trall in 1853 also suggest. Political freedom, for Trall, "though good, and great, and
glorious," was "not the *end*" but "the *means* of man's advancement."
Trall thought independence "a much abused term" and freedom
"not always well understood." "Are we not all tyrannized over by
false appetites, enslaved by wrong customs, ground down by the
usurped authority of learned bigots and ignorant professors?" he
asked. Trall went on to build a case for the enfranchisement of
women, but before he did so he had earlier made his case for constitutionalism. "Man is, and ever must be," Trall declared, "entirely dependent of the constitution of things above him, the laws
of being within him, the social relations around him, and the
sources of existence below him."[56]

Trall was not alone. In the reformist voice, republican nature
still found an echo in the water cure. Moreover, in the unpoliti-
cized world of individual caring and curing, mesmerism, too, found
an echo in the water cure. Recasting the magnetic model in moral
terms, some thought that sin was the obstruction of God's work
in the world through interference with the rhythm of natural harmonies. Less subtly, one journal, published "simultaneously" in
Rochester, New York, and Boston in 1846, could call itself *The
Magnetic and Cold Water Guide.* "Devoted to magnetism, mesemr-

ism [sic]," and "hydropathy," the journal, through an unnamed editor, excerpted "the testimony of an experienced physician of Massilon, Ohio" to underline its claims. The doctor, an A. Under-hill, waxed eloquent on his investigations of "the Water Treatment of disease" and worked his way to a concluding rhetorical flourish. "Physiology, Phrenology, and Magnetism," he summarized, "are the keys that are unlocking the great mysteries of nature and mind, and letting us in, as it were, to the inner temple, where the sun-beams of light and truth are filling the minds and understandings of all the truly devout worshippers of the Eternal principles which govern all things." [57]

By the latter part of the century, though, a number of the truly devout had left both water cure and magnetism behind. New heal-ing therapies turned not to the physicality of environmental sub-stances but to the physical frame of the body itself. In what—from a material point of view—were the most "physical" versions of physical religion, osteopathy and then chiropractic attracted new generations of seekers.

For all that, the magnetic metaphor refused to go away. Both os-teopathy and chiropractic pressed the language of obstruction and free flow into service. Certainly it was no accident that both An-drew Taylor Still, the founder of osteopathy, and D. D. (or Daniel David) Palmer, the founder of chiropractic, had once been mag-netic doctors. [58] In both the osteopathic cure of muscular manipula-tion and the chiropractic cure of spinal adjustment, a theology of flux analyzed illness and healing on the basis of what essentially was the mesmeric model. When sickness struck, there was an obstruction that had unbalanced the physical frame. When a cure occurred, it was because impediment had been removed and block-age corrected. Now the flow of nature's energy could enliven and invigorate as it was meant to do.

Will A. Potter explained the osteopathic view in typical fashion in the *Journal of Osteopathy*. Osteopathy, he wrote in 1897, "adopts . . . a system of intelligent manual operations by which all mechanical obstructions to the circulation of vital fluids are re-moved, and the inherent recuperative forces of the body are con-trolled and directed to the restoration of harmony and health, without the introduction of drugs or other agencies than the good, wholesome food prescribed by the normal appetite." And another early enthusiast made the mesmeric connection more explicit, speculating on the "healing property" of nature and the "divine presiding mind set in closest vicinage to nature, by which the tides of life, as they ebb and flow within the body, are vivified and purified." [59]

The close vicinity of nature apparently inspired late-century osteopaths as much as did obstructionist diagnostics. Andrew Taylor Still and his followers hailed the machinery of nature and nature's God, even as they promoted their new "science" of healing. "Remove all obstructions," Still exhorted. He added as quickly: "Nature will kindly do the rest." "Beginning with earth, through all its products," the founder wrote appreciatively, "man is the crowning work of the skill and wisdom of all Nature, and halts to see the beautiful workings of that unequaled laboratory of life as it operates in him." Since "the duties he [man] had to perform were to control the world and all its elements by reason," it followed for Still that "all the machinery must be higher in form and quality to suit the coming demands." If the human machinery was "self-propelling, self-sustaining, having all the machinery of strength, all the thrones of reason established, and working to perfection," then, asked Still, was it not reasonable to believe that "the Master Mechanic has provided the avenues and power to deliver . . . compounds to any part of the body?" "Nature's God," he concluded, had been "thoughtful enough to place in man all the elements and principles that the word 'Remedy' means." [60]

Still's appropriation of the late eighteenth-century language of the Enlightenment was as significant as his subtle renovation of republican discourse. Public had gone private, and the Grand Architect of state had become a Master Mechanic of personal parts. But the classical outlines of the discourse remained: reason, nature, order, a deist God—all functioned in Still's theology of health and healing. From a related perspective, the *Journal of Osteopathy* declared that the new healing method had "an immovable basis in nature itself, and that its operations are in harmonious accord with the ineradicable and irrepealable laws of nature, and that its future . . . is as illimitable as the boundless and inexplorable resources of universal life." For the journal, "man" was not only "a passive machine" and a "living organism" but, at the same time, "a microcosm—a miniature of the cosmic universe." [61]

And yet, for all the message of the Enlightenment and for all the confidence of early osteopathy in its ability to remove blockage and obstruction, an Edenic shadow remained. "We have lived under the tradition that man is made sick as a punishment for a few apples that Grandma Eve took, and has never been well since," wrote Still. "I wish she had let them alone, if that was all she knew about the chemical and biological effect of stealing apples." The difference between osteopathic analysis and that of earlier healers, however, was built on the metaphor of humans as machines. When people got sick, Christian physiologists and midcentury irregulars alike had blamed them, as moral agents, for their violation of natural law. In the osteopathic world of machines, the violation was the disorder of malfunctioning parts, a process of mechanical degeneration and breakdown. "Health and disease, life and death, are two different expressions of the one force of nature," wrote an unnamed author. If conditions were "abnormal," then disease was the result. Without imputing blame, the impersonal diagnosis could point to "unnatural, anatomic and physiological conditions" as cause for the disequilibrium that was ill health.[62]

On the other hand, the imputation of blame *was* implicit, for, if reliance on nature's law brought health, it followed that violation of the law—*by humans*—brought disease. Andrew Taylor Still offered readers of his journal an elaborate analogy that made the point:

I got ready to attend the fall races. I got up in the judges' stand where they ring the bell to "go." Nature's little pony came out on the track. He was not much bigger than a goat. He sided up by the fine steeds of drugs, and at the word "go," he lit out at full speed. I was afraid the fiery steeds would run over him. The race grew more interesting each quarter-post he passed, and he won the prize in fall diseases, because he depended upon Nature's law.[63]

More directly, the journal recommended that "clergymen should preach the importance of health culture, and that it is a sin to be sick as well as to do the wicked things so long preached against."[64]

Sin was hardly the osteopathic forte, however. Still himself had been accused of spiritualism and, alternately, of atheism;[65] and his writing sometimes suggested the kind of rationalist religion that would have appealed to the eighteenth-century founders of the republic. Moreover, the vision of osteopaths in general was perhaps more contemplative than evangelical. What Thomsonian or hydropathist would have written, for instance, the words that Helen de Lendrecie penned at the conclusion of one short essay? "The more one studies the intricate laws that govern in Osteopathic treatment, the more reverent becomes the mind, and the more intense the desire to fathom, if possible, the true relation of creature to creator, and as the study advances, the human soul seems to be absolutely absorbed in the contemplation of the founder of man, the Majesty of God." [66]

Nonetheless, contemplation did not preclude a version of millennial expectation. One commencement class at the American School of Osteopathy heard that "in these closing years of the nineteenth century, it is something to have the privilege of living and taking part in scientific efforts and movements that promise to crown civilization with its greatest glory." In prose that was somewhat purpler, Mason W. Pressly spoke of the day "not far distant when Osteopathy will be crowned by a glad and grateful public as the QUEEN SCIENCE OF HEALTH." Indeed, with apocalyptic vigor, osteopathy had "gone forth . . . panoplied in the golden armor of truth and fact." It was "now dealing its blows, thick and fast, upon the hydra-headed monster of disease, and thus winning its crown of glory." And one grateful father, whose son had been healed, spoke of "a feeling of awe and reverence, much as if we have stood in the shadow of a miracle, which the apostle of this new science, touched by the wings of divine knowledge, has accomplished." [67]

Not too long after the miracle that Still and his followers were perpetrating both at Kirksville, Missouri, and elsewhere, D. D. Palmer had stumbled his way into his personal brand of enlightened miracle. In a transformed version of magnetic theory, Palmer fused his homegrown appropriation of the Enlightenment with occult-metaphysical ideas that were tinged with the remains of sin in the biblical garden.

For Palmer and others at the end of the century, the ebb and flow of natural tides modulated into mind, tying the starkly physical to a world beyond. As Palmer, the magnetic doctor, moved toward chiropractic, he confided his ideas to his journal in short, staccato axioms. "Disease, disarrangement, is disturbed harmony," he declared. And he also noted, in his own transcription of natural sin, that "mind produces all action, conscious or unconscious" and that "moving thots [sic] produce disease." In fact, he reminded himself, he should "mentally exhibit to the wrong doer the suffering his vice or belief causes, that there is no pleasure in those beliefs. No genuine pleasure in sin." Thoughts (equivalent to "beliefs"), he decided, were "real substance," modifying all that they touched; and "as the mind so is the body."[68]

Certainly the "as above, so below" of the theory of correspondence was not difficult to find in Palmer's theoretical brief. Finally, however, Palmer moved past mental healing to understand the formerly magnetic tide as a mysterious substance called "Innate." In a healthy person, said Palmer, Innate flowed unobstructed through the spinal column and the nervous system. For the founder of chiropractic, Innate was the "Life-Force," and he called it "Universal Intelligence," "Spirit," and "God." "Innate always existed and always will," claimed Palmer. "Progression is stamped in Innate's every act. . . . Innate has a knowledge gleaned from a life of eternity; it runs the functions of the human body as readily on the first day of its habitation as in after years. It is infinite, unlimited in time and experience." Nonetheless, the results of this abstract natural theology were eminently physical. "Knowing that our physical health and the intellectual progress of Innate (the personified portion of Universal Intelligence) depend upon the proper alignment of the skeletal frame, we feel it our bounden duty to replace any displaced bones so that physical and spiritual health, happiness, and the full fruition of earthly life may be fully enjoyed."[69]

Palmer's testimony, if examined closely, is familiar. For in his explanatory system, magnetism had, in effect, been transmuted into mind. In a confusion of spirit and matter that in part had been prepared by Swedenborgian theology, Palmer—like osteopaths and homeopaths before him—had arrived at a version of nature that approximated the immaterial. Even so, natural sin and healing grace were enduring realities in chiropractic. Sin was, for the earlier Palmer, mentally caused; but by the time he came to chiropractic, in 1895, it was also a form of *physical* derangement, a contortion/blockage that pushed and strained the body out of form. Grace meant a restoration of natural flow and function. The tides of intelligence and Innate bathed the healthy body in divine benediction.

It was Joy M. Loben, however, who most succinctly expressed the theological basis for chiropractic treatment. Oral tradition had it that, after Palmer discovered the efficacy of spinal adjustment, he thought of presenting his new system of healing as religion.[70] If so, Loben would have qualified as first evangelist for the church. Writing in the early twentieth century, he reflected and summarized the nineteenth-century mentality that gave birth to Palmer's theories. "Chiropractic Philosophy," for Loben, was distinguished in that it went "far out beyond the limits of either Theology or Materialism—to the first and Absolute Cause." "Chiropractic," he continued,

has investigated and explained that mysterious and elusive thing men call the Soul; it elucidates the "Nature" which has been used for generations as a name for the unknowable; it has taken the forces and energies which move and wield and reconstruct the elements, and has shown what they are, their purpose, and how they act in absolute obedience to an Intelligence, which is all-pervading; it ventures into the realm of (so-called) occult phenomena and proves them to be simply action in obedience to easily understood laws.[71]

Nature and Nature's God lay behind Loben's formulation, but the Enlightenment reading had been remodeled to the specifications of the late-nineteenth-century occult-metaphysical world. Fusing a popular version of the science of the era to Enlightenment, magnetic, and metaphysical concepts, Loben had written an apology for chiropractic that looked toward the New Age of well over a half-century later. "The study of Chiropractic properly begins with a knowledge or conception of the ABSOLUTE," he told readers, "and proceeds by successive steps through the various steps that intervene before we arrive at a consideration of the ultimate expression of Energy in the tissue cells of man." For matter to be "affected" (i.e., for healing to take place), both "Purpose" and "Energy" were needed. Purpose came "in the determination of the Innate Mind to act." Meanwhile, Energy was "gathered in the brain, which acts as a condenser." "This energy," Loben continued significantly, "is akin to electricity except that it is a higher rate of vibration."[72]

Like Andrew Taylor Still, Loben could affirm that "man is a machine," but he hastened to add that he was "more than a mere expression of physical and chemical properties." Instead, he reiterated, "mental impulses" were "sent out through nerves to the various portions of the body." Issued "in a series of vibrations—a current continually flowing from the brain outward," in the body they were "expressed as life." Given this state of affairs, "dis-ease (the opposite of ease)" was "lack of harmony and in-co-ordination— a disturbance of equilibrium between mental creation and physical expression." In the recognizable terms of the magnetic model, it was "a swerving aside of current or a stoppage of one or more of the functions which must work together to produce complete and perfect life." [73]

If Still would have agreed with most of what Loben said, he would also have been comfortable with the relative absence of sin. More concerned with providing a theoretical ground for the *act* of chiropractic treatment than with an exploration of human nature as morally agent, Loben could relegate the moralistic attributions of earlier healers to a convenient mental attic. On the other hand, in a world of natural law such as the one that Loben had sketched, there was, finally, need for a culprit. Someone or something had to violate the law willfully if obstruction was to be convincingly explained.

Be that as it may, Loben—though evangelist for a gospel that was not Christian—was not beyond a concluding millennial flourish. "These germs of truth," he thought, "will be expanded and un-folded further and further as our minds grow more capable of grasping their details." In the future that he looked to, "Chiropractic adjustments shall have increased and broadened the scope of man's educated or objective mind," and he and others would be "blessed with more and more abundant knowledge." Loben foresaw a future of human progress, and at the apex of the future's glory there was chiropractic. "Who furthers the progress of humanity furthers his own advancement toward perfection, by laws of reciprocity, and the greatest opportunity of your life lies in the dissemnation [*sic*] of this, the grandest truth of history—Chiropractic." [74] Given all of that, D. D. Palmer's role—like that of other founder-healers before him—must have been messianic.

Depending on which nineteenth-century healer one listened to, the "grandest truth of history" might be anything from vegetarianism to water cure to physical manipulation. Beginning with the Christian physiologists and running through a series of "irregular" healing practitioners, the theology and ritual of physical religion were available to generations of ailing Americans. Alternative healing cut a wide swath through cross-sections of the population, often rural and sometimes urban, often poorer or lower middle-class, and sometimes wealthy. It throve on the incompetence of the regular medical profession, the anxieties of a society in transition, the pluralism of the political climate of liberty, and the real religious needs of the people. In keeping with its nonprofessional origins, the physical religion of the times reflected a series of confusions and inconsistencies. It was better at combining the heritages of several worlds than at sorting out contradictions and non sequiturs.

From Christian physiology to D. D. Palmer's chiropractic, "natural" forms of healing in the nineteenth century had traveled a long road. And, indeed, many of the twists in the road have necessarily been left unexamined. Nowhere have we explored eclecticism, or phrenomagnetism, or spiritualism, or occult healing of other stripes. Evangelicalism figured prominently for many of the healers we have met, and mesmerism and Swedenborgianism more subtly shaped the mental worlds of others. At the same time, the great uniting principle was the law that was nature. When the Enlightenment seemed to disappear in the nineteenth century, it had in reality only shifted shapes. It had become, in truth as in rhetoric, the heritage of the people. And, now in privatized form, it had empowered them to lay claim to the erstwhile Christian kingdom of sin and grace. Being well, it turned out, was the popular, romanticized analogue to being independent.[75]

Still further, if Nature and Nature's God had managed to stay even amid the triumph of evangelical times, the nature that stayed was decidedly multivalent. Indeed, D. D. Palmer and his successors had already suggested the range of possibilities. To designate his healing work, Palmer had selected the name *chiropractic* from several terms that a patient/friend, who was a Greek scholar, had offered at Palmer's request. Literally, *chiropractic* meant "done with the hands," and that was what Palmer wanted. But, in the mental world in which he lived, Palmer had probably chosen the new word over others after seeing references to *cheiromancy* (or *chiromancy*), the favored name for palmistry in the occult literature of his day. Reading human destiny in nature's imprint on each individual hand, the chiromancer prepared the way for the chiropractor, who read health or disease in the bony structure of the spine. Moreover, in Palmer's own small collection of pamphlets were two that were linked to the Theosophical Society, one coauthored by Annie Besant, its second leader, and the other introduced by Henry S. Olcott, one of the society's founders.[76] From 1875, Olcott, Helena P. Blavatsky, and others had pursued their new-old religion of nature in a specific quest for occult knowledge. Framed by themes of universal "brotherhood" and a syncretistic appropriation of Asian religious traditions, theosophy was one sign of a cluster of concerns that would grow through the twentieth century into our own times.[77]

On the other hand, the same year that D. D. Palmer claimed he discovered chiropractic, Wilhelm Conrad Roentgen, in Germany, discovered the X-ray. By 1909, the Palmer School in Davenport, Iowa, under the leadership of Palmer's son B. J. (Bartlett Joshua) Palmer, had acquired X-ray equipment. Perhaps half of the faculty and students left the school in protest,[78] but the acquisition was the beginning of a journey toward orthodoxy that would bring grudging medical acceptance for chiropractic by the late twentieth century. And it was also an implicit subscription to the *new* magnetic model that had dawned with the century. For the X-ray was an electromagnetic wave phenomenon, part of an electromagnetic spectrum that in its radiation ranged from cosmic waves to radio waves.

And yet again, the same year that D. D. Palmer claimed he had discovered chiropractic, another German, Max Planck, began his research on black bodies and their radiation. By 1900 Planck was reluctantly reading a paper before the German Physical Society, presenting results he could not explain in terms of Newtonian mechanics. The early nineteenth-century experiment of English scientist Thomas Young, with its double-slit apparatus, had shown light to be a wave. But now Planck told other physicists the puzzling news that light could be emitted and absorbed only in discontinuous packets of energy that he called *quanta*. Some five years later, in 1905, Albert Einstein presented a paper in which, still more radically, he proposed that radiant energy was itself composed of discrete and separate entities—tiny particles, or photons, that sped and collided as they went. Quantum theory was born. In the first thirty years of the twentieth century an international series of scientists worked to develop the theory's elegance and completeness with a mathematical language that gave it persuasive power.[79]

The news was that, at the subatomic level, electrons, which were components of atoms, behaved sometimes like particles and sometimes like waves. Matter in its subatomic reality dissolved into energy, which—as later mass-accelerator research would show—could be reconstituted as matter.[80] To make the model still more unstable, the patterns in which the transformations occurred could not be predicted accurately but could only be stated in terms of mathematical probabilities. Almost it seemed that electrons had consciousness and free will. And by 1927 the German physicist Werner Heisenberg was articulating his "unsharpness principle" or principle of uncertainty. There were limits to what humans could know about subatomic nature, and precision in one area could only be acquired at the expense of fuzziness in another. Nature, it appeared, was something of a tease, and ambiguity cloaked its presentation to human investigators. The action of the scientist altered the nature of the experiment.[81]

In such a state of affairs the firm foundations of the Newtonian world—with its absolute space and absolute time and with its commonsense laws of motion—crumbled before a universe blurred and indeterminate. Romanticism had its revenge, in earnest, on the Enlightenment world of the Great Machine. Or so it seemed. Quantum theory and the special (1905) and general (1915) theories of relativity changed the available metaphorical base for twentieth-century language. It was as though the old Swedenborgian and mesmeric worlds had, suddenly and unexpectedly, been resuscitated in new and eminently more respectable guise. Conflations of matter and energy at a subatomic level fanned the fires of metaphysical speculation at a cosmic one. The universal fluid, banished with the demise of the nineteenth-century theory of the ether, reappeared in a new physics with its "organic energy" of the quantum. Matter was, after all, "frozen light," spirit vibrating at a slower speed.[82]

Werner Heisenberg went on record with the verdict that modern physics had decided in favor of Plato. The smallest units of matter were not physical objects in the ordinary sense but forms, ideas to be expressed in mathematical language. And a "sharp separation between the world and the I" was now "impossible." The new physics was "part of a general historical process that tends toward a unification and a widening of our present world."[83]

The stage was set for a new religious synthesis in which the crack between nature as reality and nature as appearance, between ethics as harmony and ethics as mastery, could be welded more perfectly than before. And by 1948 the general historical process had found a new voice for nature on the large, environmental scale. Writing in his *Sand County Almanac,* the American Aldo Leopold, professor of game management at the University of Wisconsin, was repudiating an "Abrahamic concept of land" and calling for a land ethic. "We abuse land," he said,

because we regard it as a commodity belonging to us. When we see land as a community to which we belong, we may begin to use it with love and respect. There is no other way for land to survive the impact of mechanized man, nor for us to reap from it the esthetic harvest it is capable, under science, of contributing to culture.

Even more, land was "not merely soil" but rather "a fountain of energy flowing through a circuit of soils, plants, and animals." "Food chains" were "the living channels which conduct energy upward; death and decay return[ed] it to the soil."[84]

If so, a new twentieth-century circuit was on line. Theosophical reflection, environmental concern, and quantum physics could come together as they absorbed the past and then emitted it transformed. By the late twentieth century, Nature's God—and beside him now the Goddess—would clearly inhabit the land. With discernible enthusiasm and in new versions, religions of nature would recapitulate tales already told.

5 / Recapitulating Pieties ❧ NATURE'S
NATION IN THE LATE TWENTIETH CENTURY

In the fall of 1982, in the mid-American heartland of Nashville, Indiana, a group of young people launched *Earth Nation Sunrise.* Already organized as the Church of the Earth Nation, the six "cocreators" of the new periodical stated its purpose: "to bring light and love to all who come into contact with it. We are tired of the old and its negativity. We will let it pass on now with no further recognition from us." More explicitly, the editors proclaimed the gospel of nature's nation on the front page of their new journal. Below the photograph of a woodland lake shimmering in the rising sun, *Earth Nation Sunrise* announced:

Everywhere on planet Earth, whole kingdoms live in peace and abundance. From the plant ones to the swimmers, the crawlers, the flyers, and the four leggeds, the first creatures co-exist without war. Now, the human beings as well, have begun to learn through their brothers and sisters to live side by side cooperatively. Everywhere, all over the earth, human beings have gathered in small groups, laying down their differences and focusing on their common wisdom. They call themselves communities . . . coming into unity . . . for a new age on earth which shall be the embodiment of every positive thought we hold in our minds, just as the old age embodied our fears. The construction has begun, of a new reality, where the mysteries are revealed within each human being as s/he comes into harmony with the planet as a whole. We celebrate this sunrise . . . and the building of one earth nation.[1]

The rhetoric was disarming in its apparent simplicity. Behind it, though, lay the accumulated experience of several centuries of growth into nature's nation, this even and especially after the urban, industrialized society of the United States was flourishing. The reference to the "four leggeds" as "brothers and sisters" evoked a twentieth-century Native American consciousness tied to the American Indian heritage of the past. Impatience with the old and declaration of a "new age on earth" reiterated the Transcendental message Ralph Waldo Emerson had heralded in *Nature.* Language about "every positive thought we hold in our minds" tied the earth nation to mental healers who had mastered nature with mind. On the other hand, the vision of human beings living "side by side cooperatively" with animal and plant species, of people coming "into harmony with the planet as a whole," recalled the concerns of at least one side of the preservation and ecology movements.

Meanwhile, "small groups"-become-"communities" hinted at the formation of a new political order in the "building of one earth nation," a model of interconnectedness that also echoed the sub-atomic structure of the quantum. And, throughout, the evangelical tone linked the *Earth Nation's* proclamation to the nineteenth-century heirs of the Puritans. These Americans had experienced the new birth, often enough, in camp-meeting settings surrounded by woods or fields or near the water. From camp-meeting tents to "naturalistic" suburban tracts was not, after all, a big step; and, conversely, from the suburb to the woods was in many cases only so far as Henry David Thoreau's journey from Concord to Walden Pond.[2]

Hence, like the Hutchinson Family Singers, the Church of the Earth Nation recapitulated a "mytho-logic" of nature religion. But more than the Hutchinson Family Singers, church members in their statement recapitulated the temporal path that nature reli-gion had traveled in American history. In both of these respects, the Earth Nation's mid-American gospel was a sign of the presence of nature religion in the late twentieth century. Even the kind of cursory glance that a chapter such as this can provide reveals the existence and logic of earlier themes. The different denominations of the religion of nature flourish in our midst, and there is no sign of their abatement.

Amerindian immersion in nature lives on in a traditionalist ver-sion as well as in a New Age incarnation that is decidedly eclectic. Puritan/Calvinist awe at the violent wilderness and respect for its negative forces thrives in the work of some contemporary nature writers. Republican apotheosis of nature in a politicized ideology ranges through the present-day environmental movement, for ex-ample, as it manifests itself in the "Greens" and in ecofeminism. Transcendentalists prosper in the general harmonial-metaphysical dialectic of New Age religion and in the special case of Goddess religion. And physical religion persists in vibrational medicines that range from the contemporary laying on of hands to the quest for purity in food. All told, the recapitulating pieties move freely together, mixing and matching, bowing to new partners in a quantum dance of religious syncretism.

"I long ago lost a hound, a bay horse, and a turtle-dove, and am still on their trail," we recall that Henry David Thoreau wrote in *Walden*. "Many are the travellers I have spoken concerning them, describing their tracks and what calls they answered to."[3] Tracking the quantum energies of late twentieth-century nature religion calls to mind tracking Thoreau's hound, bay horse, and turtledove. We need to keep on the move and to speak to many travelers. Ironically, though, like Thoreau, we will never quite catch up, and we will replace experience with "ideal" construction. Moreover, the intellectual desire to control and organize will need to rest content with the record of an impressionistic trail. Like the history of nature religion that this book seeks to unfold, a survey of contemporary manifestations of the American religion of nature can only be episodic.

If we begin with the oldest Americans—those who form the continuing Amerindian population—the prominence of nature in religious symbol systems is clear. Moreover, Indian peoples have found their tongues and pens. New publications abound. Bookstores carry testimonial tales of religious experience in nature by Indian authors. And militant political activity by Native Americans often grounds itself, literally, in the earth religion of traditionalist medicine persons. Meanwhile, in their own pilgrim traditions of searching, non-Indians go to school among the natives, ritually undergoing sweats, forming medicine wheels for prayer and praise, pursuing shamanic vision journeys to the under and upper worlds.[4]

There is, of course, striking incongruity in linking traditionalists, New Age native teachers, and non-Indian seekers who often know how to turn religion to profit more than prophecy. Still, examined thematically, there is more striking congruity. Traditionalists and New Age Indians, whether native or adoptive, place nature at the center of religion and life. What unites traditionalists (who politicize the past) and New Agers (who transcendentalize it) is an abiding conviction of the centrality of nature and a continuing enactment of their concern. Nature provides a language to express cosmology and belief; it forms the basis for understanding and practicing a way of life; it supplies materials for ritual symbolization; it draws together a community. In short, like seventeenth-century Indians, contemporary Native Americans and their fellow travelers counter Euro-American Christianity with a religion of their own.

Take, for example, the religious activity of Sun Bear. Born Vincent La Duke in 1929, the son of a Chippewa (Ojibwa) father and a mother of German/Norwegian stock, Sun Bear spent his first twenty years on the White Earth Indian Reservation in northern Minnesota, where he received only an eighth-grade education. An army deserter (for reasons of conscience) in the Korean War, he spent some time in jail. He has also been an activist for Native American people and even a "Hollywood" Indian. But Sun Bear is best known today as founder of the Bear Tribe Medicine Society. Although it has been remarked sardonically that he is the only Indian in it, Sun Bear describes his intentional community as a "group of native and non-native people sharing the same vision, philosophy, and direction toward the Earth and the Creation around us."[5] With an apprenticeship program in Spokane, Washington, and a national following, that direction has become known and shared by thousands of non-Indian Americans. The nature of the vision and its direction is suggested by the Medicine Wheel Gatherings that Sun Bear and the Bear Tribe hold at various locations throughout the nation in an annual calendar of ceremonies and workshops.

Typically, medicine wheels take place over a weekend at a campground location where participants can bring sleeping bags, erect tents, or rent cabins.[6] Balancing ritual with teaching, the gatherings open with the construction of a huge circle of stones (the medicine wheel) to mark a sacred space. Sun Bear begins its consecration by placing at the center the skull of a buffalo or another sacred animal as sign of the creator and of the center of the universe. Then chosen individuals both honor and represent the powers that the stones symbolize as they place them within the wheel. Thirty-six stones, each of them for a part of the universe, become the medicine wheel as the entire community forms a circle around. People have been ceremonially smudged for purification, and they have made tobacco ties of cloth in colors to correspond to the colors

Sun Bear at a California Medicine Wheel Gathering. Photograph by Marti Kranz-
berg, 1982. (Courtesy, Bear Tribe Medicine Society.) Native American symbolism
functions as the prime carrier for forms of nature religion at Bear Tribe medicine
wheels.

of the directions. Most important, they have put into the ties their prayers.

Prayers are offered immediately again in the collective enter-prise of a pipe ceremony following the medicine wheel, the two ceremonies consecrating the weekend's activities and providing a prayer and meditation space for participants. Similarly, in the ad-aptation of a pattern common to many religious cultures, the close of the weekend's work is signaled by the Medicine Wheel Give Away in which participants bring food to give to the poor. Finally, as activities end, with its ritual disassembling the medicine wheel itself is given away.

In between, throughout the weekend, sweat lodge ceremonies offer the chance for individuals to undergo ritual purification in a traditional manner. A crystal healing ceremony provides the focus for group meditation for healing, and a children's blessing honors the contribution of the youngest members of the community. Drum-ming, chanting, dancing, and prayer form a ceremonial thread that weaves through the medicine wheel's time. Meanwhile, workshop sessions held by Bear Tribe teachers and their associates turn the campground into an outdoor school. United by a common "earth" wisdom, workshop topics may include anything from shamanism to women's "moontimes" (menstrual periods), from Hawaiian huna to star and herbal lore.

Sun Bear's Bear Tribe medicine wheels began after, according to his own account, late in the seventies Sun Bear in vision beheld a medicine wheel. Described by him as "an ancient stone circle which has been used for thousands of years by Native people as a place for prayer, ceremony and self-understanding," the medicine wheel was reborn in his new-old gatherings.[7] By 1980 the first was held at a national park campground near Mount Rainier in Wash-ington state, with an estimated six hundred people present. Later medicine wheels have sometimes attracted attendance of more than one thousand, many of the participants young but a surpris-ing number middle-aged or older.

Nor has Sun Bear stopped with oral teaching. As early as 1961 he had begun publishing in Los Angeles a monthly mimeographed sheet called *Many Smokes,* at first intended mostly for Native Americans. After at least two publication lulls, it resumed in 1972, growing and changing direction, and in the wake of many transmutations it continues today as the Bear Tribe's *Wildfire*. Meanwhile, Sun Bear himself, in a series of short books produced with the assistance of others, has communicated his latter-day version of a Native American nature religion.[8]

Perhaps the central message that Sun Bear brings is his conviction that the earth is a living being now in the midst of deep cleansing. In a prophecy that would be echoed in its own way in the New Age "harmonic convergence" of August 1987, Sun Bear sees an earth in tribulation. The Earth Mother, he believes, must heal herself of the sicknesses she has absorbed from human poisoning. "I felt the need to tell people that if they wanted to survive the coming earth cleansing," Sun Bear writes, "if they wanted to be part of the new earth, they would have to re-establish their very personal ties with the natural world." In fact, by 1983 Sun Bear believed that the time of the cleansing had already been going on some ten years. "It's plain to see," he observed, "with the volcanoes, the earthquakes, the changes in weather patterns."[9]

What does the medicine wheel have to do with the prophetic message of cleansing? It is "a means to help with the healing of the Earth Mother at this time," Sun Bear says. For it is both "a circle of stones placed on the ground" and "a set of symbols which have definite meaning in terms of your life." The medicine wheel is "similar to an astrology system," and it helps people to begin to know themselves. "Folks who don't know much about themselves, know very little about how to help save the planet."[10]

Sun Bear's need to talk of the relationship of humans to the earth had begun to coalesce perhaps as early as 1934. As a child suffering from diphtheria, Sun Bear tells, he had seen in trance a series of rolling balls of light, each a different color, that he was unable to catch. Nevertheless he remembers: "I reached out, touched the violet ball, and the others began to roll around me. They rolled faster and faster, until finally they blended; they formed a rainbow sphere around me." The vision continued as Sun Bear saw another light outside the sphere "brighter even than Father Sun." Through the light, Sun Bear relates, "an animal walked toward me; it seemed very large, and bright as the holy light." The animal was a black bear, and, as its confrontation with Sun Bear ended, "it stood on its hind legs, put its paw through the sphere and touched me gently on the hand."[11]

It was the inaugural vision of an exceptional religious man. Shaman, prophet, and teacher in one, Sun Bear claims to have experienced a number of visions.[12] This first one, though, reveals the inner dynamic of his religious activity. The bear, traditional healing animal of numerous Plains Indian societies, has become a bear of light and supplied Sun Bear his name. Sun Bear has mystically identified with its energies—and this in the context of a rainbow of colored balls that have become one sphere. Their coming together suggests the later union of Indian and non-Indian peoples in Sun Bear's Bear Tribe Medicine Society, a union that Sun Bear believes agrees with ancient prophecies.[13]

In the time of the earth cleansing—a time with prophecies of a ruined earth—walking in balance on the Earth Mother has become a kind of slogan for Sun Bear and the Bear Tribe.

The main thing I told people . . . was that in order to survive, they would have to relearn what their ancestors knew long ago. They would have to learn to walk in balance on the Earth Mother, use the earth's natural resources in a sensitive and sensible manner, without adding chemicals to everything, and pesticides, and all the other things which destroy the planet's delicate web of life.[14]

But, in a move to the metaphysical, walking in balance means attention to the internal as well as to the external environment. Repeatedly Sun Bear teaches that anger is counter to the spirit of the earth and to the spirit of his vision. Indeed, after the 1973 confrontation at Wounded Knee, South Dakota, when traditionalist holy men on the Pine Ridge (Oglala Sioux) Reservation supported Russell Means and the American Indian Movement (AIM), Sun Bear—who was there—had second thoughts. "I don't really believe in the taking up of arms. Although I believe that justice must be done, and that my brothers and sisters at Wounded Knee fought valiantly, I also believe that any act committed out of anger becomes, finally, an exercise in futility."[15]

To be angry, for the New Age Sun Bear, is to give away power, but "when you're centered in your energy and power, it's very difficult for anybody else to hurt you." And if power is not to be given away, neither does Sun Bear think it is to be held onto indiscriminately. What Sun Bear advocates is, instead, its increase and exchange. Hug a tree, he says, to begin your healing. "Trees are conductors of energy between the heavens and earth. When you hold and hug a tree, you feel the energy and it can be like a blood transfusion."[16] Meanwhile, energy exchange, for Sun Bear, happens in sexual intercourse, and it happens in a series of other human relationships. "The *sharing of energy* can be translated into sexual intercourse, as well as many other things. Another way to share energy is as a healer, and the power that helps us to make medicine is the same power as our sexual energy. It's a matter of channelling this power."[17]

Indeed, power is one's own; but power is also the property of all nature. In Sun Bear's cosmology, sharing and channeling power lead beyond oneself to the earth. "The invisible powers that are the spirit-keepers come to us, and when we lock ourselves into their energy we conduct it; we are working together, like electricity when it flows through certain kinds of crystals." Thus, Sun Bear's teaching is shamanic and mystical. We are part of the earth, he says, and so we can move and heal the wounded parts of our (earth) being.

It's very easy for me to move my fingers, to make my bones move because they're a part of me. In the same way, when you accept the fact that all creation is a part of you, you can move it, you can get it to respond to you. That's why some of us can speak with the animals and have them come to us when we call them. We can talk to the trees, to the Earth, to the Creator, and ask for what we need at a particular time. We've been doing it for thousands of years. *It's not supernatural. It's perfectly natural.*[18]

The perfectly natural, it turns out, is also the perfectly practical. Especially in the time of the cleansing, there are subtle hints of mastery within the harmonic merging. "I want my students to be able to hear the Earth when she speaks, and feel her," Sun Bear explains, "so that if an earthquake is coming or a volcano is about to erupt, or a fire is burning somewhere, they'll be ready for it. That's all part of how to survive the Cleansing, and a lot more people will survive if they learn to live in harmony."[19]

True, knowing the earth is, in Sun Bear's view, trusting the earth as, in small groups, individuals live through the cleansing. "Especially in this time of earth changes," Sun Bear counsels, "we must trust that the sudden floods, the unexpected tornadoes, the droughts, the earthquakes are all necessary happenings that will return the Earth Mother to a state in which she can bloom again cleansed of the poisons with which man has polluted her."[20] But, even so, trusting the earth does not mean passivity. Thus, *The Bear Tribe's Self Reliance Book* may begin with yet another Sun Bear vision and may be full of the message of medicine power and harmony with the earth. Nonetheless, long sections are devoted to the cultivation of intensely practical skills, with detailed instructions, for example, on how to forage for wild foods, on how to can, dry, and smoke foods, and on how to build root cellars.[21]

In sum, Sun Bear links the visionary to the down-to-earth, even as he links traditional Ojibwa and Plains Indian lore to environmental and survivalist movements and to the popular self-help religion of the New Age. How, then, are we to locate him, and what can we make of his message? Sun Bear is hardly a traditionalist: no traditionalist would tolerate his insistence on sharing sacred teachings and ceremonies with non-Indian people. (Indeed, there have been threats of violence by traditionalists against at least one full-blooded Native American who has offered workshops at Sun Bear's medicine wheels.) Still further, the substance of Sun Bear's teaching echoes the past but also syncretizes and romanticizes it. His teaching is, obviously, not specifically Ojibwa. But beyond his generalizing to a kind of Plains-Indian—and even pan-Indian—orthodoxy and orthopraxy, Sun Bear has entered a world in which the clear, defined boundaries of a Native American heritage have subtly softened. Some parts of the past (such as medicine wheels and crystals) have been lifted to new prominence. Others (such as hunting and burial practices) meanwhile decline.

Moreover, Sun Bear—product not only of a Chippewa past but of a Euro-American one as well—exercises the shaman's ultimate gift. He "makes it up as he goes along." Sun Bear, in other words, creates—out of the past, out of his construction of the past, and out of a California and West Coast present that has left him open to the twin teachings of environmentalism and the New Age. Cleaning up pollution did not figure as a motive in traditional American Indian nature religions. Hugging a tree sounds as likely to be a message from an Esalen encounter weekend as to be a message from an Indian grandfather. Sharing energies in sexual congress has a distinctly contemporary ring. And doing workshops for the uninitiated would hardly occupy the time of a nineteenth-century Ojibwa mother.

So Sun Bear, in terms of his heritage, is an innovator. That said, however, it needs to be noticed that he has kept clear touch with the past. His ceremonies and teachings, fuzzy at the seams as they are, can still be recognized as Indian in provenance. Indeed, to estimate his fidelity to the past, one need only look at any one of a number of recent non-Indian appropriations of Indian themes. The anthropologist Michael Harner, for example, spent extended periods of time (1956–57 and 1960–61) among the Jivaro and Conibo Indians of South America. His fieldwork taught him firsthand to experience the mystical journeys of a shaman by using the potent (and dangerous) medicines that the Indians gave him to alter consciousness. By 1980 Harner's highly successful *Way of the Shaman* was published, and his Harner Method of undertaking shamanic journeys—relying on sonic driving (drumming) instead of drugs to change awareness—was already being taught.[22] Gradually, Harner's Center (and then Foundation) for Shamanic Studies emphasized the worldwide nature of shamanism and shamanistic technique, heightened its reliance on the technology of the tape recorder for sonic driving, and grew away from an Indian cultural base.

Seen from the perspective of a Michael Harner, therefore, Sun Bear occupies a middle place. He would keep touch with a native past in a way that a Harner would not. Some generalizing and adapting have taken place for Sun Bear, but it is hardly the kind of universalizing and changing that Michael Harner represents. To follow Sun Bear is to be introduced to Indian people and their cultural heritage.

Indian people, or their Algonkian forebears, had once squared off against New England Puritans with their profoundly different vision of the natural world. The Puritans are gone in our time, but something of their imposing Calvinist ethos yet remains. One good place to look for it is in the reflections of sometime nature writer Annie Dillard, author of numerous literary works and, among them, the now-classic *Pilgrim at Tinker Creek*.

Dillard was born in Pittsburgh in 1945 to economically and socially privileged parents, and she inherited a Presbyterian legacy. Her father, Father Doak, "a lapsed Presbyterian and a believing Republican," had come "from an ordinary Scotch-Irish family so devotedly Presbyterian they forbade looking at the Sunday funnies." And the Presbyterian past was not lost on Dillard. With her sister, for four summers she attended a church camp where "the faith-filled theology" was "only half a step out of a tent; you could still smell the sawdust." Dillard recalls that she had "a head for religious ideas"; and at weekly Sunday school in Pittsburgh her head was fully supplied with biblical fare. "I had miles of Bible in memory: some perforce, but most by hap, like the words to songs." She remembers reading "innumerable righteous orange-bound biographies" and wondering at adult innocence regarding the prophetic opposition of the Bible to their world. And Dillard also remembers that when she attended a Unitarian friend's Sunday school once and found herself folding paper "to make little geese," it "shocked" her "to the core." [23]

The Calvinism of the heritage must have stuck, for Annie Dillard's religion of nature is played in a key distinctly different from that of Sun Bear. As a teenager, she "signed off" from Shadyside Presbyterian Church by writing the minister a self-described "fierce letter." [24] If the gesture echoed a famous nineteenth-century naturalist, so did the continuing complexity and the enduring Calvinism of her vision of nature. Like Henry David Thoreau, Annie Dillard had serious questions to address to the institutional church. But also, like him and like the Puritans before them both, she has been haunted by the relationship of God to nature.

"I used to have a cat, an old fighting tom," Dillard begins *Pilgrim at Tinker Creek*. He "would jump through the open window by my bed in the middle of the night and land on my chest. . . . He'd stick his skull under my nose and purr, stinking of urine and blood. . . . Some mornings I'd wake in daylight to find my body covered with paw prints in blood; I looked as though I'd been painted with roses." So *Pilgrim at Tinker Creek* is written under the mysterious fire sign of blood. An account of a year the author lived in the mountain valley of Tinker Creek in the Virginia Blue Ridge, Dillard's report is a meditation on violence and beauty, on fire and mystical fusion with a "spendthrift" and extravagant natural world. Significantly, the words of the ancient Greek philosopher Heraclitus form an epigraph for her work. "It ever was, and is, and shall be, ever-living Fire, in measures being kindled and in measures going out." [25]

The different (from Sun Bear) energy that moves through Dillard's work is reflected in the different ritual that forms its central ceremony. While Sun Bear and his Bear Tribe repeat natural circles in a medicine wheel suggesting harmony, Dillard's rite is linear and more strident. Dillard stalks. "Certain Indians," she says, "used to carve long grooves along the wooden shafts of their arrows." Called "lightning marks," the grooves channeled blood from a deep wound, so that if an Indian failed to kill the game there would be a trail of blood to follow. "I am an explorer, then, and I am also a stalker, or the instrument of the hunt itself. . . . I am the arrow shaft, carved along my length by unexpected lights and gashes from the very sky, and this book is the straying trail of blood." [26]

What Dillard stalks is nature, and often the "straying trail of blood" is the discipline her solitary ceremony demands. "It is ironic," she writes, "that the one thing that all religions recognize as separating us from our creator—our very self-consciousness—is also the one thing that divides us from our fellow creatures." What to do in face of the rift? "Catch it if you can. The present is an invisible electron; its lightning path traced faintly on a blackened screen is fleet, and fleeing, and gone." So stalking demands the absorption of all one's awareness in the small space that is wedge between past and future. "All I want to do is stay awake," Dillard declares, "keep my head up, prop my eyes open, with toothpicks, with trees." [27]

This kind of attentiveness does not come easily. "Learning to stalk muskrats," she says, took her "several years." Driven by her desire to see muskrats, she stalked them "day and night." "I walked up creeks and down, but no muskrats ever appeared. You must just have to be there, I thought. You must have to spend the rest of your life standing in bushes. It was a once-in-a-lifetime thing, and you've had your once." But the ritual discipline paid. "Then one night I saw another, and my life changed. After that I knew where they were in numbers, and I knew when to look." [28]

Another time, watching the maneuvers of a muskrat—with some elaborate maneuvers of her own to maintain a frozen posture for its benefit—her pains were rewarded when it climbed on the bank beside her. The muskrat was close enough for her to touch, but it foraged cheerfully without seeing her. "I was," Dillard remembers, "as purely sensitive and mute as a photographic plate; I received impressions, but I did not print out captions. My own self-awareness had disappeared; it seems now as though, had I been wired with electrodes, my EEG would have been flat." Reflecting on the process, Dillard acknowledges, "I have done this sort of thing so often that I have lost self-consciousness about moving slowly and halting suddenly; it is second nature to me now. And I have noticed that even a few minutes of this self-forgetfulness is tremendously invigorating." That she cites the Jewish mystic Martin Buber in the context of her recollection is almost an aside.[29]

Indeed, sometimes the stalking clearly happens of itself, a quality of the form of attention that Dillard, even without consciously trying, has developed. And the nature she stalks is, as clearly, red in tooth and claw—but also wildly sacred, demanding complicity in its violent beauty, union with the fire mystery it signals. Once Dillard was stalking frogs to frighten them for her amusement when she came on a frog being sucked up alive by a huge water bug. "The spirit vanished from his eyes as if snuffed. His skin emptied and drooped; his very skull seemed to collapse and settle like a kicked tent. . . . Soon, part of his skin, formless as a pricked balloon, lay in floating folds like bright scum on top of the water: it was a monstrous and terrifying thing." [30]

With violence less apparent, on a day she would never forget Dillard experienced a cosmic awareness that was light and fire. Inspired by reading about a blind girl who, with vision newly created by an operation, saw in her garden "the tree with the lights in it," Dillard herself saw the tree. She had been searching for it, she said, "for years."

Then one day I was walking along Tinker Creek thinking of nothing at all and I saw the tree with the lights in it. I saw the backyard cedar where the mourning doves roost charged and transfigured, each cell buzzing with flame. I stood on the grass with the lights in it, grass that was wholly fire, utterly focused and utterly dreamed. It was less like seeing than like being for the first time seen, knocked breathless by a powerful glance.[31]

The vision faded but did not fade, a touch point for the time ahead. "The flood of fire abated, but I'm still spending the power. . . . The vision comes and goes, mostly goes, but I live for it, for the moment when the mountains open and new light roars in spate through the crack, and the mountains slam." Nonetheless, another form of awareness roars through the crack for Dillard, and she acknowledges the destructive, almost trivial conjunction that brought her vision. Meditating on the omnivorousness that is nature's unkept secret, on the unmitigated feeding of species on species, she thinks again of the tree with the lights in it. This time she thinks about the presence on it of galls, of swellings of tissue caused by fungi or insect parasites. "Were the twigs of the cedar I saw really bloated with galls? They probably were; they almost surely were. I have seen those 'cedar apples' swell from that cedar's green before and since: reddish-gray, rank, malignant." [32]

There is cancer in the cosmos, and Dillard must come to terms with it. She cannot deny the vision and its power. Neither can she deny the galls. "Can I say then that corruption is one of beauty's deep-blue speckles, that the frayed and nibbled fringe of the world is a tallith, a prayer shawl, the intricate garment of beauty? It is very tempting, but I honestly cannot." [33]

What, then, *can* Dillard do? She can think long thoughts about corruption being something that eats around the edges while beauty is firm at the core. And she can ponder her place as a "frayed and nibbled survivor in a fallen world." She can see herself as a "sacrifice bound with cords to the horns of the world's rock altar, waiting for worms." But, like the Christian tradition, and especially its Calvinist incarnation, she is stuck with the problem of evil. There is a depth, a capacity for pain, in her religion of nature that is not matched in the vision of the healing bear. Dillard, we might say in the language of William James, has been "twice born," while Sun Bear and his followers—despite all of *their* pain—have survived by being born only once. [34]

Pain, for Dillard, means life lived on the cutting edge. And she can exult even in malignancy as she waits for the knife to cut. "Looking, I see there are worms in the horns of the altar like live maggots in amber, there are shells of worms in the rock and moths flapping at my eyes. A wind from noplace rises. A sense of the real exults me; the cords loose; I walk on my way." Or again, in a flashback to an earlier experience, creeping malignancy becomes cosmic devourment. Dillard sees with mystical sight that the giant water bug sucking life out of the frog "ate the world." Her response is as decisive: "I go my way, and my left foot says 'Glory,' and my right foot says 'Amen': in and out of Shadow Creek, upstream and down, exultant, in a daze, dancing, to the twin silver trumpets of praise."[35]

What is real, what is firm at the core for Dillard, is the Holy. And for her the Holy comes often enough violent, incongruent, and monstrous. Even in childhood Dillard was touching the edges of the mystery. She remembers the schooltime incident concerning a huge polyphemus moth. One of her friends had brought a moth co-coon to school, and the teacher encouraged the children to pass it around. The warmth of their hands caused the creature inside to warm and squirm; the delighted children held it only tighter. Fi-nally, the teacher interrupted to put the disturbed cocoon in a jar. Slowly, agonizingly, the moth clawed its way out. Then the horror:

He couldn't spread his wings. There was no room. The chemical that coated his wings like varnish, stiffening them permanently, dried, and hardened his wings as they were. He was a monster in a Mason jar. Those huge wings stuck on his back in a torture of random pleats and folds, wrinkled as a dirty tissue, rigid as leather. They made a single nightmare clump still wracked with useless, frantic convulsions.[36]

The teacher intervened again to let the moth out of the jar onto an asphalt driveway. "He heaved himself down the asphalt drive-way by infinite degrees, unwavering. His hideous crumpled wings lay glued and rucked on his back, perfectly still now, like a col-lapsed tent." In her autobiographical account of her childhood, Dillard recalls knowing "that this particular moth, the big walking moth, could not travel more than a few more yards before a bird or a cat began to eat it, or a car ran over it." Yet there was something vital at its creature core. "Nevertheless, it was crawling with what seemed wonderful vigor, as if, I thought at the time, it was still ex-cited from being born."[37]

The flash of pain is the flash of life. In *Holy the Firm* Dillard tells readers that "nothing is going to happen in this book. There is only a little violence here and there in the language, at the corner where eternity clips time." The violence erupts, again, under the fire sign. There is, for the beginning, another moth, this one flying into a nighttime candle. "The moth's wings vanished in a fine, foul smoke. At the same time her six legs clawed, curled, blackened, and ceased, disappearing utterly. And her head jerked in spasms, making a spattering noise; her antennae crisped and burned away and her heaving mouth parts crackled like pistol fire."[38]

Even then the epiphany of death was incomplete:

And then this moth-essence, this spectacular skeleton, began to act as a wick. She kept burning. The wax rose in the moth's body from her soaking abdomen to her thorax to the jagged hole where her head should be, and widened into flame, a saffron-yellow flame that robed her to the ground like any immolating monk. That candle had two wicks, two flames of identical height, side by side. The moth's head was fire. She burned for two hours, until I blew her out.[39]

What hovers in and behind the flame is the inscrutable deity that demands the sacrifice, that watches—and burns—the martyr at the stake. And the flame sears human nature as well. There is one Julie Norwich, seven years old. (Is the name a coincidence, or does it consciously hark back to that other Julie, Julian of Norwich, fourteenth-century English mystic who found in divine love the answer to evil?)[40] Living alone on northern Puget Sound in the state of Washington, Dillard one day saw a small plane fall out of the sky. "The fuel exploded; and Julie Norwich seven years old burnt off her face." That she has met the child and has found echoes of herself in her does not help. "Her face is slaughtered now, and I don't remember mine." So the accident brings bitter pondering, a skeptic's challenge to the forbidding (and hauntingly Calvinist) force that imposes itself on the world. "It is the best joke there is, that we are here, and fools—that we are sown into time like so much corn, that we are souls sprinkled at random like salt into time and dissolved here, spread into matter, connected by cells right down to our feet, and those feet likely to fell us over a tree root or jam us on a stone."[41]

For Dillard, skeptic's challenge becomes Job-like complaint. "God despises everything, apparently." Anger becomes another kind of flame at the "evidence of things seen: one Julie, one sorrow, one sensation bewildering the heart, and enraging the mind." "Of faith I have nothing," Dillard asserts, "only of truth: that this one God is a brute and traitor, abandoning us to time, to necessity and the engines of matter unhinged." Yet anger transmutes to philosophical question; and answer, to a mystical and catholic Christ. "The question is, then, whether God touches anything. Is anything firm, or is time on the loose?" And answer comes in a landscape aflame. "Each thing in the world is translucent, even the cattle, and moving, cell by cell. I remember this reality."[42]

It is the "one glare of holiness," the Christ interfused with all the world.

I see, blasted, the bay transfigured below me, the saltwater bay . . . the bay and the islands on fire and boundless beyond it, catching alight the unraveling sky. Pieces of the sky are falling down. Everything, everything, is whole, and a parcel of everything else. I myself am falling down, slowly, or slowly lifting up. On the bay's stone shore are people among whom I float, real people, gathering of an afternoon, in the cells of whose skin stream thin colored waters in pieces which give back the general flame.[43]

Holy the Firm is the substratum of the world, "in touch with the Absolute, at base." A concept borrowed from "esoteric Christianity," something like the prime matter of Aristotle, it is "matter at its dullest." Dillard embraces the idea. Still "there is Julie Norwich. Julie Norwich is salted with fire. She is preserved like a salted fillet from all evil, baptized at birth into time and now into eternity, into the bladelike arms of God. For who will love her now, without a face?" The answer is uneasy. "Julie Norwich; I know. Surgeons will fix your face. This will all be a dream, an anecdote, something to tell your husband one night."[44]

So there is Holy the Firm, and there is a cosmic Christ—a kind of communion fused with all the world. There is a plane that has fallen out of the sky, obedient to the natural law of gravity's force; and there is little Julie Norwich. They are all, for Dillard, "showings" of the divine, revelations of the fire. But the tension is unresolved, the stridency still present. Something of a Puritan brooding over evil remains. Nature is not simple, as it is for Sun Bear—in need only of a cleansing from the pollution humans have wrought. Nature is accomplice to what we read as evil, malignant itself. The home of demons and demonic force, the Puritans would have said. Dillard's estimate, less personified, is not less sensitive to a negative power, almost a negative sacred, within the natural world. On the level of gross nature, Newton—not the quantum—rules, and the communion ceremony is also the interconnectedness of devourment.

Annie Dillard in later life surely unsigned her adolescent "signing off" from the church. She has written of attending Congregational and Roman Catholic churches, and a fascination with Roman Catholicism is apparent in her work.[45] But the violent beauty that meets her in nature is product of a different legacy. Heir to the general Christian problem of evil, she confronts it in a recognizably Calvinist way. If her writing suggests a quality of mind and act that is shared (and the steady market for her books suggests that it does), in one form or another the seventeenth-century Puritan struggle with nature is alive in late twentieth-century American society.

Yet for all that, Dillard's vision is a distinctly private one. Set beside the medicine wheels of Sun Bear, with their public and political potential, her religion of nature is acted out in solitude. Others in contemporary America, however, have been quick to read their nature religion as political, not merely in the Bear Tribe's gentle and implicit way but loudly and actively so. Ideological linkage of nature to nation came strongly in the eighteenth-century language of the republic. In the closing years of the twentieth century, a new form of politicized myth, played out for different reasons, can still be found. Indeed, the twentieth-century linkage between nature and nation flourishes on many fronts; and it is tempting, for example, to examine the national park movement or the wilderness movement as more or less recent American incarnations. Here, though, for the sake of the very contemporary case, we look to the growing political movement known familiarly as the Greens.

"Imagine, if you will, an alternative political party that gives highest priority to the interconnectedness of all life on Earth—indeed, a party that sees the Earth as a living being, whose life we must help sustain and replenish." So wrote Stephan Bodian and Florence Windfall in a 1988 issue of a popular New Age journal.[46] By that time the alternative political party was, clearly, more than imaginary. In nations such as England, West Germany, Italy, Austria, Belgium, and Switzerland, there were Green political parties, and Greens had held elective office.

Less than four years earlier, in 1984, however, the organizational beginnings of Green politics in the United States were just becoming apparent. With an invitational meeting of sixty-two concerned individuals at Macalester College in St. Paul, Minnesota, a loose coalition emerged. They named themselves the Committees of Correspondence (after the grass-roots network that worked for the patriot cause in the American Revolution), and they hammered out their collective agreement in a statement they called

Ten Key Values. By March of 1986, the language of their list included ecological wisdom, grass-roots democracy, personal and social responsibility, nonviolence, decentralization, community-based economics, postpatriarchal values, respect for diversity, global responsibility, and future focus.[47]

"How can we operate human societies with the understanding that we are *part* of nature, not on top of it?" asks the Green document. "How can we replace the cultural ethics of dominance and control with more cooperative ways of interacting?"[48] In fact, the ethic of being part of the whole and never on top extends even to the institutionalization of Green concerns. It is for this reason, among others, that Greens are loosely joined in a network of local organizations, perhaps one hundred of them. They work together through federations that operate regionally and through a nationwide clearinghouse of the Committees of Correspondence in Kansas City, Missouri. And in the late eighties they have concentrated on local organizing around a series of environmental and human issues: toxic wastes and nuclear power plants, economic democracy and agricultural reform, a technology of renewable resources and the needs of homeless people. Yet, despite the repugnance toward hierarchy, the Green agenda looks to the formation of a national political party by the last decade of the century.

What fuels the Greens in these and similar matters is a vision and active commitment that are essentially religious. And what is as surprising is the degree of Green awareness of the religious dimension of their work. Bodian and Windfall write insightfully of the sources of Green spirituality in a series of world traditions. Citing Buddhist emphasis on "the interconnectedness of all life," they say that from the Buddhists Greens "draw their emphasis on inner peace, non-grasping, right livelihood, and the inseparability of body, heart, and mind." From the Christians, they continue, Greens "draw their emphasis on the poor and lowly inheritors of the Earth." Most of all, they declare, "Greens owe their spirituality to Native Americans and other indigenous peoples." Bodian and Windfall go on to note that "many Greens practice some form of paganism, neo-paganism, shamanism, or goddess religion, and many worship the Earth as a spiritual being."[49]

In the summer of 1987 a Green National Conference in Amherst, Massachusetts, revealed a division between "spiritual" and "leftist" Greens. But most of those present, argue Bodian and Windfall, thought that "an implicit spiritual orientation was quintessentially Green." Beyond that, a Bioregional Conference Spirituality Committee has encouraged ceremonial honoring of seasonal cycles. "Learn from the Earth," the committee urges. "Learn the names, identities, and habits of the other species who share our regions and the lessons they have to teach us; attuning to the cycles of the sun, the moon, and the other elemental forces; finding and protecting the sacred places and power points of our regions." [50]

Perhaps the most studied expression of the nature religion that permeates Green politics comes from Charlene Spretnak. In her *Spiritual Dimensions of Green Politics,* Spretnak, an organizer of the 1984 Minnesota meeting and a founder of the Committees of Correspondence, notes Green ideas for "sustainable" systems in economy, democracy, and the like. To these she links a question: *"What is sustainable religion?"* Spretnak finds answers in both the context and substance of Green thinking. Green politics, for Spretnak, reject "the anthropocentric orientation of humanism." "We need only consider the proportions of the environmental crisis to realize the dangerous self-deception contained in both religious and secular humanism," she writes. "It is *hubris* to declare that humans are the central figures of life on Earth and that we are in control. In the long run, *Nature is in control.*" [51]

Spretnak declares that Green politics counter modernity in favor of a vision that "goes beyond." Modern culture, she argues, "is based on mechanistic analysis and control of human systems as well as Nature, rootless cosmopolitanism, nationalistic chauvinism, sterile secularism, and monoculture shaped by mass media." And Greens, she continues, counter patriarchal values, which include "not only injustice toward women but also . . . love of hierarchical structure and competition, love of dominance-or-submission modes of relating, alienation from Nature, suppression of empathy and other emotions, and haunting insecurity about all of these matters." [52]

Casting an eye toward the classical background, Spretnak reads the coming of Indo-European culture (ca. 4500 B.C.) as a major negative event in world history. At that time, she says, early neolithic culture, with its "sophisticated understanding of our interrelatedness with Nature and her cycles," met its demise. "Once reverence for the mysteries of the life force was removed from Nature and placed in a remote judgmental sky god—first Zeus, then Yahweh—it was only a matter of time before the 'Great Chain of Being' would place the sky god at the top of 'natural order' and Nature at the bottom (trailing just behind white women, white children, people of color, and animals)." In this context, Spretnak eschews the Enlightenment—for her the source of contemporary cultural problems—and quotes poet Gary Snyder with approval: "'Our troubles began with the invention of male deities located off the planet.'"[53]

Given this analysis of contemporary life, Spretnak looks to Green politics to embody posthumanist, postmodern, and postpatriarchal values. "Sustainable religion," therefore, is religion that—pluralistic like our society—yet expresses and advances these values. And Spretnak describes its substance by articulating her own notion of spirituality. It is "the focusing of human awareness on the subtle aspects of existence, a practice that," she affirms, "reveals to us profound interconnectedness." What follows is a clear statement of one contemporary form of nature religion. Faulting Newtonian physics for its inability to model the behavior of matter beyond a "middle range," she writes:

At the subatomic and astrophysical levels . . . Newtonian explanations are inadequate. Similarly, our perceptions at the gross levels—that we are all separate from Nature and from each other—are revealed as illusion once we employ the subtle, suprarational reaches of mind, which can reveal the true nature of being: all is One, all forms of existence are comprised of one continuous dance of matter/energy arising and falling away, arising and falling away.[54]

Hovering behind this affirmation is assuredly at least an acquaintance with popular accounts of quantum theory. The unpredictable behavior of the smallest particles of "matter," dancing in and out of existence, acting now like particles and now like waves, has impressed Spretnak as it has many others. But hovering behind the Spretnak affirmation, too, is a more than passing acquaintance with the traditional language of Christian theology. Thus, Spretnak can go on to declare that what she is describing is "'God consciousness.'" "Such experiential, rather than merely intellectual, awareness of the profound connectedness is what I hold to be the true meaning of being in 'a state of grace.' Awe at the intricate wonders of creation and celebration of the cosmic unfolding are the roots of worship." [55]

However, if Spretnak seeks to come to terms with the Judeo-Christian tradition, she also seeks, from her own perspective, to correct it and to move beyond it. So far as she is concerned, church religion has not sufficiently noticed human bodies. "Much could be gained by *paying attention* to our body wisdom rather than seeking transcendence 'above' the body to realms of the sky god." And again: "We have not yet recognized the teachings I call 'body parables,' which are inherent in our sexuality." Nor has church religion cared sufficiently about the environment. There is, for Spretnak, a "disparity between Judeo-Christian religion and ecological wisdom." She tells us that suspicion of nature as the domain of paganism—shame of its own "'pagan' inheritance"—runs through the tradition. Spretnak warns: "Religion that sets itself in opposition to Nature and vehemently resists the resacralizing of the natural world on the grounds that it would be 'pagan' to do so is not sustainable over time." [56]

Thus, nature religion, in Spretnak's Green incarnation of it, plays itself out in the body wisdom of individuals but, as clearly, extends outward into the environmental body of the world. And the world is alive: it is *she,* the female presence of the deity. It is Gaia.

From the eternal Void, Gaia danced forth and rolled Herself into a spinning ball. She molded mountains along Her spine, valleys in the hollows of Her flesh. A rhythm of hills and stretching plains followed Her contours. From Her warm moisture She bore a flow of gentle rain that fed Her surface and brought life. Wriggling creatures spawned in tidal pools, while tiny green shoots pushed upward through Her pores. She filled oceans and ponds and set rivers flowing through deep furrows. Gaia watched Her plants and animals grow. In time She brought forth from Her womb six women and six men. [57]

In the end, Spretnak argues that the Green conception of sustainable religion means emphasizing "spiritual development through inner growth, ecological wisdom, gender equality, and social responsibility." Available to some degree in the nation's religious traditions, these values-become-goals need to be stressed for growth "toward deeply meaningful religion that does not separate itself from Nature, from our bodies, and from women." In this formula,

Spretnak has voiced an agenda for organized religious bodies in American society. However, that fact should not obscure the prior religiousness out of which she writes, a religiousness personified in the sacred claims of Gaia but present in more "secular" garb in notions of "deep ecology" and the like.[58] The (deep-ecological) gospel of interconnectedness, its radical leveling of humans with other species, its repudiation of human dominance over the environment as being fraught with violence for the ecosystem—all of this constitutes a religious vision already at the core of Green politics.

The vision fans out from the Committees of Correspondence, as Green politics merge with a series of movements in our times. Indeed, the vision of Gaia as living person has received scientific bolstering of sorts in James Lovelock's "Gaia hypothesis" that the earth behaves as a single entity.[59] And the vision of Gaia is uppermost for ecofeminists, who sometimes work in concert with the Greens but who also move in their own different directions. That Spretnak herself has edited the massive and often-cited *Politics of Women's Spirituality* is but one straw in the wind.[60] For the women's spirituality movement finds concrete expression in new ecofeminist endeavors, linking women to earth and to a religion of nature.

The term *ecofeminism* dates at least to 1980, when the University of Massachusetts at Amherst became the site for a three-day conference of perhaps four hundred women. Titled "Women and Life on Earth: EcoFeminism in the 80's," the meeting drew women concerned about practical issues such as nuclear power, toxic waste dumps, and runaway technology. But it also affirmed "the importance of women's energy in healing the Earth."[61] And the opening statement for the meeting, coauthored by Grace Paley and Ynestra King, was revealing.

We here are part of a growing movement of women for life on Earth. We come from the feminist movement, the anti-nuclear movement, the disarmament movement, the holistic health movement. We have come because life on Earth and the Earth itself is in terrible danger. We feel a great urgency. . . .
We're here to say the word ECOLOGY and announce that for us as feminists it's a political word—that it stands against the economics of the

destroyers and the pathology of racist hatred. It's a way of being, which understands that there are connections between all living things and that indeed we women are the fact and flesh of connectedness.[62]

The ecofeminist way of being has spawned a series of conferences, threading together, as the Greens have done, an implicit religion of nature with political concerns. When measured against the republican religion of the revolutionary era, of the writings of Thomas Jefferson and even—later—of the populist Davy Crockett almanacs, this contemporary wearing of the green is surely ironic. The spontaneous and still self-conscious appropriation of nature for the needs of the republic in the late eighteenth century has yielded unlikely descendants. Eighteenth-century republicans yoked nature to their essentially conservative revolution, creating ideology through their studied use of natural themes, orchestrating the enthusiasm of a populace with the sacred banner of earth and sky. Jefferson, after all, was on *top* and looking down at Natural Bridge. On the other hand, the contemporary greening of America *begins* with a radical religious impulse, with nature, if anywhere, on top. The greening is a gesture of estrangement from received religion, a revolution in mentality spilling over into politics. There is little—or no—ideology of the nation as such in the new environmental politics. Much more, there is a pragmatic willingness to use politics for the sake not of nation but of nature itself.

Put another way, while the direction of the first revolution was essentially centripetal—if one understands the center to be on the American side of the Atlantic—the direction of the second is centrifugal. Present-day Committees of Correspondence and their fellow-travelers may attempt self-consciously to repeat the networking structure of colonial patriots. In our own society, they hardly achieve the colonial result. In fact, it is not too much to say that what the eighteenth century preached rhetorically, with a nature mysticism linked to the political destiny of the republic, contemporary nature politicians live out with a kind of literalism, a fundamentalism of the earth, that is decidedly new and decidedly twentieth century. For all the quantum talk of interconnectedness, political bonds of affection are formed warily, with a distrust of traditional government power. Tremendous continuity flourishes in the instinct that links nature to politics and that makes of politics a religious process. As tremendous a gulf separates the nature politics of the eighteenth from those of the late twentieth century. In the eighteenth century, Gaia had not yet broken away from existence as a literary conceit, a romanticized personification of the classical past come to new birth as Columbia, the infant republic of the United States. In our own time, Gaia is the Goddess, and the nation is suspect.

To name the Goddess, however, is to move from her exclusively green incarnation to a more metaphysical view. For in the late twentieth century the Goddess functions at the center of an immanentist transcendentalism that puts earth—as earth—squarely in the camp of heaven. The Goddess commands a theology and promotes a ritual. She encourages an ethic born in devotion to her, and she brings together a community. Gaia, in short, presides over an authentically American form of paganism.

In *Drawing Down the Moon,* her encyclopedic account of contemporary paganism in the United States, Margot Adler keeps to the centrifugal theology. In company with the movement she represents, Adler understands paganism to mean "the pre-Christian nature religions of the West." In America, she includes in their number "the feminist goddess-worshippers, new religions based on the visions of science-fiction writers, attempts to revive ancient European religions—Norse, Greek, Roman, Celtic—and the surviving tribal religions."[63]

Adler herself worships the Goddess, and she considers herself a modern-day witch. Many others—perhaps the majority—who honor the Goddess do not call themselves witches; and, conversely, the Goddess is not so prominent in some forms of contemporary paganism as in others. Still, the Goddess reigns over a fairly widespread American religious movement, a particular form of nature religion. Estimating the number of the Goddess's followers, Adler suggests that roughly ten thousand Americans "identify themselves with the broad Neo-Pagan phenomenon, with its journals and newsletters, its covens, groves, and groups." She adds that "many other groups and individuals may exist without such links."[64] And if we count in their number a host in the women's spirituality movement and still others in the New Age movement, we begin to find in the entourage of the Goddess a group of considerable size.

What can the Goddess mean to these people, and what does she expect of them? The short answer that can be given here is the general word that does not distinguish subtleties defining different constituencies. Still, the short answer suggests the power of the Goddess in the lives of her adherents and discloses the commands she lays on them. In fact, the Goddess is no doubt among the most self-conscious of deities who have inhabited the minds and worlds of human beings. She is pervasively understood as a symbol even as she bestows life and receives praise. In a society that values religious literalness, she champions religious metaphor.

What the Goddess means is earth and its energies, but earth transformed and transfigured by its capacity for magic. For the Goddess exalts religious imagination and pushes it consistently into act. In her classic incarnation in the collective memory of European shamanism, she is "related to the ancient Mother Goddess in her three aspects of Maiden, Mother, and Crone."[65] Her consort is the Horned God, the lord of animals and forests, associated with hunting and the forces of death. Thus, the Goddess through all of her history embodies fertility, the creativity of the seed and the springtime, and also, reflecting that larger environment, the creativity of the human mind.

In this context, the Goddess focuses the attentive consciousness that enables magic to happen. She collects energy and concentrates it, as any powerful symbol does. She charges her devotees with the energy she bears, and she provokes them to ritual and practical activity in keeping with her values. She is of the earth, immanent in all that exists, consciously recognized there as symbol. Yet, in the end, she is as transcendental as Emersonian idealism had been. Magic happens through human imagination: mind, in other words, creates the Goddess's world. The Goddess, therefore, embodies an ambiguity that recalls the one that the nineteenth-century Transcendentalists lived with. Pushed one way, she celebrates the reality, the concreteness, of matter. Her teaching is harmony; and, if her teaching is woman, it is because in the collective Western consciousness woman has always stood closest to earth. Pushed another way, though, she tells us that matter is only a form of energy, that it can be shifted and changed by spirit. Her teaching is mastery; and, since her teaching is woman, she points to the strength of a rising feminist consciousness.

So the Goddess is ecologist and mental healer at once. Straddling the two energies, living out of the double vision, consider one articulate representative—one leader—among those who call on the Goddess. Consider Starhawk. Born Miriam Samos, master's graduate from Antioch University West, sometime lecturer there and elsewhere, frequent workshop leader, feminist psychotherapist and antinuclear activist (she has been arrested numerous times), Starhawk is a contemporary American witch. She teaches and practices the Old Religion of the Goddess, has founded two covens and a witchcraft collective in San Francisco, and has even been licensed as minister of the Covenant of the Goddess, legally recognized as a church.

Starhawk admires the work of Roman Catholic priest Matthew Fox at his Institute in Culture and Creation Spirituality in Oakland, California, and has continued to teach in his Creation Spirituality program. She has appeared at regional and national meetings of the American Academy of Religion. And her first two books, with her workshops, have probably constituted the strongest attraction to feminist witchcraft in the nation. By the close of 1985, according to Margot Adler, Starhawk's *Spiral Dance* (1979) had sold about fifty thousand copies, while her second book, *Dreaming the Dark* (1982), had sold roughly thirty thousand copies.[66]

Starhawk calls witchcraft "Goddess religion" and explains that her covens are "based on the Faery Tradition, which goes back to the Little People of Stone Age Britain." She adds that "we believe in creating our own rituals, which reflect our needs and insights of today." She is eager to affirm that witchcraft is the "Old Religion," but she also owns that "it is undergoing so much change and development at present that, in essence, it is being recreated rather than revived."[67]

Be that as it may, Starhawk emphasizes, as do others in the Craft, that the religion of the Goddess is a religion of nature. She pays tribute to "the pulsating rhythm that infuses all life, the dance of the double spiral, of whirling into being, and whirling out again." Indeed, in the ecological poetry of Starhawk's Goddess, "all things are swirls of energy, vortexes of moving forces, currents in an ever-changing sea. Underlying the appearance of separateness, of fixed objects within a linear stream of time, reality is a field of energies that congeal, temporarily, into forms. In time, all 'fixed' things dissolve, only to coalesce again into new forms, new vehicles." [68]

Ralph Waldo Emerson would have agreed, for the language of "currents in an ever-changing sea" and "fixed things" that "dissolve" parallels his own formulations. Meanwhile, there are hints of the quantum energy that has stirred Charlene Spretnak and so many other followers of nature religion in our time. "The spiral motion is revealed in the shape of galaxies, shells, whirlpools, DNA," writes Starhawk. "Sound, light, and radiation travel in waves—which themselves are spirals viewed in a flat plane. The moon waxes and wanes, as do the tides, the economy, and our own vitality." And always there is the theme of interconnectedness: "Our growing awareness of ecology, the impending environmental apocalypse, has forced on us a realization of our interconnectedness with all forms of life, which is the basis of Goddess religion." [69]

From this point of view, matter—the earth—is no illusion. It is ever moving, ever changing, but it is real, the very stuff of human existence. Castigating the Judeo-Christian view of the world that "sees spirit and matter as separate and that identifies matter with evil and corruption," Starhawk preaches a different word. "The flesh, the material world, are not sundered from the Goddess, they are the manifestation of the divine. Union with the Goddess comes through embracing the material world." Put differently, the Goddess herself is the symbol of the material world as sacred. In fact, "She *is* the world," for she means "choosing to take this living world, the people and creatures on it, as the ultimate meaning and purpose of life, to see the world, the earth, and our lives as sacred." [70]

And if matter, which is real, is constantly in motion, there is a pulsating pattern behind and through its spiral dance. Starhawk calls it "the on-off pulse, the alternating current of the two forces in perfect balance." "Unchecked," she warns, "the life force is cancer; unbridled, the death force is war and genocide." "Together, they hold each other in the harmony that sustains life, in the perfect orbit that can be seen in the changing cycle of the seasons, in the ecological balance of the natural world, and in the progression of human life from birth through fulfillment to decline and death—

and then to rebirth." Like universe, so humans: balance means life lived between both forces, and "the energy created by the push-pull of forces flows within each of us."[71]

In this context, sex becomes "far more than a physical act." Rather, it embodies "a polarized flow of power between two people." Still more, for Starhawk, human sexuality reflects the prior sexuality of the earth. Writing near a lake in the high Sierras, her statement is explicit:

The still water is a perfect mirror, reflecting the rounded outcroppings of pink and gray granite, which have been molded into forms that undulate and are sexual. Cracks suggest vaginas and their stony, clitoral protrusions. The line where rock meets water becomes the body's line of symmetry. The Goddess stretches out Her arms: a fallen log and its mirror image, to protect Her hidden clefts. Her pendulous breasts, looked at from the opposite side, become uprising penises. Up here, it seems clear that earth is truly Her flesh and was formed by a sexual process: Her shakes and shudders and moans of pleasure, the orgasmic release of molten rock spewing forth in fiery eruptions, the slow caress of glaciers, like white hands gently smoothing all that had been left jagged.[72]

From one point of view, Starhawk's observations only apply the ancient doctrine of correspondence—the legacy of the metaphysical tradition and the teaching of the American Transcendentalists. But, from another point of view, the erotic energy in Starhawk's work is striking. In its "broadest sense," she confirms, sexuality is the "essence" of witchcraft mysteries. And sexual connection, for Starhawk, always leads to community where, in a public realm, her cares and concerns come home. The "work of making community" means "weaving the mantle of the Goddess."[73]

In practical terms, the work means a politics of eroticism. And such a politics, for Starhawk, "cannot be based on hierarchical structures" but must rely instead on "small groups." It must be, in an image that reflects the Goddess's mantle, "strengthened by an underlying network of human connections, a weaving of close relationships that bind it like warp and weft." Finally, an erotic politics must lead to "an erotic relationship with the earth."

We can love nature, not just aesthetically, but carnally, with our meat, our bones. That sort of love threatens all the proprieties of estranged culture. Love that mirrors the wildness of nature can move us into the struggle to protect her, and can give us the deep strength we need. That love is connection. When we feel it deeply, perhaps with an oak, when we feel the tree's aura move into our bodies, feel our energy flow through the ground into its roots, let ourselves merge and feel at one with its tree-ness, we are sustained in the fight to keep the ax from its trunk, the radiation from its leaves.[74]

Sun Bear's advice to hug a tree assumes heightened passion in Starhawk's telling. And here is sexual energy that leads not to private communion but to outright political deed. Witchcraft, in sum, is a "religion of ecology," with an environmentalism that is radical and cosmic but also intensely pragmatic. The vision leads Starhawk to move with Greens and with ecofeminists, and it is as violent in its mystical embrace as the other violence of nature that Annie Dillard saw. The universe is totally present, totally real: the task is to create balance and to keep it in the midst of the universal spiral dance. Starhawk's religion of the Goddess gives us, therefore, an immanent divinity; it parallels the side of the Transcendentalist ambiguity that exalts the life force in the here and now.

Nonetheless, Starhawk's religion of the Goddess is a religion that exalts the world of mind as much. As witch and feminist psychotherapist, Starhawk is a late twentieth-century mental healer. So in a certain sense her world that is real is also a world that is unreal, a world that has the capacity to be molded and changed by the capacity of mind. That, after all, is what magic is about, and Starhawk reflects the connection. "Magic functions within natural law," she writes. "But natural law may be broader and more complex than we realize." It is a complexity, moreover, that demands attention. "It is through study and observation of nature, of the visible, physical reality, that we can learn to understand the workings of the underlying reality." [75]

To return to the underlying reality is to return to the principle of interconnectedness and to the spiral dance of all matter. The witchcraft explanation for magic, says Starhawk in her own quantum allusion, "coincides in many ways with the 'new' physics." She goes on to explain that "the physical world is formed by . . . energy as stalagtites are formed by dropping water. If we cause a change in the energy patterns, they in turn will cause a change in the physical world—just as, if we change the course of an underground river, new series of stalagtites will be formed in new veins of rock." Enter the power of mind to alter the physical pattern: "When our own energy is concentrated and channeled, it can move the broader energy currents. The images and objects used in spells are the channels, the vessels through which our power is poured and by which it is shaped. When energy is directed into the images we visualize, it gradually manifests physical form and takes shape in the material world."[76]

Typically, it is ritual that generates the energy, that focuses attention so that magic can be made. Its importance, therefore, is primary—and its meaning is at least double. From one perspective, ritual is "a patterned movement of energy to accomplish a purpose"; but, from another, the rituals of the Goddess are wild and free. "Every real ritual at some point goes out of control, breaks the plan, does the unexpected." Indeed, the classic witches' ritual as carefully reconstructed by Starhawk exists, above all, to "raise energy." In the midst of the coven mysteries, the priestess guides and directs a cone of energy that rises from the group, knowing how to foster its rise and enabling it to come down at the moment of climax to ground and strengthen members of the coven.[77]

It is not hard to see the orchestration of erotic energies in the portrait Starhawk paints. Nor, as important, is it hard to see that, given her initial understandings, she can enormously widen the space of ritual. Starhawk can find the natural home of ritual not merely in the coven circle but also in the private space of the individual psyche and in the public space of politics.

Thus, Starhawk can teach coven sister or client to summon magical forces for ritual journeys through inner space, where problems and fears become monsters to tame or overcome. Or the magic that ritual generates can be "very prosaic," as Starhawk insists that "a leaflet, a lawsuit, a demonstration, or a strike can change consciousness." Yet, even in the prose that governs politics, there is poetry and a fundamentally mystical vision. If politics is about power-in-connection and if magic's first principle is "connection," Starhawk's world of ritual energy permeates political work. Indeed, whether as private therapist or as public activist, Starhawk never forgets her picture of the universe as "a fluid, ever-changing energy pattern, not a collection of fixed and separate things." And it follows, with ecological vision, that "what affects one thing affects, in some way, all things." For Starhawk, one of the basic disciplines of magic, "the simplest and most natural," involves *moving* energy, directing its changes in the way one wants the energy to go.[78] Healing the self and doing politics, therefore, become cases of moving energy either in private or in public paths. The roles of ritual and of focused awareness in the transaction are paramount.

Yet, ultimately, whether in the intimate circle of the coven or in the large circle of the world, it is the concrete power of mind in imaginative act that works the change.

To work magic, we begin by making new metaphors. Without negating the light, we reclaim the dark: the fertile earth where the hidden seed lies unfolding, the unseen power that rises within us, the dark of sacred human flesh, the depths of the ocean, the night—when our senses quicken; we reclaim all the lost parts of ourselves we have shoved down into the dark. Instead of *enlightenment,* we begin to speak of *deepening.* . . . We remember that in the old myths, the entrance to the realm of spirit was through the fairy mound, the cave, the crack, the fissure in the earth, the gate, the doorway, the vaginal passage. We call it *the underworld,* and we go within for our visions.[79]

Mind, clearly, rules. But mind comes with a concreteness, a focused sense of body energy, that veers strikingly away from the Transcendentalist dilemma. The Neoplatonic idealism that drained Transcendentalist forces, leaving so wide a gap between harmony and mastery, finds no echo in Starhawk's magic caverns. Perhaps she is freed by the otherness of being woman and witch in the public realm; perhaps by something so vague as the "climate of the times"; perhaps by her Jewish heritage (she is Jewish) that puts its premium on tangible act and deed. Perhaps, finally, she is freed by a popular appropriation of the new science, claiming that matter and energy are different but continuous modes of being. At any rate, in her consummate paganism, Starhawk negotiates the divide between ideal and real with grace. But even as she does, her dance of energy is a dance with partners outside the world of Goddess religion. For all the powers of mind, healing *begins* for most with material attention to the suffering human body. Starhawk leaves us on the doorstep of late twentieth-century physical religion.

One need not make an exhaustive study of the holistic health movement of our time to discover a cornucopia of cures that link nineteenth-century nature healing to the present. The huge "HerbaLife" sign, visible by airplane over Los Angeles, suggests one theme for exploration. The manifest presence of a small army of chiropractors, hypnotherapists, homeopaths, pure-water advocates, and diet and exercise enthusiasts promises numerous others. Not surprisingly, what all of these have in common is a strong attachment to a point of view. Each healing method comes connected, if you will, to a nature theology: a theology articulated as foundation for practical action on behalf of the sick and a theology that, in the busyness of action, forges community and transforms practicality to ritual. For healing the sick and, in many cases, improving the well become focused and concentrated magical events, as powerful symbolic doing as found in the coven ceremonies of a Starhawk.

Beyond these, increasing contact with East and South Asia has brought healing modalities that resonate, at least as they are understood, with the nineteenth-century legacy. Already in their time Emerson and Thoreau had avidly read the translations of classics from India and China that became available to them; and the Transcendentalists played no small role in the introduction of Eastern themes to other Americans.[80] Roughly a century and a half later, herbs from the Indian Ayurvedic tradition and from Chinese five-element medicine join forces with a Native American botanic garden and with the Thomsonian pharmacy. Techniques of Indian chakra balancing and of Chinese acupuncture and acupressure combine with Western forms of body manipulation. An old-fashioned laying on of hands finds roots in mesmerism but also in Japanese and new American sources.

In an American world in which East has met West, let two cases suffice to show the continuity with an indigenous past and, at the same time, the purchase on a syncretistic, Eastern-inspired present. And let the cases be Japanese. For if some contemporary Americans buy Japanese cameras and computers and drive Japanese cars, some also turn to healing forms of nature religion imported originally from Japan. Old theories of energy and vibration, mingled with new ones derived from the ever-present quantum, share the physician's theater with the teachings of Japanese healers. In one case, there is Reiki; in another, macrobiotics.

According to Virginia Samdahl—the first mainland American Reiki master—the founder of Reiki had studied at the old University of Chicago in the late 1800s. As minister and president of a Christian school in Kyoto, Mikao Usui had been challenged by his students to heal the sick and to raise the dead as it was claimed that Jesus had done. When he could not testify to gospel grace by healing deed, he set forth for America where in a Christian land he thought he would find the answers. Samdahl recounts that he enrolled in the theological seminary at Chicago and attended there "for seven years until he got his Doctorate in Theology."[81]

Mikao Usui found no answers in America, relates Samdahl, and returned to his native Japan. There, after an exhaustive search of the Buddhist monasteries in his land, he took up residence in a Zen monastery outside Kyoto. After an arduous process that took years and meant learning Chinese and Sanskrit, Usui found, in a Sanskrit version of the Buddhist sutras, the secret of healing the sick. He had discovered what Samdahl calls the "keys," but he still did not have the power he needed to use them. For that, says Samdahl, Usui undertook a twenty-one day fast on a mountain outside of Kyoto. On the morning of the final day, weakened and still without empowerment, he saw a small point of light that began to move toward him. He was terrified as it gathered speed, but he held his ground and was finally knocked unconscious by the light. In Samdahl's words:

The next thing he knew, he saw bubbles . . . millions and millions of bubbles all moving from right to left in every color of the rainbow. From the palest pink to the deepest cerise; from the palest green to the deepest emerald; palest aqua to the deepest blue. And after all these gorgeous colors the gold came, and in the gold the white lights. And in the center of every white bubble was a gold figure in the Sanskrit that he had learned and read in the Sutras.

And the bubble would come and stop, as though it would say "Here, Usui, learn this so you will know it always and be able to use it." And it would go. And then another would come and stop.[82]

Subsequently, says Samdahl, Mikao Usui was able to heal the sick by placing his hands on them. And subsequently, too, he taught his healing methods to others, acquired disciples—some eighteen of them—and, at his death, left his colleague Chugio Hayashi as master. Hayashi transmitted the knowledge and power of the mastership to Hawayo Takata, a Japanese-Hawaiian woman who had been healed by Reiki. She, in turn, initiated Virginia Samdahl but died in 1980 without, at least according to Samdahl, leaving a head master. "However, she did leave keys to make masters," Samdahl declares, and therefore "Reiki will never die."[83]

Reiki might never die, but the land in which it would flourish became the United States. And it flourished not without division and contest between competing "sects." But more important here than the "church" history of Reiki and its divisions is its practitioners' fundamental explanation of what it is and how it works.

For those who teach and use Reiki, the mysterious "substance" they employ is universal life-force energy. It is, they believe, a "white-light" energy that balances and restores, that is natural and available to all living things.[84] Practically considered, it becomes a force to heal the sick when a Reiki initiate places his or her hands, in prescribed fashion, on an individual who is ill. A Reiki treatment typically lasts an hour or longer, and giver and receiver of the healing may claim to experience tingling sensations or feelings of warmth or cold in hands or body parts, respectively. Reiki is administered with receiver fully clothed, and it may even be administered without actually touching the person receiving it. It can be given to pets or plants, and—while the sequence of positions to follow is more or less normative—it can be given as spot treatment for, say, a sprained ankle or burned leg.

Reiki healers say that their treatment is effective for sudden and dramatic illness, as in the case of an accident. But they also say that treatment can heal the chronically ill, although the healing may take longer. And they speak of Reiki energy working slowly through the history of an illness, so that in the process of being cured the sick person may experience earlier phases of the disease. Practitioners claim that they know, by the rise and fall of energy in their hands, when to move from one body healing position to the next. The energy, they insist, is not their own: it is a natural and universal force and, indeed, say Samdahl and others, it is God. Thus, they say they do not feel fatigue from administering Reiki but are themselves energized by the process. When the energy of the universe enters them in an attuned and focused way for the process of healing, they cannot help but be strengthened by its passage.

Reiki, they explain, is both power and knowledge. The knowledge is taught, as is any knowledge, through lectures, diagrams, reading material, and less formal contact and conversation. The power, though, must be transmitted by a Reiki master who has the appropriate "keys" to initiate the would-be healer. The process of initiation is short and simple, understood as an "attunement" or series of attunements that aligns the individual with the natural energy present all around. Once the attunement is completed, Reiki initiates attest that a person can give Reiki to him- or herself as well as to others. Its effectiveness does not depend on personal belief, either the healer's or the receiver's. Nor does it depend on their conscious attention to the process. And it works, say Reiki practitioners, because it "brings the body into harmony by relieving physical and emotional blockages." It "heals the cause and eliminates the effects of an imbalance."[85]

Such explanations place Reiki in a conceptual lineage connecting it to the mesmeric model of the nineteenth century. The language of blockages, of energy to remove obstructions, of power and vibration moving within is, as we have seen, basic to the alternative-healing tradition of the American past. But the language is also supported by popular grasp of quantum theory, a fact that is not lost, at least, on Reiki master Barbara Weber Ray. In her book *The Reiki Factor,* in a chapter that begins by quoting the familiar energy equation of Albert Einstein, Ray announces: "From the scientific community comes the information that all things are energy and the essence of energy is *light*." Against the background of the "new physics," she tells us, in a statement that closely follows French physicist Jean Charon, "matter when examined and broken down is energy. And when examined further, energy is transparent—is light." Ray continues:

Now modern science is placing increased importance on light. In humanity's New Age of expanded knowledge and consciousness, light brings together the worlds of science and spirit. Einstein's famous formula . . . tells you that light and matter are interchangeable. Light appears to be at the heart of all things. Just before this century, the Impressionists made an entire art form of light. The mystics have always known about it and have reminded us through the centuries that we are, in truth, Light. The scientist now becomes the mystic.[86]

The vibration of light brings Reiki full circle, back to its founder Mikao Usui, stunned on a Japanese mountain by light, empowered by the many colors of his vision. As surely as in the nineteenth century, matter is spiritual, and the "physicalized" spirit is the enlivening force in matter. Physic and metaphysic are intertwined, and syncretism thrives.

Physic and metaphysic are intertwined, too, in a second healing method that originated in Japan and that grew strong in a hospitable America. One need only glance at the title of Aveline Kushi's definitive macrobiotic cookbook—*Aveline Kushi's Complete Guide to Macrobiotic Cooking: For Health, Harmony, and Peace*—to know that more than recipes is at issue. Macrobiotics, Kushi explains in a preface, "requires only that you eat in harmony with your environment. By eating well, you will create order and balance in your daily life. Your peaceful spirit will extend to your family and community and eventually influence the whole world." In the phrase that, more and more, has become a watchword for the contemporary movement, macrobiotics is intent on building "one peaceful world." [87]

The Japanese lecturer, writer, and social activist George Ohsawa (1893–1966) is usually considered the founder of macrobiotics (meaning "long" or "great life"). Ohsawa had inherited from the past a Japanese tradition of "food philosophy" and was for many years the central figure in the Japanese Shoku-Yō—a philosophical and even political movement that advocated proper food as cure for social as well as physical ills. Tireless in writing about his own food philosophy and zealous for his views, he subsequently organized a worldwide network of macrobiotic centers where the principles he taught would be practiced.

However, in America and even the world, the man who eventually became the acknowledged leader of the macrobiotic movement was Ohsawa's Japanese student Michio Kushi. Born in 1926 in Wakayama Prefecture, Kushi had matriculated in politics and law at Tokyo Imperial University during and after the Second World War. It was at this time that he visited a study house ("Student World Government Association") run by Ohsawa in Hiyoshi and spoke with him regarding Kushi's concern for world peace. "Have you ever considered the dialectical application of dietary principles to the problem of world peace?" Ohsawa asked. [88]

Although initially Kushi neither understood nor was impressed by Ohsawa—nor by the food served him at the center—the younger man thereafter began to study with him and then, with Ohsawa's encouragement, came to the United States. Kushi at first enrolled at Columbia University as a student in international law, but later he devoted all of his efforts to the spread of macrobiotic teaching, joined by the young Japanese woman Tomoko Yokoyama ("Aveline")—also an Ohsawa student—who became his wife. Other Ohsawa students arrived—notably Herman Aihara and then Chiiko ("Cornellia") Yokota, who married him. Subsequently the Kushis moved to Boston, and the Aiharas moved to the West Coast; East West Centers began to spring up in various cities, staffed by former students of the Kushi Institute in Boston; and public acceptance, slow in coming, grew. By 1985 the *East West Journal,* launched under macrobiotic auspices in 1970, reached a circulation of near eighty thousand. In the late eighties, the macrobiotic movement was a vigorous, growing enterprise with, as a conservative estimate, close to one hundred thousand adult adherents in America.[89]

What was it that these individuals were about? To what teaching did they subscribe, and what did the teaching have to do with physical religion? To begin to understand macrobiotics is to begin where the movement and its converts do—with the physical substance of food. For, as in many religious groups, it is diet that is the visible badge of commitment, here a diet that emphasizes grains and vegetables, locally grown and in season, and mostly cooked. Macrobiotic eating generally spurns what are regarded as dietary extremes, such as red meat and commercial salt, alcohol, drugs, and sugar. On the other hand, it is not purely vegetarian, countenancing white-fleshed fish and, in some versions, very occasionally chicken or eggs (even, in an extremely cold climate such as Alaska, red meat). Nor does the diet avoid sea salt and other condiments that contain it. The staple macrobiotic drink is bancha tea, which contains minute amounts of caffeine. Some macrobiotic recipes include the use of mirin, a sweet cooking wine; and, for holidays, Japanese sake or the equivalent may occasionally be used. On the other hand, dairy products are almost totally avoided, and "health-food" vitamin and mineral preparations are regarded with considerable suspicion.[90]

Diet fans out into ritual in the concept of "macrobiotic practice"

Aveline and Michio Kushi. Photograph by Leon Zawicki. (Courtesy, Leon Zawicki and Michio Kushi.) The Kushis lead the macrobiotic movement in the United States, in the terms of this study a form of nature religion.

and in the public activities that have come to support it. Cooking classes form an almost obligatory introduction to the preparation of macrobiotic fare. In addition to the practical instruction that one would expect, they typically contain lectures on the religious philosophy that undergirds food preparation. Macrobiotic communities of any size sponsor regular potlucks, where food provides both ceremonial focus for the discussion of principles and support for a macrobiotic life-style. Meanwhile, counselors offer dietary advice for sick individuals, providing detailed guidance as to what to eat within the standard macrobiotic diet and how to prepare it. An active center may sponsor a regular lecture program, may bring in "stars" such as the Kushis, the Aiharas, or a senior counselor for a weekend, may offer a restaurant or food store to the community. More national in scope, summer camps, traditional since the sixties, continue to flourish.

It is impossible to estimate how many people have been drawn to macrobiotics because of serious health problems, but the number is surely the majority.[91] And, indeed, at the heart of macrobiotic food ritual is the ritual of cure. When a person who has been eating the standard American diet turns to macrobiotics, whether sick or well by conventional medical diagnosis, he or she is understood by macrobiotic practitioners to be out of balance. Visible illness is only the far end of a continuum that includes a series of states of being less than fully well. According to macrobiotic teaching, disease manifests itself slowly, and the human body has various ways to throw off poisons before the stage of serious illness comes. Virtually everyone who begins the practice of macrobiotics stands in need of some kind of cure.

To be sick or out of balance, in macrobiotic terms, is to have an improper relationship to the cosmic principles of yin and yang that derive from the One—the Tao, the Order of the Universe, or God. In a variation of the general Chinese teaching, yin is seen as the centrifugal, expanding power, earth's force, the energy of the rising seed and growing plant. Yang, conversely, is the centripetal, contracting power, heaven's force, the energy of the compact and contained seed, the germ from which life begins. Yin is understood as female, cold, passive, spiritual; yang as male, hot, active, physical. Each individual, to exist in peace and harmony and, therefore, health, must be balanced between yin and yang forces. Moreover, each individual comes into the world with a preponderance of yin or yang (here more than gender) that determines whether the person has a generally yin or a generally yang constitution. Subsequently, because of individual history, including eating habits, a person develops in a direction that either confirms or counters original constitution. Meanwhile, all foods are classified as either yin or yang, in a taxonomical system that locates some ("extreme foods") on the far ends of a spectrum and others ("balanced foods") closer to the center.

The macrobiotic ritual of healing, therefore, becomes an intricate plan to make balance for the individual given his or her present condition. For some, who are relatively healthy, the ritual may stop with the standard macrobiotic diet and its careful balance of yin and yang foods. For others, who are more seriously ill, the plan becomes a complex choreography that compensates for present imbalances by subtly stressing foods believed to contain certain energies or properties and by more or less avoiding others. Throughout the process, macrobiotic teaching stresses the "energetics of food"— that is, that food is living matter with a vast array of different energy vibrations; that food is altered in its energy by the way it is cleaned and cut, by the quality and duration of the fire to which it is subjected, by the cooking methods that are employed. Indeed, Aveline Kushi speaks often of the "peace" that the individual cook must put into the food—by conscious preparation and, as well, by mental and spiritual condition.

Presiding over the choreography of yin and yang is the spiral dance that embodies the order of the universe. In a cosmology that resonates with the Goddess wisdom of a Starhawk as well as with a popular wisdom based on the new physics, Michio Kushi writes of beginnings:

In the beginningless beginning . . . there was only endless motion which moved with infinite speed in all directions. Because of this infinite speed, there was no past nor future, nor [were there] any relative phenomena whatsoever.

However, whenever and wherever the infinite motion, which moves in all directions, intersects, spirallic movements begin to form in a process of differentiation. . . .

From the motion of galaxies to the motion of preatomic particles, from invisible spiritual movement to visible physical constitutions, all are spirallically formed and governed by two antagonistic, complementary forces: yin . . . and yang.[92]

From the macrobiotic community, the peace that humans seek can only be found by consciously joining the dance. And since humans—because they are materialized—are yang, they join by attending, first, to a proper relationship with the physical world, especially that part of it that reaches them most tangibly. Richard France and Jerome Carty explain:

Food is the mechanism whereby one's *view of life, of reality,* is actually embodied in flesh. Your heaven/earth environment actually becomes your psycho/physical being through your daily food! A carrot, for example, is the composite expression (or hologram) of all of the unique characteristics of its garden environment, woven into a singular and in each case unique pattern by the spiral "weaver," which is its ancestral/environmental pattern. The seed dictates *tendency,* but heaven and earth supply the material *possibility.* And when one's daily diet is in conscious conformity to local and seasonal patterns, one becomes a conscious expression of the environment and a home for all of nature. One knows what time it is, and one knows where he is. In the Real Present![93]

Thus, when, in a cookbook, Aveline Kushi tells novices that "for daily cooking, slowly stirring the tofu by hand gives the most peaceful, steady vibration," she writes out of a cosmic religious vision.[94] "Very peaceful," she repeats again and again in cooking classes as she stirs or puts food under a low gas flame. "More peaceful," macrobiotic practitioners say, as they explain why they cook with gas (or wood fire) instead of with electricity (with its far speedier cycles of heat energy) and never with microwave.

Beyond that, macrobiotic eating is only the beginning of a macrobiotic way of life—one lived in attempted harmony with the cosmic principles of yin and yang and dedicated, by practical means, to what macrobiotic people believe will help to create a peaceful world. Practical means include such personal conventions as avoiding synthetic clothing, especially next to one's skin; retiring before midnight and rising early; and even, because of its physical effects, chanting. Practical means also include work to bring balance back to an environment that is seen as disturbed.

Writing in a 1988 issue of the Aihara-inspired monthly *Macrobiotics Today,* counselor John David Mann declares that he challenges "the premise that the best we can do in the face of a global

shakedown is to hoe our own gardens and make 'ourselves' healthy."
In a strident confession he responds to a (macrobiotic) reader's
question about what he has been eating:

I have been eating the experiences of people I watch who "eat well" and
still don't feel better or *get* better . . . of farmers who, confronted with
hopes grown as barren as their net worth and the groaning soil at their
feet, wed desolation to suicide . . . of porpoises that wash up on the Atlantic shores in a wave of a thousand used syringes discarded by hospitals
who could do no more for their diseased patients than could the porpoises
for themselves . . . of millions of acres of trees, trees that die without first
being reborn as the next season's saplings.

"'What am I eating?'" Mann continues. "Indeed! I'm eating the
days of the latter Twentieth Century. They're pretty hard to di-
gest; let's chew them well, and not swallow them whole." [95]

Mann's is the strong statement, but it expresses the logic of macrobiotic thought and points to its everyday ethic beyond the rituals
of food and cure. To practice macrobiotics is to begin (in spirit if
not in substance) like the nineteenth-century Grahamite William
A. Ghaskins who, we saw in chapter 4, "subsisted on a quantity of
coarse bread." And it is to parallel, in an Oriental rhetoric, the
mesmeric vocabulary of tides of energy and the problem of their
obstruction. But to practice macrobiotics is to end with a social
and political vision that clearly moves beyond the nineteenth century. Writing on the theme of "World Peace through World Health,"
Michio Kushi sums up the physical religion that is macrobiotics:

Nature is always realizing harmony and making balance. The sun, the
moon, and the seasons cycle in perfect order. Yet within this wonderful
harmony, humanity is suffering from a plague of degenerative diseases
and trembling on the brink of war. Why is humanity suffering from internal and external disease and chaos?
   Pollution, crime, and the threat of war mirror the condition of our own
internal health. Those who can solve the problem of illness are really
those who can solve the problem of war. Those who cannot solve the problem of illness cannot solve the problem of war. [96]

Sun Bear and Annie Dillard, Charlene Spretnak and Starhawk,
Virginia Samdahl and Michio Kushi—all in one way or another

speak a similar language. It is a language of centering and connection, of energy vibration and flow, of piety and harmony spoken with a passion that, in some cases, becomes a violence. That language is distinctive in each case—different enough to evoke an identifiable theme from the past explored earlier in this book—but demonstrably similar in privileging the symbol of nature and in finding in it a key to mastery and empowerment. And mastery and empowerment are discovered often enough in metaphors that, blending a variety of cultural goods, look especially to the quantum as bridge between contrary visions inherited from the past.

Yet, for all the centered, connected talk of their vocabulary, for all the common privileging of nature, it could be argued that the speakers we have met are extreme proponents of a point of view. Even if one accepts the most generous of estimates, the numbers who follow Sun Bear and others hardly add up to a significant dent in the nation's population. And it is unlikely that in the near future the majority—or even a large minority—of Americans will enter a medicine wheel or stalk muskrats in the wild. It is improbable that most of them will follow the Goddess or join a Green political party or practice macrobiotics or become Reiki initiates. Nevertheless, in another sense our speakers give us important clues to the people in the ideational center.

It is a truism that voting patterns and political surveys show serious concern regarding the environment among many, if not most, late twentieth-century Americans. It is another truism that to call a substance "natural" is to promote its sales in marked ways; and it is yet again a truism that those who support food irradiation would like, for fear of popular rejection, to have their product go to market unlabeled. To take only the case of macrobiotics, brown rice, miso, and rice cakes have become readily available commodities in a food industry that caters to more than isolated tastes. Meanwhile, national parks and wilderness areas have felt the need to regulate use of their open spaces—for a public that loves nature so well that it may love it away. Bicycle paths and hiking trails abound; romanticized Native Americans flourish in and out of the film industry; positive thinking shows no sign of abatement in an era that celebrates "natural" intuition and trusts the inner voice.

Given all of this, the late twentieth-century report on nature religion in America is that it is alive and well, growing daily, and probably a strong suit for the century to come. In the face of its continuing technological commitment—perhaps even *because* of its continuing technological commitment—Nature's nation is unlikely to desert the God or Goddess in any future that can be foreseen.

Epilogue

"Catch it if you can," wrote Annie Dillard. And at last report Henry David Thoreau was still on the trail of his hound, his bay horse, and his turtledove. Heartened by such company, in this book I have searched for an elusive form of religion that has graced American history. Unorganized and unacknowledged as religion, it is—given the right places to look—everywhere apparent. But it is also a form of religion that slips between the cracks of the usual interpretive grids—or that, more slippery still, evades and circumvents even adventurous ways to name it.

One reason it does so is that it contains its own pluralism readymade. Nature religion in the United States is actually nature religions—the matter-of-fact reality of different "denominations" within what is unorganized, noninstitutionalized, and largely intuitive. So there have been many trails to follow, and it has not been possible to follow each to its end or to probe the many side trails that invited. Republican religion, for example, did not die after the Davy Crockett almanacs of the mid-nineteenth century to be resurrected in our own time. Calvinist ambivalence toward nature did not vanish after the Puritans, then echo mysteriously and ambiguously among the Transcendentalists, and experience sudden rebirth in Annie Dillard. Physical religion did not hibernate from the last day of the nineteenth century until it awoke in the holistic health movement of the present day.

Given all of that, I have looked for significant cultural pathways in key historical contexts; and in so doing I have offered a kind of plot. Nature religion was present early; it was lived out by Indian inhabitants who owned (in their sense) the land and was experienced ambiguously by Puritan newcomers who strove for place and dominance. By the time of the American Revolution, nature religion specialized in self-conscious mythmaking, and the dominance it promised became the politics of being on top. Thereafter, as the young republic grew, the New England Transcendentalists authoritatively set forth a classic American double vision of nature as reality and nature as appearance; and they provided a double ethic to accompany it. Mastery of nature hid behind harmony with it, while Emerson, Thoreau, and others worked to fill a conceptual crack that would not go away. Preservationists pushed hard on one side to lessen the gap, and mental healers pushed hard on the other. Together they could not force or wish it away. Meanwhile, harmony and mastery cheerfully accommodated decades of nineteenth-century Americans who made the territory of their physical bodies the field for natural religious practice.

Then, with the dawn of the twentieth century, the mysterious half-lives of the quantum resolved the conceptual conflict between nature real and nature ideal. At least in the subatomic world, the crack looked like it had been healed. And outside the atom there were new metaphorical possibilities of interconnection for harmony and mastery. By the late twentieth century a new-old piety in the land was taking advantage of the situation. Theosophical currents and ecological ones were joining the quantum to fund a purchase on nature. Dominance, it seemed, could now be an entirely harmonious enterprise.

Whatever the grace of the twentieth-century version of master harmony, however, the search for it had been there from at least the seventeenth century. Hence, my hope is that I have followed enough trails to convince that nature has provided a compelling religious center for many Americans throughout our history. And to show more: that nature as religious symbol has become so effectively a culture broker that the study of nature religion can cast important light on persistent patterns in past and present American life.

Moreover, I have tried to suggest that these patterns are more than "thought" pure and simple. As I have searched for the different denominations and the different historical periods, I have tried to show that nature religion is just that: religion. Therefore, it is embodied and enacted, not simply pondered. The study of comparative religions makes it clear that religions are *action* systems as much as—if not more than—they are thought systems. Given that assumption, I have avoided, as much as possible, treatment of theorists or schools of theorists—unless and until I could find evidence that their ideas had found a ritual base and had inspired some kind of ethic for everyday living. So the Transcendentalists could mix and mingle in these pages, because of their sustained ritualization of their views in their own lives and, more, because of their ability to encourage action systems in the wilderness preservation and mind-cure movements. Annie Dillard, a favorite twentieth-century Puritan, could appear because, for all her reading and writing, she had learned to stalk.

A philosopher friend once told me, with only some oversimplification, that the difference between religion and philosophy was that you could find religion in the telephone book and you could not find philosophy there. I would be hard put to find religions of nature in any American city's Bell Telephone listings, but the observation still has its point for what I am calling nature religion. To be religion, the symbol of nature must, so to speak, get out on the street. It must leave the philosopher's armchair and the mystic's roost, to touch flesh, blood, and action. Inevitably, then, the symbol of nature had to become the property of everybody's people. And, that said, it has been appropriate to look for it not just among the elite but, as much and more, among the democratic many who struggled to name and express it. The homespun quality of what they produced, the do-it-yourself edge to their ideas and practice, should not deter us from acknowledging the seriousness of the religious mentality among nonspecialists.

Having said that, I am drawn here to the words of at least one specialist. Sidney Mead, no novice at religion or history, once wrote that "we can find a stable identity only through an imaginative grasp that we are one with all of life in time and space, and, recognizing that there is no marked boundary between what we call organic or inorganic, that human life *is* the planet become conscious of itself."[1] Late-twentieth-century nature religionists would no doubt agree, and so, with a series of provisos, might earlier ones.

At the same time, for all their universal vision nature religionists have tackled a major problem that has plagued their culture, and, in doing so, they have shown a surprising specificity about their own society and about their "place" in history. While it is an easy path in nature to the wilderness that avoids the human community, the tangled road back to the city and society has more often been taken. Those who have followed nature religion in American history have given consistent witness to the other, extraordinary world to which much of religion points, *and* they have also witnessed to the ordinary bonds of religion in this one. The presence of nature religion in America is one more sign that, in a "secular" society, the search for the sacred refuses to go away.

Notes

Introduction

1. I owe a large debt to Dale Cockrell of William and Mary College in Williamsburg, Virginia, who introduced me to the Hutchinsons. Basic information on the Hutchinsons that is related in this chapter may be found in John Wallace Hutchinson, *Story of the Hutchinsons (Tribe of Jesse),* 2 vols. (1896; reprint, New York: Da Capo Press, 1977). For the Hutchinson genealogy, see, esp., ibid. 1:5–6; and, for the quotation—a comment by N. P. Willis—see ibid., 46.

2. Quoted ibid., 52–53, 118, 85.

3. Ibid. 2:298–300.

4. Ibid., 299–300.

5. Ibid. 1:271, 263, 109. For "maddening Second Advent tunes," see the review by N. P. Rogers, quoted ibid., 77. The line by John Wallace Hutchinson is from his song "The Fatherhood of God and the Brotherhood of Man," quoted ibid., 1 (see, also, 447–48).

6. See ibid., esp. 272, 285, 134, 318, 470. For material on John's conversion and on Jesse Jr.'s clairvoyance, as well as on the relationship of the Hutchinsons to Andrew Jackson Davis, I am indebted to Dale Cockrell.

7. For references to the brothers and hydropathy, see Hutchinson, *Story of the Hutchinsons* 1:125, 288, 318. For the song, see Jesse Hutchinson, Jr., "Cold Water," in Asa B. Hutchinson, comp., *The Granite Songster; comprising the songs of the Hutchinson Family, without the music* (Boston: A. B. Hutchinson, 1847), 33 (emphasis in original).

8. Hutchinson, *Story of the Hutchinsons* 1:87. For the reference to the private journal of Asa Hutchinson (for 6 June 1843), I am indebted to Dale Cockrell, in his unpublished edition of the Hutchinson family journals, "The Journals of the Hutchinson Family," a copy of which he has generously supplied me. As this work goes to press, Dale Cockrell's edition of the journals is being published as *Excelsior: Journals of the Hutchinson Family Singers,* The Sociology of Music Series, no. 5 (Stuyvesant, N.Y.: Pendragon Press, 1989). And, for the song, see J. J. Hutchinson, "'Go Call the Doctor, & Be Quick'! or Anti-Calomel," in *Songs of the Hutchinson Family* (New York: Firth & Hall, 1843), 206:3–5. Punctuation and spelling here and elsewhere reflect the source from which the material is transcribed.

9. Asa Hutchinson, 22 and 23 July 1842, in Cockrell, "The Journals of the Hutchinson Family." See, also, Judson Hutchinson, 9 and 29 August 1842, ibid.

10. Asa Hutchinson, 11 May 1843 and 2 January 1844, ibid.; Hutchinson, *Story of the Hutchinsons* 1:302, 282; Asa Hutchinson, 5 March 1845 and 15 January 1844, in Cockrell, "The Journals of the Hutchinson Family."

11. Asa Hutchinson, 5 March 1845, ibid., Hutchinson, *Story of the Hutchinsons* 1: 132, 315, 288, 265–66, 275–78.

12. I have more fully discussed ordinary and extraordinary religion and the concept of religious boundaries in Catherine L. Albanese, *America: Religions and Religion* (Belmont, Calif.: Wadsworth Publishing, 1981), 3–7.

13. For his classic discussion, see Mircea Eliade, *The Sacred and the Profane: The Nature of Religion,* trans. Willard R. Trask (New York: Harcourt, Brace & World, 1959).

14. Robert N. Bellah introduced the term *civil religion* into recent scholarly discourse through his well-known article "Civil Religion in America," *Daedalus* 96 (Winter 1967): 1–21. In a later reflection on this article, Bellah, following the sociology of knowledge of Peter Berger and Thomas Luckmann, called civil religion "a social construction of reality." See Robert N. Bellah, "American Civil Religion in the 1970s," in Russell E. Richey and Donald G. Jones, eds., *American Civil Religion* (New York: Harper & Row, 1974), 256; and, for Berger and Luckmann, see Peter L. Berger and Thomas Luckmann, *The Social Construction of Reality: A Treatise in the Sociology of Knowledge* (Garden City, N.Y.: Doubleday, Anchor Books, 1967).

15. For religions of the cosmos and of history, see Mircea Eliade, *Cosmos and History: The Myth of the Eternal Return,* trans. Willard R. Trask (New York: Harper & Row, 1959). My interest in issues of dominance and mastery has been encouraged by the work of both Michel Foucault and Pierre Bourdieu, although I read dominance in a different and ultimately less sinister key than they. For Foucault, see especially his *Discipline and Punish: The Birth of the Prison,* trans. Alan Sheridan (New York: Random House, Vintage Books, 1979). For Pierre Bourdieu, see his *Outline of a Theory of Practice,* trans. Richard Nice, Cambridge Studies in Social Anthropology, no. 16 (Cambridge: Cambridge University Press, 1987).

16. Hutchinson, *Story of the Hutchinsons* 1: 63–64.

17. Davis's many works make his materialistic theology clear. See, especially, Andrew Jackson Davis, *The Principles of Nature, Her Divine Revelations, and a Voice to Mankind* (New York: S. S. Lyon and W. Fishbough, 1847).

18. See the discussion in Mircea Eliade, *Myth and Reality,* trans. Willard R. Trask (New York: Harper & Row, Harper Torchbooks, 1968), 54–74.

19. This formulation, of course, owes something to Claude Lévi–Strauss. See Claude Lévi–Strauss, *The Raw and the Cooked,* vol. 1 of *Introduction to a Science of Mythology,* trans. John Weightman and Doreen Weightman (New York: Harper & Row, Harper Torchbooks, 1970).

20. Clarence J. Glacken, *Traces on the Rhodian Shore: Nature and Culture in Western Thought from Ancient Times to the End of the Eighteenth Century* (1967; reprint, Berkeley: University of California Press, 1976), 15. Glacken uses the phrase to refer to astrology.

21. For "history of the present," see Foucault, *Discipline and Punish,* 31. For alerting me to Foucault's usage and theme, I am indebted to Gary Laderman of the University of California, Santa Barbara.

Chapter One

1. Paul le Jeune, "Relation of What Occurred in New France, in the Year 1634," in Reuben Gold Thwaites, ed., *The Jesuit Relations and Allied Documents: Travels and Explorations of the Jesuit Missionaries in New France, 1610–1791,* 73 vols. (Cleveland: Burrows Brothers, 1896–1901), 7 : 103.

2. The Indian's exhortation may have been literal as well as metaphorical, for le Jeune was having trouble learning the language of the Montagnais.

3. Mary Rowlandson, "A Narrative of the Captivity and Restauration of Mrs. Mary Rowlandson" (1682), in Charles H. Lincoln, ed., *Narratives of the Indian Wars, 1675–1699,* Original Narratives of Early American History (1913; reprint, New York: Barnes & Noble, 1959), 121.

4. For an insightful discussion of the Rowlandson narrative in the context of other captivity narratives, see Richard Slotkin, "Israel in Babylon: The Archetype of the Captivity Narratives (1682–1700)," in Richard Slotkin, *Regeneration through Violence: The Mythology of the American Frontier, 1600–1860* (Middletown, Conn.: Wesleyan University Press, 1973), 94–115.

5. See H. F. Dobyns et al., "Estimating Aboriginal American Population," *Current Anthropology* 7 (1966): 395–449; Harold E. Driver, *Indians of North America,* 2d ed., rev. (Chicago: University of Chicago Press, 1969), 63; Peter Farb, *Man's Rise to Civilization: The Cultural Ascent of the Indians of North America,* rev. 2d ed. (New York: E. P. Dutton, 1978), 231. These are recent estimates, which—with growing awareness of the impact of European microbes in decimating Indian populations at the beginning of the contact period and with a growing sense, too, of the biases built into earlier projections—have moved decidedly upward.

6. Farb, *Man's Rise to Civilization,* 8, 219; Driver, *Indians of North America,* 35–47.

7. A. Irving Hallowell, "Ojibwa Ontology, Behavior, and World View" (1960), in Dennis Tedlock and Barbara Tedlock, eds., *Teachings from the American Earth: Indian Religion and Philosophy* (New York: Liveright, 1975), 147. (Emphasis in original.)

8. For the Tewa origin myth, see Alfonso Ortiz, *The Tewa World: Space, Time, Being, and Becoming in a Pueblo Society* (Chicago: University of Chicago Press, 1969), 13–17.

9. Nicolas Perrot, "Memoir on the Manners, Customs, and Religion of the Savages of North America" (1864), in *The Indian Tribes of the Upper Mississippi Valley and Region of the Great Lakes as Described by Nicolas Perrot, French Commandant in the Northwest,* trans. and ed. Emma Helen Blair (1911; reprint, New York: Kraus Reprint, 1969), 1 : 31–37, 37. I am indebted to James P. Ronda of Youngstown State University for alerting me to this and other Algonkian sources.

10. For the Winnebago Trickster, see Paul Radin, *The Trickster: A Study in American Indian Mythology* (1956; New York: Schocken Books,

1972); for a pact with the animals and for the keeper or owner of the game, see Ruth M. Underhill, *Red Man's Religion: Beliefs and Practices of the Indians North of Mexico* (Chicago: University of Chicago Press, 1965), 41–44; and, also, the more controversial Calvin Martin, *Keepers of the Game: Indian-Animal Relationships and the Fur Trade* (Berkeley: University of California Press, 1978), 69–76.

11. For the Eastern Cherokee, see Catherine L. Albanese, "Exploring Regional Religion: A Case Study of the Eastern Cherokee," *History of Religions* 23 (May 1984): 353. For the Kiowa, see N. Scott Momaday, *The Way to Rainy Mountain* (Albuquerque: University of New Mexico Press, 1969), 8.

12. See the account of the Kiowa origin myth in Momaday, *Way to Rainy Mountain*, 16.

13. See Edmund Nequatewa, *Truth of a Hopi* (1936; reprint, Flagstaff, Ariz.: Northland Press with the Museum of Northern Arizona, 1967), 7–23, 63–77.

14. For Navajo etiology of disease, see Donald Sandner, *Navaho Symbols of Healing* (New York: Harcourt Brace Jovanovich, Harvest/HBJ Book, 1979), 33–35. For the Cherokee, see James Mooney, *Myths of the Cherokee*, Smithsonian Institution, Bureau of American Ethnology Nineteenth Annual Report, 1897–98, pt. 1 (Washington, D.C.: Government Printing Office, 1900), 250–52; and Albanese, "Exploring Regional Religion," 348–50. For Amerindian violation of the ecological perspective at a time of cultural crisis, see the provocative explanation of the fur trade in Martin, *Keepers of the Game*, 40–65, 113–49. And, for a rebuttal of Martin's thesis of Amerindian war with the animals, see Shepard Krech III, ed., *Indians, Animals, and the Fur Trade: A Critique of "Keepers of the Game"* (Athens: University of Georgia Press, 1981).

15. For a useful discussion in the context of Algonkian manitou belief, see Elisabeth Tooker, "Introduction," in Elisabeth Tooker, ed., *Native North American Spirituality of the Eastern Woodlands: Sacred Myths, Dreams, Visions, Speeches, Healing Formulas, Rituals, and Ceremonials*, The Classics of Western Spirituality (New York: Paulist Press, 1979), 13–29.

16. Joseph Epes Brown, ed., *The Sacred Pipe: Black Elk's Account of the Seven Rites of the Oglala Sioux* (1953; Baltimore: Penguin Books, 1971), 3–9.

17. Mooney, *Myths of the Cherokee*, 291–92; Tooker, ed., *Native North American Spirituality*, 93–94.

18. For an informative discussion of sacred clowns, including the Oglala Sioux *heyoka*, see Peggy V. Beck and A. L. Walters, "Sacred Fools and Clowns," in Peggy V. Beck and A. L. Walters, *The Sacred: Ways of Knowledge, Sources of Life* (Tsaile, Ariz.: Navajo Community College, 1977), 301–25. For the best account of the Tewa healing Bears, see Vera Laski, *Seeking Life*, Memoirs of the American Folklore Society, vol. 50 (Philadelphia: American Folklore Society, 1959), 112–17.

19. Brown, ed., *Sacred Pipe*, 58.

20. Recent estimates have been adjusted strikingly upward from ear-

lier ones (see n. 5 above). Francis Jennings proposed a native population of seventy-two thousand to ninety thousand for southern New England in 1600 (Francis Jennings, *The Invasion of America: Indians, Colonialism, and the Cant of Conquest* [Chapel Hill: University of North Carolina Press for the Institute of Early American History and Culture, 1975], 29). Still more recently, Neal Salisbury has argued for a range between 126,000 and 144,000 (Salisbury, *Manitou and Providence: Indians, Europeans, and the Making of New England, 1500–1643* [New York: Oxford University Press, 1982], 26–27). The data on the English population is supplied by William Cronon, *Changes in the Land: Indians, Colonists, and the Ecology of New England* (New York: Hill and Wang, 1983), 42. (Cronon's estimate of Amerindian populations in *all* of New England in 1600 is seventy thousand to one hundred thousand.)

21. For a discussion of the epidemics, see Salisbury, *Manitou and Providence,* 101–9, 190–92, passim.

22. Sources for general secondary material on Eastern Algonkian culture in southern New England include Bert Salwen, "Indians of Southern New England and Long Island: Early Period," in Bruce G. Trigger, ed., *Northeast,* vol. 15 of *Handbook of North American Indians* (Washington, D.C.: Smithsonian Institution, 1978), 160–76; William S. Simmons, "Narragansett," ibid., 190–97; Regina Flannery, *An Analysis of Coastal Algonquian Culture* (Washington, D.C.: Catholic University of America Press, 1939); Cronon, *Changes in the Land,* 19–156; Salisbury, *Manitou and Providence,* 13–49; and Howard S. Russell, *Indian New England before the Mayflower* (Hanover, N.H.: University Press of New England, 1980).

23. On "personal initiative," see Henry W. Bowden and James P. Ronda, "Introduction," in Henry W. Bowden and James P. Ronda, eds., *John Eliot's Indian Dialogues: A Study in Cultural Interaction,* Contributions in American History, no. 88 (Westport, Conn.: Greenwood Press, 1980), 9–12.

24. Roger Williams, *A Key into the Language of America* (1643), in Roger Williams, *The Complete Writings of Roger Williams* (1866; reprint, New York: Russell & Russell, 1963), 1: 123. For patterns of ownership, sovereignty, and work, see Cronon, *Changes in the Land,* 58–67.

25. See Salisbury, *Manitou and Providence,* 47, which criticizes the thesis of individualism.

26. Williams, *Key,* 165; William Wood, *New England's Prospect* (1634), ed. Alden T. Vaughan (Amherst: University of Massachusetts Press, 1977), 90, 91, 92–93. For Wood's probable non-Puritanism, see the introduction by Vaughan, ibid., 4–5.

27. Salisbury, *Manitou and Providence,* 10, 34–35.

28. Williams, *Key,* 157–58, 23 (emphasis in original); Daniel Gookin, *Historical Collections of the Indians in New England* (1792; reprint, New York: Arno Press, 1972), 6–7.

29. Williams, *Key,* 114. (Emphasis in original.)

30. Wood, *New England's Prospect,* 100. The reference to Proserpine is

particularly striking, since in the myth of Ceres and Proserpine (Demeter and Persephone) there is a strong link between the goddess of grain and Hades or death.

31. Williams, *Key*, 150 (emphasis in original); Gookin, *Historical Collections*, 14; Thomas Mayhew to the Corporation in London [Society for Propagation of the Gospell in New England], 22 October 1652, in [John] Eliot and [Thomas] Mayhew, "Tears of Repentance: Or, A Further Narrative of the Progress of the Gospel Amongst the Indians in New-England" (1653), in *Collections of the Massachusetts Historical Society*, 3d ser., vol. 4 (Cambridge: Charles Folsom, 1834), 202. For a summary of other references, see Flannery, *Coastal Algonquian Culture*, 153; and, for manitou in English ships and great buildings, see Williams, *Key*, 151. William Jones's observations are from his essay "The Algonkin Manitou," *Journal of American Folk-Lore* 18 (January–March 1905): 187, 183–84.

32. Williams, *Key*, 148 and n269, 149; Thomas Mayhew to Henry Whitfield, 7 September 1650, in Henry Whitfield, "The Light appearing more and more towards the perfect Day; Or, A farther Discovery of the present state of the Indians in New-England, Concerning the Progresse of the Gospel amongst them" (1651), in *Collections of the Massachusetts Historical Society*, 3d ser., vol. 4 (Cambridge: Charles Folsom, 1834), 111; Mayhew to the Corporation in London, in Eliot and Mayhew, "Tears of Repentance," 201–2; Gookin, *Historical Collections*, 14.

33. Salisbury, *Manitou and Providence*, 136.

34. John Josselyn, *An Account of Two Voyages to New-England* (1675), as cited in Salisbury, *Manitou and Providence*, 35 (the language of "gesture of reciprocity" is Salisbury's, ibid.); Williams, *Key*, 190; Wood, *New England's Prospect*, 85; John Eliot to ?, 2 December 1648, in I. D., "The Glorious Progress Of The Gospel, Amongst The Indians in New England" (1649), in *Collections of the Massachusetts Historical Society*, 3d ser., vol. 4 (Cambridge: Charles Folsom, 1834), 91 (emphasis in original).

35. Salisbury, *Manitou and Providence*, 47; Williams, *Key*, 151, 153, 197; John W. De Forest, *History of the Indians of Connecticut, From the Earliest Known Period to 1850* (1851; reprint, Hamden, Conn.: Archon Books, 1964), 29. (See, also, Flannery, *Coastal Algonquian Culture*, 70, 133, 135, 143–44.)

36. Cronon, *Changes in the Land*, 43; Flannery, *Coastal Algonquian Culture*, 95; Williams, *Key*, 149–50, 24.

37. The best discussion of shamanism and the role of Hobbamock may be found in William S. Simmons, "Southern New England Shamanism: An Ethnographic Reconstruction," in William Cowan, ed., *Papers of the Seventh Algonquian Conference, 1975* (Ottawa: Carleton University, 1976), 217–56. (The cultural limitations of the English sources are especially handicapping in trying to make religious sense of the shamanistic material.) For a brief but useful discussion, in a Euro-American context, of the relationship between witchcraft and anxiety, see Peter W. Williams, *Popu-*

lar Religion in America: Symbolic Change and the Modernization Process in Historical Perspective (Englewood Cliffs, N.J.: Prentice-Hall, 1980), 151–55.

38. Mayhew to the Corporation in London, in Eliot and Mayhew, "Tears of Repentance," 202; Thomas Mayhew to Henry Whitfield, 16 October 1651, in Henry Whitfield et al., "Strength Out Of Weaknesse; Or a Glorious Manifestation Of the further Progresse of the Gospel among the Indians in New-England" (1652), in *Collections of the Massachusetts Historical Society,* 3d ser. vol. 4 (Cambridge: Charles Folsom, 1834), 187 (emphasis in original), 186.

39. Wood, *New England's Prospect,* 101; Simmons, "Southern New England Shamanism," 231–32, 236–38; Mayhew to the Corporation in London, in Eliot and Mayhew, "Tears of Repentance," 204.

40. William Scranton Simmons, *Cautantowwit's House: An Indian Burial Ground on the Island of Conanicut in Narragansett Bay* (Providence: Brown University Press, 1970), 59–60. (There is evidence of belief in at least two souls.)

41. Williams, *Key,* 154; Wood, *New England's Prospect,* 111.

42. John Eliot, in Bowden and Ronda, eds., "Dialog I," *John Eliot's Indian Dialogues,* 73; Wood, *New England's Prospect,* 97; Gookin, *Historical Collections,* 70 (Gookin, ibid., cited the "averseness" of native sachems and the "bad example of the English" in government and religion as reasons for the Rhode Island lack of success). For a useful discussion of the Puritan failure, see Henry Warner Bowden, *American Indians and Christian Missions: Studies in Cultural Conflict,* Chicago History of American Religion (Chicago: University of Chicago Press, 1981), 113–15.

43. William Bradford, *Bradford's History: "Of Plimoth Plantation," From the Original Manuscript, with a Report of the Proceedings Incident to the Return of the Manuscript to Massachusetts* (Boston: Wright & Potter, 1901), 95.

44. Roderick Nash, *Wilderness and the American Mind,* 3d ed. (New Haven: Yale University Press, 1982), 8–9, 1–22. The discussion that follows is based on Nash's seminal study.

45. Gookin, *Historical Collections,* 83.

46. Salisbury, *Manitou and Providence,* 11. For a revealing discussion of the Satanic character of the Indians as perceived by the Puritans, see Peter N. Carroll, *Puritanism and the Wilderness: The Intellectual Significance of the New England Frontier, 1629–1700* (New York: Columbia University Press, 1969), 76–79.

47. Gookin, *Historical Collections,* 14.

48. Gookin summarizes the laws and orders of the General Court of Massachusetts, including the prohibition under penalty of "powwows, or wizards and witches," in ibid., 38.

49. Ibid., 5; I. D., "Glorious Progress of the Gospel," 94.

50. On the prevalence of the notion that the Indians were descended

from the ten tribes of Israel, see the discussion in Charles M. Segal and David C. Stineback, *Puritans, Indians, and Manifest Destiny* (New York: G. P. Putnam's Sons, 1977), 143.

51. See Ex. 11 : 1–35 : 29 for the central events in the biblical account.

52. For Jesus in the wilderness, see Matt. 4 : 1–11. For Antony of Egypt, see the account in Herbert B. Workman, *The Evolution of the Monastic Ideal, from the Earliest Times Down to the Coming of the Friars: A Second Chapter in the History of Christian Renunciation* (1913; reprint, Boston: Beacon Press, 1962), 92–101, esp. 94–95; and St. Jerome, "The Life of St. Paul the First Hermit," in Helen Waddell, trans., *The Desert Fathers: Translations from the Latin with an Introduction* (London: Constable, 1936), 44–52. For a brief, general discussion of the relationship of Christianity to wilderness, see Nash, *Wilderness and the American Mind*, 18–20. And for a more extensive treatment of Jewish and Christian history that is also classic, see George H. Williams, *Wilderness and Paradise in Christian Thought: The Biblical Experience of the Desert in the History of Christianity and the Paradise Theme in the Theological Idea of the University* (New York: Harper & Brothers, 1962).

53. See the discussion in Carroll, *Puritanism and the Wilderness*, 117–19; and see, also, Williams, *Wilderness and Paradise*, 5–19.

54. John Winthrop to his wife [Margaret Winthrop], 10 March 1629 [/30], quoted in Carroll, *Puritanism and the Wilderness*, 27. George Williams argued that the Exodus theme appealed largely to "the Revolutionary generation and their descendants." In his reading, colonial New Englanders were more commonly drawn to "the eschatologically oriented conception of the wilderness in Revelation 12 : 6 and the mystically saturated imagery of the wilderness in Canticles and the allied texts of the pre-exilic prophets" (Williams, *Wilderness and Paradise*, 98–99).

55. Bradford, *"Of Plimoth Plantation,"* 90–91, 92–93.

56. Carroll, *Puritanism and the Wilderness*, 29–31.

57. Wood, *New England's Prospect*, 27, 33, 36–37.

58. See the discussion in Carroll, *Puritanism and the Wilderness*, 17, 109–12; see, also, 87–90, 104–6.

59. Carroll's book *Puritanism and the Wilderness* explores the antithesis between these two visions. For a succinct summary of his thesis of concurrent Puritan impulses toward cohesion and expansiveness, see *Puritanism and the Wilderness*, 1–4.

60. Joseph Caryl, in John Eliot, "A Late and Further Manifestation of the Progress of the Gospel amongst the Indians in New-England" (1655), in *Collections of the Massachusetts Historical Society*, 3d ser., vol. 4 (Cambridge: Charles Folsom, 1834), 266–67. (Emphasis in original.)

61. Cecelia Tichi, *New World, New Earth: Environmental Reform in American Literature from the Puritans through Whitman* (New Haven: Yale University Press, 1979), 7. Tichi argues that the "ideology of environmental reform" (ix) originated with the Puritans. And for mystical leanings, see the discussion in Williams, *Wilderness and Paradise*, 98–108.

62. Conrad Cherry, "New England as Symbol: Ambiguity in the Puritan Vision," *Soundings* 58 (Fall 1975): 349, 352–55.

63. Jennings, *Invasion of America*, 15–31. On the move from sacred to ordinary (or profane), see Salisbury, *Manitou and Providence*, 238–39; and, on commodity orientation, see Cronon, *Changes in the Land*, 20–21.

64. Cotton Mather, *The Christian Philosopher: A Collection of the Best Discoveries in Nature, with Religious Improvements* (1721; reprint, Gainesville, Fla.: Scholars' Facsimiles & Reprints, 1968), 8, 2. (Emphasis in original.) For Mather as scientist and poet, see Kenneth B. Murdock, "Introduction," in Kenneth B. Murdock, ed., *Selections from Cotton Mather* (New York: Harcourt, Brace, 1926), lii–liv.

65. Mather, *Christian Philosopher*, 111, 114, 115–16. (Emphasis in original.)

66. Ibid., 128, 130–31. (Emphasis in original.)

67. Ibid., 139, 295 (emphasis in original); for the coda, see 297–304.

68. Clyde A. Holbrook, *Jonathan Edwards, The Valley and Nature: An Interpretative Essay* (Lewisburg, Pa.: Bucknell University Press; London and Toronto: Associated University Presses, 1987), 33.

69. See Jonathan Edwards, "Personal Narrative," in Clarence H. Faust and Thomas H. Johnson, eds., *Jonathan Edwards: Representative Selections*, American Century Series, rev. ed. (New York: Hill and Wang, 1962), 57.

70. Ibid., 60–61 (emphasis in original). For "cosmic consciousness," see Richard Maurice Bucke, *Cosmic Consciousness: A Study in the Evolution of the Human Mind* (1901; reprint, New York: E. P. Dutton, 1969), esp. 3–4, 61–82.

71. For a useful discussion of Puritan Platonism and the Ramean logic, see the introduction in Perry Miller and Thomas H. Johnson, eds., *The Puritans*, rev. ed. (New York: Harper & Row, Harper Torchbooks, 1963), 1: 27–40.

72. Perry Miller, "Introduction," in Jonathan Edwards, *Images or Shadows of Divine Things*, ed. Perry Miller (1948; reprint, Westport, Conn.: Greenwood Press, 1977), 28.

73. Edwards, *Images or Shadows*, 109; Miller, in ibid., 36.

74. Edwards, *Images or Shadows*, 44 (brackets in Miller edition). For a classic account of at least one side of the relationship between Edwards and the Transcendentalist leader Ralph Waldo Emerson, see Perry Miller, "From Edwards to Emerson," in Perry Miller, *Errand into the Wilderness* (1956; reprint, New York: Harper & Row, Harper Torchbooks, 1964), 184–203.

75. Edwards, *Images or Shadows*, 45, 50–51, 79, 94, 91–92.

76. Ibid., 69; Mason I. Lowance, Jr., *The Language of Canaan: Metaphor and Symbol in New England from the Puritans to the Transcendentalists* (Cambridge: Harvard University Press, 1980), 178–207 (see, also, Lowance's instructive reading of Edwards's *Images or Shadows* in ibid., 258–72); Sacvan Bercovitch, *The Puritan Origins of the American Self* (New Haven: Yale University Press, 1975), 153–56; and Sacvan Bercovitch, *The*

American Jeremiad (Madison: University of Wisconsin Press, 1978), 93–131. For Edwards's American millennium, see the material from Jonathan Edwards, "Some Thoughts concerning the Present Revival of Religion in New England" (1742), in Alan Heimert and Perry Miller, eds., *The Great Awakening* (Indianapolis: Bobbs-Merrill, 1967), 264–90, esp. 273. For the largest corpus of Edwards's apocalyptic and millennial writings, see Jonathan Edwards, *Apocalyptic Writings,* ed. Stephen J. Stein, The Works of Jonathan Edwards, vol. 5 (New Haven: Yale University Press, 1977).

77. Miller, "From Edwards to Emerson," in Miller, *Errand,* 184–203.

78. Jonathan Edwards, "The Mind," in Jonathan Edwards, *Scientific and Philosophical Writings,* ed. Wallace E. Anderson, The Works of Jonathan Edwards, vol. 6, (New Haven: Yale University Press, 1980), 351; Jonathan Edwards, "Things to be Considered an[d] Written fully about," in ibid., 235. For useful discussions of Edwards's philosophical idealism that are germane to the treatment here, see Wallace E. Anderson, "Editor's Introduction," in ibid., 53–75; and Holbrook, *Jonathan Edwards,* 55–72.

79. John Wise, *A Vindication of the Government of New-England Churches* (1717; reprint, Gainesville, Fla.: Scholars' Facsimiles & Reprints, 1958), 3, 30, 31.

80. Ibid., 31–32, 35, 37, 40, 44.

Chapter Two

1. For material regarding Royall Tyler and the early history of his play *The Contrast,* I have relied on Ada Lou Carson and Herbert L. Carson, *Royall Tyler* (Boston: Twayne Publishers, 1979), 15–43.

2. Quoted ibid., 29, 31.

3. On a British model for *The Contrast* (Richard Brinsley Sheridan's *The School for Scandal* [1777]), see Carson and Carson, *Royall Tyler,* 31, 34, 35; and Arthur Hobson Quinn, *A History of the American Drama: From the Beginning to the Civil War,* 2d ed. (New York: Appleton-Century-Crofts, 1951), 69–70.

4. See Royall Tyler, *The Contrast: A Comedy in Five Acts,* Introduction by James Benjamin Wilbur (1920; reprint, New York: AMS Press, 1970), 50, 79. I owe the phrase "nature's nation" to the title of Perry Miller's posthumously published collection of essays *Nature's Nation* (Cambridge: Harvard University Press, Belknap Press, 1967), although I use the phrase here in a context different from that in Miller's work.

5. See Tyler, *Contrast,* 112, 48, 26, 32. "Chesterfield" was Philip Dormer Stanhope, the fourth earl of Chesterfield, whose letters to his son on well-bred etiquette and worldly wisdom were published after his death in 1773. So popular did the letters become that they were printed in a fifth edition within a year. For a relatively recent edition, see the Fourth Earl of Chesterfield, Philip Dormer Stanhope, *Letters to His Son and Others,* Everyman's Library, no. 823 (London: J. M. Dent, 1973). Samuel Richardson's seven-volume novel *The History of Sir Charles Grandison* was

published in 1753–54. For a useful study of the themes reflected here, see Richard L. Bushman, "American High-Style and Vernacular Cultures," in Jack P. Greene and J. R. Pole, eds., *Colonial British America: Essays in the New History of the Early Modern Era* (Baltimore: Johns Hopkins University Press, 1984), 345–83.

6. Tyler, *Contrast,* 32. I have quoted the third stanza of the four-stanza song.

7. Ibid., 38–39, 66, 54.

8. For a discussion of these themes, see Catherine L. Albanese, *Sons of the Fathers: The Civil Religion of the American Revolution* (Philadelphia: Temple University Press, 1976), esp. 81–111, 19–27.

9. J. Hector St. John Crèvecoeur, *Letters from an American Farmer* (1782; Gloucester, Mass.: Peter Smith, 1968), 57–59. For the Exodus theme and the New World wilderness during the revolutionary era, see George H. Williams, *Wilderness and Paradise in Christian Thought: The Biblical Experience of the Desert in the History of Christianity and the Paradise Theme in the Theological Idea of the University* (New York: Harper & Brothers, 1962), 111–13; and see, also, Albanese, *Sons of the Fathers,* 24, 29, 88–90, passim.

10. For the classic account of the sacred as the wholly Other, see Rudolf Otto, *The Idea of the Holy: An Inquiry into the Non-Rational Factor in the Idea of the Divine and Its Relation to the Rational [Das Heilige],* trans. John W. Harvey (New York: Oxford University Press, Galaxy Book, 1958), esp. 25–30.

11. Samuel Eliot Morison, *The Oxford History of the American People* (New York: Oxford University Press, 1965), 198. See, also, Morison's discussion of John Dickinson's "Farmer's Letters," ibid., 191. The Dickinson letters appeared in the *Pennsylvania Chronicle* from November 1767 to January 1768. (Emphasis on "farmer" in the text is mine.)

12. David Ramsay, *The History of the American Revolution* (1789; Lexington, Ky.: Downing and Phillips, 1815), 1:83–84 (emphasis mine). For a fuller discussion of the Liberty Tree in a religious context, see Albanese, *Sons of the Fathers,* 58–68.

13. See the discussion in Albanese, *Sons of the Fathers,* 58–60. For a fuller account, on which my own work draws, see Mircea Eliade, *Patterns in Comparative Religion,* trans. Rosemary Sheed (Cleveland: World Publishing, Meridian Books, 1963), 265–78, 309–18; and, for the classic account of maypoles, see Sir James Frazer, *The Golden Bough: A Study in Magic and Religion,* abr. ed. (New York: Macmillan, 1963), 139–56.

14. For a discussion of the "state of nature" with reference to the American colonists, see Albanese, *Sons of the Fathers,* 48–55.

15. Marjorie Hope Nicolson, *Mountain Gloom and Mountain Glory: The Development of the Aesthetics of the Infinite* (1959; reprint, New York: W. W. Norton, Norton Library, 1963), 3.

16. See the discussion ibid., esp. 134–43, 157–59.

17. Joseph Butler, *The Analogy of Religion, Natural and Revealed, to the*

Constitution and Course of Nature, Everyman's Library, no. 90 (1736; London: J. M. Dent, 1906), xxx; William Wollaston, *The Religion of Nature Delineated* (London: Printed by Samuel Palmer, 1726), 26 (emphasis in original); Samuel Clarke, "A Discourse concerning the Unchangeable Obligations of Natural Religion, and the Truth and Certainty of the Christian Revelation" (1705), in *The Works of Samuel Clarke, D.D.* (1738; reprint, New York: Garland Publishing, 1978), 643–44 (emphasis in original). The definitive study of the American Enlightenment is the nuanced and illuminating work by Henry F. May, *The Enlightenment in America* (New York: Oxford University Press, 1976).

18. John Adams, *The Works of John Adams, the Second President of the United States,* ed. Charles F. Adams, 10 vols. (Boston: Little, Brown, 1850–56), 2:370–71. Reportedly the debate occurred on 8 September 1774.

19. Bernard Faÿ, *Revolution and Freemasonry, 1680–1800* (Boston: Little, Brown, 1935), 315; C. W. Moore, according to Robert Frike Gould, *Gould's History of Freemasonry throughout the World,* ed. Dudley Wright et al. (New York: Charles Scribner's Sons, 1936), 4:277; Faÿ, *Revolution and Freemasonry,* 241–42; Philip Davidson, *Propaganda and the American Revolution, 1763–1783* (Chapel Hill: University of North Carolina Press, 1941), 101; Herbert M. Morais, *Deism in Eighteenth-Century America* (1934; reprint, New York: Russell & Russell, 1960), 148.

20. Captain George Smith, *The Use and Abuse of Freemasonry; A Work of the Greatest Utility to the Brethren of the Society, to Mankind in General, and to the Ladies in Particular* (1783; New York: Macoy Publishing & Masonic Supply, 1914), 134. The sun-reason-truth analogy here is strikingly consonant with Mircea Eliade's assessment of connecting themes in sun symbolism and sun religion. See Eliade, *Patterns in Comparative Religion,* 124–51, esp. 125–26, 150–51.

21. Smith, *Use and Abuse of Freemasonry,* 16–17; Thomas Paine, "Origin of Freemasonry" (1805), in *The Complete Writings of Thomas Paine,* ed. Philip S. Foner (New York: Citadel Press, 1945), 2:832–33; Smith, *Use and Abuse of Freemasonry,* 147 (and see Smith's quotation from Hermes Trismegistes, ibid., 150).

22. Paine, "Origin of Freemasonry," 835–36; Smith, *Use and Abuse of Freemasonry,* 156–58; Paine, "Origin of Freemasonry," 840, 834, 836–37. On the floor and roof of lodges, see, also, Smith, *Use and Abuse of Freemasonry,* 148, 72–73; and, for another pointed comment on the Johannine festivals, see Gould, *Gould's History of Freemasonry,* 2:38.

23. For further discussion of the Freemasonic mythic model for moral development, see Albanese, *Sons of the Fathers,* 133–36.

24. Smith, *Use and Abuse of Freemasonry,* 11, 147–48.

25. Max Weber, *The Protestant Ethic and the Spirit of Capitalism* (1904–5), trans. Talcott Parsons, 2d ed. (New York: Charles Scribner's Sons, 1958).

26. Edmund Burke, *A Philosophical Enquiry into the Origin of Our Ideas*

of the Sublime and Beautiful, ed. J. T. Boulton (London: Routledge and Kegan Paul, 1958), 39, 57, 64, 72–73, 77–79. (Boulton's text is that of the second edition in 1759.)

27. Otto, Idea of the Holy [Das Heilige], esp. 12–40.

28. Jedidiah Morse, The American Geography; Or, A View of the Present Situation of the United States of America (1789; reprint, New York: Arno Press and The New York Times, 1970), esp. 34–126; Roderick Nash, Wilderness and the American Mind, 3d ed. (New Haven: Yale University Press, 1982), 67, 69 (emphasis in original), 46.

29. Charles Coleman Sellers, Charles Willson Peale, vol. 2, Later Life, 1790–1827 (Philadelphia: American Philosophical Society, 1947), 229; Edgar P. Richardson, "Charles Willson Peale and His World," in Edgar P. Richardson et al., Charles Willson Peale and His World (New York: Harry N. Abrams, 1983), 87; Sellers, Charles Willson Peale, 224, 228, 235, passim; Hans Huth, Nature and the American: Three Centuries of Changing Attitudes (Berkeley: University of California Press, 1957), 17.

30. William Bartram, The Travels of William Bartram, ed. Francis Harper, Naturalist's ed. (New Haven: Yale University Press, 1958), 31, 48, 212, 229, 154–55.

31. Crèvecoeur, Letters from an American Farmer, 192.

32. Philip Freneau, "The Philosopher of the Forest," no. 1, Freeman's Journal (November 1781), in The Prose of Philip Freneau, ed. Philip M. Marsh (New Brunswick, N.J.: Scarecrow Press, 1955), 198; Philip Freneau, "The American Village" (1772), in The Poems of Philip Freneau: Poet of the American Revolution, ed. Fred Lewis Pattee, 3 vols. (New York: Russell & Russell, 1963), 3:386; Philip Freneau, "Neversink" (1791), ibid., 3. ("The American Village" was Freneau's first distinct published poem.)

33. See the Tomo Cheeki papers from the Jersey Chronicle (1795) and The Time Piece, and Literary Companion (1797), in Freneau, Prose, 331–53, 357–62. (Freneau's philosophical Tomo Cheeki took his name and a tenuous identity from the Creek chief Tomo-Chi-Chi who, in 1734, traveled with his wife to England.) For nature's God in Freneau's poetry, see, e.g., "The Pictures of Columbus, the Genoese" (1788), in Freneau, Poems, 1:117; "On a Book Called Unitarian Theology" (1786), ibid., 2:307–9; and "Ode to Liberty" (1793), ibid., 3:95. For Freneau's late poems, cf. "On the Universality and Other Attributes of the God of Nature" (1815) and "On the Uniformity and Perfection of Nature" (1815), in Philip Freneau, Poems of Freneau, ed. Harry Hayden Clark, Hafner Library of Classics, no. 19 (1929; reprint, New York: Hafner Publishing, [1960]), 422–24. For a useful introduction to Freneau's thought, pointing to its complexity, see Nelson F. Adkins, Philip Freneau and the Cosmic Enigma: The Religious and Philosophical Speculations of an American Poet (1949; reprint, New York: Russell & Russell, 1971).

34. Timothy Dwight, "Greenfield Hill (1794)," in The Major Poems of Timothy Dwight, ed. William J. Mc Taggart and William K. Bottorff (Gainesville, Fla.: Scholars' Facsimiles & Reprints, 1969), 510; Joel Bar-

low, "The Vision of Columbus" (1787), in *The Works of Joel Barlow,* ed. William K. Bottorff and Arthur L. Ford (Gainesville, Fla.: Scholars' Facsimiles & Reprints, 1970), 135, 142.

35. Nash, *Wilderness and the American Mind,* 44.

36. [Thomas Jefferson], "The Declaration of Independence" [draft form], in J. R. Pole, ed., *The Revolution in America, 1754–1788: Documentaries and Commentaries* (Stanford: Stanford University Press, 1970), 30, 33, 31, passim. For a recent and succinct summary of the Adams anecdote, see Charles B. Sanford, *The Religious Life of Thomas Jefferson* (Charlottesville: University Press of Virginia, 1984), 17.

37. By "inactive creator deities," I intend reference to the kind of high god known to historians of religions as the *deus otiosus.* See Mircea Eliade, *The Sacred and the Profane: The Nature of Religion,* trans. Willard R. Trask (New York: Harcourt, Brace & World, Harvest Book, 1959), 121–25. For alienation from the past, see Daniel J. Boorstin, *The Lost World of Thomas Jefferson* (1948; reprint, Boston: Beacon Press, 1960), 169. And, for an insightful comprehensive account of Jefferson's thought regarding nature, see the new study by Charles A. Miller, *Jefferson and Nature: An Interpretation* (Baltimore: The Johns Hopkins University Press, 1988). Writes Miller: "Nature was Jefferson's myth for all purposes, a flexible idea that gathered together his deepest beliefs. It was uncritically accepted, pervasively invoked. Nature was the source of all that existed and all that was worthwhile" (ibid., 251). Unfortunately, Miller's work appeared too late to inform the treatment of Jefferson here.

38. Thomas Jefferson to Peter Carr, 10 August 1787, in *The Portable Thomas Jefferson,* ed. Merrill D. Peterson (New York: Viking Press, 1975), 424–25, 424.

39. Sanford, *Religious Life of Thomas Jefferson,* 47. For the concreteness of the Jeffersonian cosmology, cf. Boorstin, *Lost World of Thomas Jefferson,* 43–44. For Jefferson's two New Testament compilations—"The Philosophy of Jesus" (1804) and "The Life and Morals of Jesus" (1819–20?)—see *Jefferson's Extracts from the Gospels: "The Philosophy of Jesus" and "The Life and Morals of Jesus,"* ed. Dickinson W. Adams et al., vol. 1 of *The Papers of Thomas Jefferson, Second Series,* ed. Charles T. Cullen (Princeton: Princeton University Press, 1983); and, for an insightful discussion of these extracts in the context of Jefferson's religion as a whole, see the introduction, by Eugene R. Sheridan, to the volume (3–42). See, also, the useful discussion of the so-called Jefferson Bible, in Sanford, *Religious Life of Thomas Jefferson,* 102–40.

40. Thomas Jefferson to John Adams, 15 August 1820, in *The Adams-Jefferson Letters: The Complete Correspondence between Thomas Jefferson and Abigail and John Adams,* ed. Lester J. Cappon, 2 vols. (Chapel Hill: University of North Carolina Press for the Institute of Early American History and Culture, 1959), 2:567, 568 (emphasis in original). See, also, Thomas Jefferson to John Adams, 14 March 1820, ibid., 562; Thomas

Jefferson to John Adams, 8 January 1825, ibid., 606. And, for a short and helpful discussion of Jefferson's materialism, see Sanford, *Religious Life of Thomas Jefferson*, 147–52.

41. Boorstin, *Lost World of Thomas Jefferson*, 118; Adrienne Koch, *The Philosophy of Thomas Jefferson* (1943; reprint, Gloucester, Mass.: Peter Smith, 1957), 190. For a series of masterful interpretations of religion as an expression of human labor, see the essays in Jonathan Z. Smith, *Imagining Religion: From Babylon to Jonestown*, Chicago Studies in the History of Judaism (Chicago: University of Chicago Press, 1982), esp. 43–44, 89, 100–101.

42. Thomas Jefferson to John Banister, Jr., 15 October 1785, in *Portable Thomas Jefferson*, 393–94; Thomas Jefferson, *Notes on the State of Virginia* ([1784] 1861; reprint, New York: Harper & Row, Harper Torchbooks, 1964), 157.

43. Ibid.

44. Boorstin, *Lost World of Thomas Jefferson*, 231; Thomas Jefferson, "First Inaugural Address (4 March 1801)," in *Portable Thomas Jefferson*, 292.

45. Boorstin, *Lost World of Thomas Jefferson*, 232, 233.

46. Thomas Jefferson to Maria Cosway, 12 October 1786, in *Portable Thomas Jefferson*, 404. (These are the words of the "heart" in Jefferson's literary dialogue "between my Head and my Heart" [ibid., 400] for Cosway's benefit.)

47. Ibid.

48. Jefferson, *Notes on the State of Virginia*, 16.

49. Ibid., 17.

50. Ibid., 21.

51. Garry Wills, *Inventing America: Jefferson's Declaration of Independence* (Garden City, N.Y.: Doubleday, 1978), 264; Jefferson, *Notes on the State of Virginia*, 21.

52. Jefferson, *Notes on the State of Virginia*, 38, 39, 41, 45–55. In his essay "De la Dégénération des Animaux," in volume 14 of his massive *Histoire Naturelle, Générale et Particulière* (1749–1804), Georges-Louis Leclerc, the Count de Buffon, pointing to the effects of climate and of food, had argued for the "degeneration" of animals in the New World.

53. The account in the next several paragraphs is based on Catherine L. Albanese, "David Crockett," in Joel Myerson, ed., *Antebellum Writers in New York and the South*, vol. 3 of *Dictionary of Literary Biography* (Detroit: Gale Research, 1979), 94–96. For the underlying interpretation presented here, see, also, Catherine L. Albanese, "Citizen Crockett: Myth, History, and Nature Religion," *Soundings* 61 (Spring 1978), 87–104; Catherine L. Albanese, "King Crockett: Nature and Civility on the American Frontier," *Proceedings of the American Antiquarian Society* 88, pt. 2 (October 1979): 225–49; and Catherine L. Albanese, "Savage, Sinner, and Saved: Davy Crockett, Camp Meetings, and the Wild Frontier," *American Quar-*

terly 33 (Winter 1981): 482–501. My work on the Davy Crockett almanacs was supported by a Fred Harris Daniels Fellowship granted by the American Antiquarian Society during the summer of 1977.

54. Crockett's autobiography, written with the assistance of Thomas Chilton, has been reprinted in facsimile. See David Crockett, *A Narrative of the Life of Davy Crockett of the State of Tennessee*, ed. James A. Shackford and Stanley J. Folmsbee (Knoxville: University of Tennessee Press, 1973).

55. For an insightful work that links hunter, warrior, and politician through a study of selected American literary materials, see Richard Slotkin, *Regeneration through Violence: The Mythology of the American Frontier, 1600–1860* (Middletown, Conn.: Wesleyan University Press, 1973), esp. 517–65.

56. *Davy Crockett's Almanac, 1845* (Boston: James Fisher, n.d.), 5; *Crockett's Almanac, 1851* (Philadelphia, New York, and Boston: Fisher & Brother, n.d.), 14; *Crockett's Almanac, 1848* (Boston: James Fisher, n.d.), 9; *Crockett's Almanac, 1850* (New York, Philadelphia, and Boston: Turner and Brothers, n.d.), 23. (Page numbers are missing in most of the almanacs, but I have supplied them as necessary.)

57. *Davy Crockett's Almanack, of Wild Sports in the West, Life in the Backwoods, & Sketches of Texas* (Nashville: Published by the heirs of Col. Crockett, 1837), 40. (Emphasis in original.)

58. Slotkin, *Regeneration through Violence*, esp. 124–25.

59. *Davy Crockett's Almanac, 1847* (New York and Philadelphia: Turner & Fisher, n.d.), 13; *Crockett's Yaller Flower Almanac, for '36* (Snagsville: Boon Crockett, and Squire Downing [New York: Elton], n.d.), 4–6; *The Crockett Almanac, 1841* (Nashville: Ben Harding, n.d.), 10. (Ben Harding is a fictional character.)

60. *Davy Crockett's Almanac, 1845*, 4; *Crockett's Almanac, 1846* (Boston: James Fisher, n.d.), 20.

61. *Crockett's Almanac, 1854* (New York: Philip J. Cozans, n.d.), 25. Crockett had probably acquired his title as colonel because of the popular identification of him with Colonel Nimrod Wildfire in James K. Paulding's play *Lion of the West* (1830).

62. For Crockett's legendary thumbnail and its use, see, e.g., *The Crockett Almanac 1841* (Boston: J. Fisher, n.d.), 11; and *Crockett's Almanac, 1848* (Boston: James Fisher, n.d.), 18; and, for the notorious episode in which Crockett ends by eating two Indian chiefs he killed along the Oregon, see *Crockett Almanac, 1849* (Boston: James Fisher, n.d.), 9.

63. For history and its "terror," see Mircea Eliade, *Cosmos and History: The Myth of the Eternal Return*, trans. Willard R. Trask (New York: Harper & Row, Harper Torchbooks, 1959), esp. 141–62.

64. William Cullen Bryant, "Thanatopsis," in *The Poetical Works of William Cullen Bryant*, ed. Parke Godwin (1883; reprint, New York: Russell & Russell, 1967), 1: 17. For a discussion of Bryant germane to this account, see Huth, *Nature and the American*, 30–36.

65. Ralph Waldo Emerson, quoted in Parke Godwin, *A Biography of William Cullen Bryant, with Extracts from His Private Correspondence* (1883; reprint, New York: Russell & Russell, [1967]), 2:216, 217.

Chapter Three

1. Ralph Waldo Emerson, "Self-Reliance," in *Essays: First Series,* vol. 2 of *The Collected Works of Ralph Waldo Emerson,* ed. Alfred R. Ferguson et al. (Cambridge: Harvard University Press, Belknap Press, 1971–), 33.

2. Perry Miller, "Nature and the National Ego," in Perry Miller, *Errand into the Wilderness* (1956; New York: Harper & Row, Harper Torchbooks, 1964), 204.

3. Ralph Waldo Emerson to William Emerson, 28 June 1836, in *The Letters of Ralph Waldo Emerson,* ed. Ralph L. Rusk (1939; reprint, New York: Columbia University Press, 1966), 2:26.

4. Rusk, ibid., n. 76; Ralph Waldo Emerson to William Emerson, 8 August 1836, ibid., 32; James Elliot Cabot, *A Memoir of Ralph Waldo Emerson* (Boston: Houghton Mifflin, 1887), 1:259; Robert E. Spiller, "Introduction," in *Nature, Addresses, and Lectures,* vol. 1 of *The Collected Works of Ralph Waldo Emerson,* xiii–xiv. (I am, in general, indebted to Spiller for my reading here.)

5. Gail Thain Parker, *Mind Cure in New England: From the Civil War to World War I* (Hanover, N.H.: University Press of New England, 1973), 20.

6. Ralph Waldo Emerson, *Nature,* in *Collected Works,* 1:7–9.

7. Ibid., 9–10.

8. Ibid., 10, 12, 19, 17, 26.

9. Barbara Novak, *Nature and Culture: American Landscape and Painting, 1825–1875* (New York: Oxford University Press, 1980), 269.

10. Emerson, *Nature,* 29–30.

11. Ibid., 30.

12. Ibid., 36.

13. Ibid., 35–36.

14. Ibid., 36–37, 41–42.

15. Ibid., 42–43.

16. Ibid., 43.

17. Ibid., 45.

18. See, e.g., Philip F. Gura, *The Wisdom of Words: Language, Theology, and Literature in the New England Renaissance* (Middletown, Conn.: Wesleyan University Press, 1981), 107–44; Victor Carl Friesen, *The Spirit of the Huckleberry: Sensuousness in Henry Thoreau* (Edmonton: University of Alberta Press, 1984); Donald Worster, *Nature's Economy: A History of Ecological Ideas* (Cambridge: Cambridge University Press, 1977), 58–111; and Charles E. Headington, "Americans in the Wilderness: A Study of Their Encounters with Otherness from the Initial Contact through Henry David Thoreau" (Ph.D. diss., University of Chicago, 1985), 236ff.

19. Gura, *Wisdom of Words,* 137.

20. Henry D. Thoreau, *Walden,* ed. J. Lyndon Shanley, The Writings of Henry D. Thoreau (Princeton: Princeton University Press, 1971), 210; Henry David Thoreau, *Huckleberries,* ed. Leo Stoller (Iowa City: Windhover Press of The University of Iowa and The New York Public Library, 1970), 23 (emphasis in original).

21. Cecelia Tichi, *New World, New Earth: Environmental Reform in American Literature from the Puritans through Whitman* (New Haven: Yale University Press, 1979), 167.

22. Mircea Eliade, *The Sacred and the Profane: The Nature of Religion,* trans. Willard R. Trask (New York: Harcourt, Brace & World, Harvest Book, 1959), 11–12, 20–24; Henry D. Thoreau, *The Maine Woods,* ed. Joseph J. Moldenhauer, The Writings of Henry D. Thoreau (Princeton: Princeton University Press, 1972), 179, 181. The phrase "a community of love" is taken from Henry D. Thoreau, *Journal* (29 January 1840), ed. John C. Broderick et al., The Writings of Henry D. Thoreau (Princeton: Princeton University Press, 1981–), 1:105. For Worster's lucid discussion, to which I am much in debt, see *Nature's Economy,* 84, and his entire chapter on Thoreau, 77–111.

23. For readings of Thoreau that stress his Puritan heritage, see, e.g., William J. Wolf, *Thoreau: Mystic, Prophet, Ecologist* (Philadelphia: United Church Press, Pilgrim Press, 1974), as well as—in briefer references— Mason I. Lowance, Jr., *The Language of Canaan: Metaphor and Symbol in New England from the Puritans to the Transcendentalists* (Cambridge: Harvard University Press, 1980), 245, 250, 278–95; Sacvan Bercovitch, *The Puritan Origins of the American Self* (New Haven: Yale University Press, 1975), 162; and Sacvan Bercovitch, *The American Jeremiad* (Madison: University of Wisconsin Press, 1978), 185–90. Bercovitch—and Perry Miller before him—also emphasizes Emerson's Puritan roots. See Bercovitch, *Puritan Origins,* 157–86; Bercovitch, *American Jeremiad,* 182–85, 199–203; and Perry Miller, "From Edwards to Emerson," in *Errand into the Wilderness,* 184–203.

24. Thoreau, *Walden,* 213–14.

25. Ibid., 218–20.

26. Ibid., 221–22.

27. Ibid., 222.

28. See Sherman Paul's insightful discussion in *The Shores of America: Thoreau's Inward Exploration* (1958; reprint, Urbana: University of Illinois Press, 1972), 234–92, esp. 259.

29. Thoreau, *Walden,* 17. For Thoreau's own comment on the passage, see Henry D. Thoreau to B. B. Wiley, 26 April 1857, in *The Correspondence of Henry David Thoreau,* ed. Walter Harding and Carl Bode (Washington Square, N.Y.: New York University Press, 1958), 478.

30. Henry D. Thoreau, "Walking," in *Excursions* (1863; reprint, Gloucester, Mass.: Peter Smith, 1975), 161, 169, 190.

31. Ibid., 187, 185, 204–5, 201, 207.

32. Ibid., 210–11, 214.

33. Worster, *Nature's Economy,* 107.

34. Thoreau, "Walking," 185; Thoreau, *Huckleberries,* 31, 32, 34–35.

35. John Muir, 11 July 1890, in Linnie Marsh Wolfe, ed., *John of the Mountains: The Unpublished Journals of John Muir* (1938; reprint, Madison: University of Wisconsin Press, 1979), 317; Novak, *Nature and Culture,* 15; Miller, "Nature and the National Ego," 209. See, also, Myra Jehlen's introduction to *American Incarnation: The Individual, the Nation, and the Continent* (Cambridge: Harvard University Press, 1986), esp. 5–18. For the Puritanism, see Bercovitch, *Puritan Origins,* 151–52; and Lowance, *Language of Canaan,* ix. For "biocentric" romanticism, see Worster, *Nature's Economy,* 85.

36. Miller, "Nature and the National Ego," 209.

37. For Thoreau's "perfect body," see his *Journal,* 13 September 1839, 1:138, although the context indicates quite clearly that the body existed as the "fruits" of the "Soul." For a brief but useful discussion of cultural millennialism during the middle period of the nineteenth century, see Novak, *Nature and Culture,* 4–6.

38. For a related discussion, to which this one is at least partially indebted, see Novak, *Nature and Culture,* 7–8, 34–44.

39. Lee Clark Mitchell, *Witnesses to a Vanishing America: The Nineteenth-Century Response* (Princeton: Princeton University Press, 1981). For a discussion of George Catlin's national park idea, see 96–97, and, for Mitchell's words quoted here, see xiv. For a discussion of preconditions for the conservation movement, see Roderick Nash, "The American Invention of National Parks," *American Quarterly* 22 (Fall 1970): 726–35.

40. Mitchell, *Witnesses to a Vanishing America,* 53; Michael P. Cohen, *The Pathless Way: John Muir and American Wilderness* (Madison: University of Wisconsin Press, 1984), 366.

41. For a perceptive discussion of Muir's rhetorical strategy, see Christine Oravec, "John Muir, Yosemite, and the Sublime Response: A Study in the Rhetoric of Preservationism," *The Quarterly Journal of Speech* 67 (August 1981): 245–58, esp. 256.

42. Linnie Marsh Wolfe, *Son of the Wilderness: The Life of John Muir* (1945; Madison: University of Wisconsin Press, 1978), 3. "A Stern Heritage" is Wolfe's title for part I of the biography.

43. For a more detailed discussion, see Wolfe, *Son of the Wilderness,* esp. 188–348; Roderick Nash, *Wilderness and the American Mind,* 3d ed. (New Haven: Yale University Press, 1982), 122–40, 156–81; Stephen Fox, *John Muir and His Legacy: The American Conservation Movement* (Boston: Little, Brown, 1981).

44. For nature as the book of God, see, e.g., Muir's reflections, in Wolfe, *John of the Mountains,* 47 (21 March 1870), 153–54 (20 August 1873?), and his words to Jeanne Carr, in Cohen, *Pathless Way,* 109. For the Old Testament mold of Muir's language, see Cohen, *Pathless Way,* 149, and, for his

Yosemite experience as religious awakening, see ibid., 65–83, esp., for the quotation, 66.

45. John Muir, *The Mountains of California* (1894; reprint, New York: Century, 1903), 61–64. (Emphasis in original.)

46. Ibid., 64–65.

47. Cohen, *Pathless Way,* 127; Muir, in Wolfe, *John of the Mountains,* 86 (ca. October 1871).

48. Muir, in Wolfe, *John of the Mountains,* 43–44 (18 January 1870).

49. John Muir, *To Yosemite and Beyond: Writings from the Years 1863 to 1875,* ed. Robert Engberg and Donald Wesling (Madison: University of Wisconsin Press, 1980), 51 (6 June 1869); Henry David Thoreau to Lucy Brown, 21 July 1841, in Thoreau, *Correspondence,* 45 (but cf., ibid., Thoreau's assertion to Brown: "I grow savager and savager every day, as if I fed on raw meat, and my tameness is only the repose of untamableness"); Muir, *To Yosemite and Beyond,* 51 (6 June 1869); Muir, as quoted in Wolfe, *Son of the Wilderness,* 124. For Muir's attitudes toward hunting and animal slaughter, see the discussion in Cohen, *Pathless Way,* 179–84.

50. Wolfe, *Son of the Wilderness,* 267; Muir, in Wolfe, *John of the Mountains,* 83 (October 1871); Muir to Jeanne Carr, as quoted in Wolfe, *Son of the Wilderness,* 161; Muir, in Wolfe, *John of the Mountains,* 137–38 (15 March 1873).

51. Muir, in Wolfe, *John of the Mountains,* 138 (15 March 1873).

52. Muir, ibid., 118 (16 February 1873).

53. Muir, ibid., 313 (11–21 July 1890); Muir to Jeanne Carr, undated (Fall 1870), in Cohen, *Pathless Way,* 122 (the letter is printed in full, 122–23).

54. Muir to Jeanne Carr, in Cohen, *Pathless Way,* 122. (Emphasis in original.)

55. Wolfe, *Son of the Wilderness,* 166; Oravec, "John Muir, Yosemite, and the Sublime Response" (for fuller background, see, also, Oravec's "Studies in the Rhetoric of the Conservation Movement in America, 1865–1913" [Ph.D. diss., University of Wisconsin, 1979]).

56. Nash, *Wilderness and the American Mind,* 125; Wolfe, *Son of the Wilderness,* 77–79, 146–47. Cohen, e.g., calls Emerson's visit "a terrible disappointment" (Cohen, *Pathless Way,* 131). For Muir's account of the meeting, see John Muir, *Our National Parks* (1901; reprint, Madison: University of Wisconsin Press, 1981), 131–36; and, for Muir's recollection of a snatch of conversation between the two, 235–36.

57. Muir, *Our National Parks,* 131–32; Muir, in Wolfe, *John of the Mountains,* 436; for Emerson's encouragement of Muir, see Wolfe, *Son of the Wilderness,* 153; and, for Muir's reading of Emerson, see Cohen, *Pathless Way,* 38, 51–54, and Fox, *John Muir and His Legacy,* 6; for Emerson's list, see Wolfe, *Son of the Wilderness,* 151.

58. Wolfe, *Son of the Wilderness,* 256; Cohen, *Pathless Way,* 132–33, 140–42; Muir, quoted ibid., 350. For Thoreau's affirmation—"For many

years I was self-appointed inspector of snow storms and rain storms"—see *Walden*, 18.

59. Cohen, *Pathless Way*, 59; for the "domestic embrace," see Tichi, *New World, New Earth*, 167; and, for Muir's acquaintance with Hinduism, see Fox, *John Muir and His Legacy*, 365.

60. Fox, *John Muir and His Legacy*, 82.

61. Muir, in Wolfe, *John of the Mountains*, 102–3 (6 January 1873). Muir seems to depart at least partially from the Transcendentalists, though, in repudiating "bookmaking out of material I have already eaten and drunken" (ibid., 102).

62. Muir, ibid., 84 (October 1871); ibid., 438 (1913?) (emphasis in original); ibid., 226 (1 September 1875).

63. Ibid., 16 (19 January 1869); ibid., 92 (1872?); Muir, *Mountains of California*, 144. For other harmonial observations, see, e.g., Muir, in Wolfe, *John of the Mountains*, 107 (16? January 1873); and Muir, ibid., 318 (11 July 1890).

64. For his critique of Muir's refusal to hunt, see Cohen, *Pathless Way*, 182–84; for the Mount Whitney experience, see Muir, as quoted in Wolfe, *Son of the Wilderness*, 169; and, for Wolfe's assessment, see ibid., 170.

65. The incidents and Muir's words are related in Wolfe, *Son of the Wilderness*, 151–52, 122, 233, 269, 257, 277.

66. Fox, *John Muir and His Legacy*, 333–57, 116.

67. "Back to Nature," *The Outlook* 74 (6 June 1903): 305.

68. Ibid., 306.

69. Parker, *Mind Cure in New England*, 8.

70. Novak, *Nature and Culture*, 134.

71. Near-contemporary (1888) summaries of Phineas P. Quimby's life, one by his son George Quimby and one by an early unnamed biographer, may be found in Phineas Parkhurst Quimby, *The Complete Writings*, ed. Ervin Seale, 3 vols. (Marina del Rey, Calif.: Devorss, 1988), 1: 19–29. For a longer account of Quimby's life and thought, see Horatio W. Dresser, ed., *The Quimby Manuscripts* (1921; reprint, Secaucus, N.J.: Citadel Press, 1969); and Horatio W. Dresser, *Health and the Inner Life: An Analytical and Historical Study of Spiritual Healing Theories, with an Account of the Life and Teachings of P. P. Quimby* (New York: G. P. Putnam's Sons, Knickerbocker Press, 1906). Horatio Dresser was the son of Quimby's former students and patients Julius and Annetta Dresser.

72. Franz Anton Mesmer, "Dissertation on the Discovery of Animal Magnetism" (1779), in George Bloch, trans. and comp., *Mesmerism: A Translation of the Original Scientific and Medical Writings of F. A. Mesmer* (Los Altos, Calif.: William Kaufmann, 1980), 67–68. For a useful discussion of mesmerism, see Stefan Zweig, *Mental Healers: Franz Anton Mesmer, Mary Baker Eddy, Sigmund Freud* (1932; reprint, New York: Frederick Ungar Publishing, 1962), esp. 15–33, in which Zweig notices a lack of conceptual coherence between the cosmological teaching of planetary in-

fluence and the practical ability of the "animal" magnetist. See, also, Robert C. Fuller, *Mesmerism and the American Cure of Souls* (Philadelphia: University of Pennsylvania Press, 1982).

73. Horatio W. Dresser, in the editorial fashion of an earlier day, "corrected," anthologized, and collated Quimby's writings to produce the collection contained in *The Quimby Manuscripts*. In so doing, he frequently omitted words or sentences without indicating ellipses, and he joined numerous short pieces to form "chapters" in what thus became essentially nontexts. Recently, a complete, though not critical, edition has become available (Quimby, *Complete Writings*), which is far more respectful of the integrity of Quimby's text. Unfortunately, it appeared too late to be used in my work here. However, a comparison of the two editions suggests that, in spite of Dresser's editorial hand, Quimby's thought is not seriously misrepresented in what the Dresser volume contains and insofar as it goes. Dresser's status close to the Quimby tradition did much to guarantee fidelity to the teaching of Quimby's texts, and Dresser seems to have tried to eliminate what he felt was rough, embarrassing, or inconsistent.

74. Phineas P. Quimby, in Dresser, *Quimby Manuscripts*, 253–55, 257. Cf. Quimby, *Complete Writings*, 3:93–95. It is evident in this edition that Quimby is thinking of spiritualism too.

75. Ibid., 258 (brackets in Dresser text).

76. Ibid., 175, 335–36.

77. Ibid., 299, 414, 393.

78. Ibid., 263 (a footnote after "chemical change," not identified clearly as to source, adds, "This term includes bodily changes, as well"), 313, 267. Horatio Dresser vigorously denies any Swedenborgian influence on Quimby, although he cites one reference to Swedenborg in Quimby's lecture notes (see Dresser, *Quimby Manuscripts*, 18, 56–57). For the reference that he may have had in mind, see Quimby, *Complete Writings*, 1:151.

79. See, e.g., Emanuel Swedenborg, *Heaven and Its Wonders and Hell, from Things Heard and Seen*, trans. J. C. Ager (1852; reprint, New York: Swedenborg Foundation, 1964), 6–7; Emanuel Swedenborg, *The True Christian Religion, Containing the Universal Theology of the New Church*, trans. John C. Ager, 2 vols. (1853; reprint, New York: Swedenborg Foundation, 1970), 2:244–46, 100–101; Swedenborg, *Heaven and Its Wonders and Hell*, 100–101, 19, 184, 261, 354. Gail Thain Parker thought that "Swedenborg's definition of 'influx' was invaluable" to mind curists (Parker, *Mind Cure in New England*, 42). Swedenborg's doctrine of "conjugial love" is most fully treated in Emanuel Swedenborg, *The Delights of Wisdom Pertaining to Conjugial Love after Which Follow the Pleasures of Insanity Pertaining to Scortatory Love*, trans. Samuel M. Warren and rev. trans. Louis H. Tafel (1856; reprint, New York: Swedenborg Foundation, 1980). For the quotations, see Swedenborg, *Heaven and Its Wonders and Hell*, 257 (cf. 41ff.); and Swedenborg, *True Christian Religion*, 1:367.

80. Quimby, in Dresser, *Quimby Manuscripts*, 61.

81. Ibid., 180, 213–14, 272. For "spiritual matter," see, also, e.g., ibid., 118, 227, 231, 235, 246, 334. For Dresser's words, see ibid., 66.

82. Quimby, ibid., 118; Quimby to Miss G. F., 27 December 1860, ibid., 140–41; Quimby to Mrs. Ware, 25 January 1861, ibid., 143; Quimby, ibid., 225. Cf. Quimby, *Complete Writings*, 3 : 401, 408; 2 : 388.

83. Quimby to Mrs. Ware, ibid., 143. Cf. Quimby, *Complete Writings*, 3 : 408. This edition reads: "Like a seed in the earth it grows or develops either in matter or spirit just the same."

84. Quimby, ibid., 75, 186 (brackets in Dresser text).

85. Ibid., 232, 169, 379. Horatio Dresser wrote that Quimby "felt no antagonism to the Church in his early years, but the churches seem to have had no direct influence upon him" (Horatio W. Dresser, *A History of the New Thought Movement* [New York: Thomas Y. Crowell, 1919], 22).

86. Quimby, in Dresser, *Quimby Manuscripts*, 185. For my understanding of misreading or "misprision" in what follows, I am indebted to the literary critic Harold Bloom, in *Agon: Towards a Theory of Revisionism* (New York: Oxford University Press, 1982). (See, esp., 16–22.)

87. Quimby, in Dresser, *Quimby Manuscripts*, 237, 375.

88. Ibid., 346, 289.

89. Charles S. Braden, *Spirits in Rebellion: The Rise and Development of New Thought* (Dallas: Southern Methodist University Press, 1963), 73; Stewart W. Holmes, "Phineas Parkhurst Quimby: Scientist of Transcendentalism," *The New England Quarterly* 17 (1944): 357, 367–68.

90. Dresser, *History of the New Thought Movement*, 135, 8; Braden, *Spirits in Rebellion*, 35; Parker, *Mind Cure in New England*, 5 (cf. Parker's statement that "it is hard to find anything in the New Thought creed which Emerson did not say first" [ibid., 58]).

91. Mary Baker Eddy, "The Oak on the Mountain's Summit," in Mary Baker Eddy, *Miscellaneous Writings, 1883–1896* (Boston: Trustees under the Will of Mary Baker G. Eddy, 1896), 392; Mary Baker Glover [Eddy], *Science and Health* (1875; reprint, Freehold, N.J.: Rare Book Company, n.d.), 229, 225 (emphasis mine). For metaphors of harmonizing and governing, see, e.g., [Eddy], *Science and Health* (1875), 295, 330, 339; and, for the characterization of Jesus, see Mary Baker G. Eddy, *Historical Sketch of Metaphysical Healing* (1885; reprint, New York: Rare Book Company, n.d.), 8.

92. Mary Baker Eddy, *Science and Health with Key to the Scriptures* (Boston: Trustees under the Will of Mary Baker G. Eddy, 1906), 183.

Chapter Four

1. *The Health Journal and Independent Magazine* 1, no. 2 (April 1843): 57–58.

2. On the revivals—the First and Second Great Awakenings—the best short recent account is contained in William G. McLoughlin, *Revivals, Awakenings, and Reform: An Essay on Religion and Social Change in Amer-*

ica, 1607–1977, Chicago History of American Religion (Chicago: University of Chicago Press, 1978), 45–140.

3. For Mathews's definitive essay on the concept, see Donald G. Mathews, "The Second Great Awakening as an Organizing Process, 1780–1830," *American Quarterly* 21 (1969): 23–43.

4. The classic locus for this idea is John Locke's *Two Treatises on Civil Government* (1690).

5. For American diet, see the short but useful summary in Richard Harrison Shryock, *Medicine and Society in America, 1660–1860* (New York: New York University Press, 1960), 88–89; and, for American drinking habits in the context of the temperance crusade, see the account in Alice Felt Tyler, *Freedom's Ferment: Phases of American Social History from the Colonial Period to the Outbreak of the Civil War* (1944; reprint, New York: Harper & Row, Harper Torchbooks, 1962), 308–12. Probably the most famous nineteenth-century literary consumptive was Little Eva, in Harriet Beecher Stowe's *Uncle Tom's Cabin; or, Life among the Lowly* (1852), but the number of literary consumptives was legion. And, for a discussion of nervous Americans, see George Beard, *American Nervousness* (New York: G. P. Putnam, 1881).

6. For nineteenth-century heroic practice in America, see William G. Rothstein, *American Physicians in the Nineteenth Century: From Sects to Science* (Baltimore: Johns Hopkins University Press, 1972), 41–62.

7. Robert C. Fuller, *Mesmerism and the American Cure of Souls* (Philadelphia: University of Pennsylvania Press, 1982).

8. For a useful study of the communications network for these ideas, see Donald M. Scott, "The Popular Lecture and the Creation of a Public in Mid-Nineteenth-Century America," *Journal of American History* 66 (1980): 791–809.

9. Ralph Waldo Emerson's *Nature* (1836), his new gospel of the Transcendental theory of correspondence, owed considerably to Emanuel Swedenborg. Emerson had been influenced by Swedenborgian thought through the work of Sampson Reed in his *Observations on the Growth of the Mind* (1826).

10. For an introduction to Sylvester Graham and his work, see Stephen Nissenbaum, *Sex, Diet, and Debility in Jacksonian America: Sylvester Graham and Health Reform* (Westport, Conn.: Greenwood Press, 1980). For William Andrus Alcott, see James C. Whorton, *Crusaders For Fitness: The History of American Health Reformers* (Princeton: Princeton University Press, 1982), 49–61.

11. James C. Whorton, "'Christian Physiology': William Alcott's Prescription for the Millenium" [*sic*], *Bulletin of the History of Medicine* 49 (1975): 466. I am grateful to Leonard I. Sweet for bringing this essay to my attention.

12. For millennial readings of the health reformers, see Whorton, "'Christian Physiology,'" 466–81; and Harvey Green, *Fit for America:*

Health, Fitness, Sport, and American Society (New York: Pantheon Books, 1986), 10–12, 28–29, 319–20.

13. John B. Blake, "Health Reform," in Edwin Scott Gaustad, ed., *The Rise of Adventism: Religion and Society in Mid-Nineteenth-Century America* (New York: Harper & Row, 1974), 37.

14. Whorton, *Crusaders for Fitness*, 4.

15. Ibid., 4–5.

16. See Nissenbaum, *Sex, Diet, and Debility in Jacksonian America*, 9, 13.

17. William Andrus Alcott, *Forty Years in the Wilderness of Pills and Powders* (1859), quoted in Whorton, *Crusaders for Fitness*, 54.

18. *Health Journal and Advocate of Physiological Reform* 1, no. 13 (July 15, 1840): 49; ibid., no. 7 (June 3, 1840), 27; ibid. 2, no. 15 (December 4, 1841): 58; ibid. 1, no. 1 (April 1, 1840): 1 [Charles G. Finney, "An Appeal to Ministers," from the *Oberlin Evangelist*].

19. *Health Journal and Advocate of Physiological Reform* 1, no. 4 (May 13, 1840): 16.

20. Nissenbaum, *Sex, Diet, and Debility in Jacksonian America*, 19. Nissenbaum was quoting from Sylvester Graham's *A Lecture to Young Men, on Chastity* (1834).

21. *Health Journal and Advocate of Physiological Reform* 2, no. 10 (September 25, 1841): 37. (Emphasis mine.)

22. *The Teacher of Health, and the Laws of the Human Constitution* 1, no. 1 (January 1843): 9, 10–11.

23. S. Graham, "Letter from Mr. Graham," *Health Journal and Advocate of Physiological Reform* 1, no. 33 (February 10, 1841): 130. (Emphasis in original.)

24. "Grahamism *alias* Millennialism," ibid. (Emphasis in original.)

25. Ibid., no. 2 (April 15, 1840): 7. (Emphasis in original.)

26. Ibid. 2, no. 14 (November 20, 1841): 53–54; ibid. 1, no. 11 (July 1, 1840): 42.

27. For a discussion of the connection between myths of the end and myths of the beginning, see Mircea Eliade, *Myth and Reality*, trans. Willard R. Trask (New York: Harper & Row, Harper Torchbooks, 1968), 54–74.

28. Fred Somkin, *Unquiet Eagle: Memory and Desire in the Idea of American Freedom, 1815–1860* (Ithaca, N.Y.: Cornell University Press, 1967).

29. John Duffy, *The Healers: A History of American Medicine* (Urbana: University of Illinois Press, Illini Books, 1979), 111.

30. Ibid., 111–12 (see, also, Rothstein, *American Physicians in the Nineteenth Century*, 140).

31. *The Thomsonian Recorder, or Impartial Advocate of Botanic Medicine: And the Principles Which Govern the Thomsonian Practice* 2, no. 14 (April 12, 1834): 216; "Thomsonism Dying Away," *Boston True Thomsonian* 1, no. 3 (October 1, 1840): 41 (emphasis in original); Aaron Douglass,

"'Regular' Murder," *Boston Thomsonian Manual and Lady's Companion* 9, no. 1 (December 1, 1842): 14; *Thomsonian Recorder* 2, no. 8 (January 18, 1834): 114.

32. "Dyspepsia and Its Causes" [Letter from J. M. A., to his brother; reprinted from the *Philadelphia Saturday Courier*], *Boston Thomsonian Manual* 9, no. 1 (December 1, 1842): 9.

33. *The Thomsonian Scout* 1, no. 20 (September 1, 1842): 156–57; *Boston True Thomsonian* [From Bell's *Anatomy and Physiology of the Teeth*] 2, no. 23 (August 1, 1842): 359; "Tea and Coffee Deadly Poisons" [From the *Health Journal* (extract of a letter from a Dr. Burdell, New York, January 27, 1842)], *Boston True Thomsonian* 3, no. 16 (November 15, 1842): 86; "A Memorial to the Medical Faculty," *The Boston Thomsonian Medical and Physiological Journal* 1, no. 9 (February 1, 1846): 136–37.

34. "An Apology," *Boston Thomsonian Medical and Physiological Journal* 1 (April 15, 1846): 219 (uppercase in original). And, for Thomsonian enthusiasm regarding the "electric" and magnetism, see, e.g., James C. Olcott, "Correspondence: The Electric System," in *Boston Thomsonian Manual* 8, no. 14 (June 1, 1842): 220.

35. "Extracts from an Address of Prof. I. M. Comings, M.D., Delivered before the Southern Botanico-Medical Society" [From the *Southern Medical Reformer*], *Boston Thomsonian Medical and Physiological Journal* 1, no. 16 (May 15, 1846): 246; *Boston Thomsonian Medical and Physiological Journal* 1, no. 11 (March 1, 1846): 170; L. S. K., "For the *Thomsonian Scout*," *Thomsonian Scout* 1, no. 15 (June 15, 1842): 118.

36. For the masthead, see *Thomsonian Advertiser* 1, no. 1 (October 1, 1844). The motto, of course, echoes John Locke's *Letters concerning Toleration* (1689). On the "regulars," see J., "The Changing of Times," *Thomsonian Scout* 1, no. 22 (October 1, 1842): 175; and "Regularism and Paganism" and S., "Changes," *Boston True Thomsonian* 2, no. 24 (August 15, 1842): 370 (emphasis in original; the material was reprinted from the *Poughkeepsie Thomsonian* and the *Thomsonian Scout*, respectively).

37. Douglass, "'Regular' Murder," 14; S., "Thomsonism Progressing," *Thomsonian Scout* 1, no. 14 (June 1, 1842): 108.

38. "Preface," *Thomsonian Recorder* 2 (October 12, 1833–September 16, 1834): v; Cassiopea, "Superior Merit When Assumed Is Lost," *Thomsonian Scout* 1, no. 21 (September 15, 1842): 163–64; *Thomsonian Recorder* 2, no. 9 (February 1, 1839): 139.

39. For brief accounts of the life and work of Samuel Hahnemann, see Rothstein, *American Physicians in the Nineteenth Century,* esp. 52–57; and, with a contemporary holistic reading, Richard Grossinger, *Planet Medicine: From Stone Age Shamanism to Post-Industrial Healing,* rev. ed. (Boulder, Col.: Shambhala, 1982), esp. 204–23. (Significantly, Grossinger identifies Hahnemann with a "German occult tradition" [*Planet Medicine,* 205].)

40. O. A Woodbury, "Homoeopathy the Only True Medical Practice,"

The Homoeopathic Advocate and Guide to Health 1, no. 5 (August 1851): 65–66. (Emphasis in original.)

41. Ibid., 66. (Emphasis in original.)

42. Ibid., "Our Journal," 1, no. 1 (April 1, 1851): 9; ibid., "Prospectus of *The Homoeopathic Advocate and Guide to Health,* 16; ibid., 1, no. 5, 76–77.

43. O. A. Woodbury, "Homoeopathy the Only True Medical Practice," *Homoeopathic Advocate* 1, no. 6 (September 1851): 81 (emphasis in original); ibid., 1, no. 1, 10; Woodbury, "Homoeopathy the Only True Medical Practice," 1, no. 6, 81.

44. Ibid. (emphasis in original); Charles Niedhard, M.D., "An Address Delivered before the Rhode Island Homeopathic Society, May 7th, 1851," *Homoeopathic Advocate* 1, no. 11 (February 1852): 168.

45. I. H., "Opposition, Hybredism" [*sic*], ibid. 1, no. 6, 84; "Communication from 'A Medical Student,'" *The North-Western Journal of Homeopatheia* 1, no. 9 (June 1849): 191; "Homoeopathy," *Homoeopathic Advocate* 1, no. 1, 1.

46. "To the Friends of Homoeopathy," *The Homoeopathic News* 1, no. 5 (January 31, 1855): 33; "Cincinnati Toasts," ibid., no. 7 (October 1855): 51 (emphasis in original). (Of nine published toasts, only two—the two quoted—were printed in italics. Significantly, only one other—to the "Legislature of Michigan," which had established a chair of homeopathy at the state university at Ann Arbor—contained any political reference.)

47. For a brief and useful recent introduction to water cure, see Jane B. Donegan, *"Hydropathic Highway to Health": Women and Water-Cure in Antebellum America,* Contributions in Medical Studies, no. 17 (Westport, Conn.: Greenwood Press, 1986), xi–xx, 3–17, 185–201. (Donegan suggests the upper- and middle-class background of institutional patients [ibid., xiii].) And, for a still later and more extensive discussion of the general water-cure movement, see Susan E. Cayleff, *Wash and Be Healed: The Water-Cure Movement and Women's Health* (Philadelphia: Temple University Press, 1987). (For a discussion of who could afford an institutional water cure, see ibid., 75–108. It should not be forgotten, though, that—as Cayleff emphasizes—"the most common forum of education and cure through water therapy was the home" [ibid., 44].)

48. "Our Platform," *The Water-Cure World* 1 (April 1860): 5.

49. W. T. Vail, "Origin of Human Diseases," ibid. (May 1860): 10–11; ibid. (July 1860): 27 (emphasis in original).

50. "Wash and be Healed," in fact, appeared as the motto that opened issue after issue of Joel Shew's *Water-Cure Journal.*

51. M. S. Gove Nichols, "A Word to Water-Cure People," *The Water-Cure Journal* 13, no. 1 (January 1852): 8; "To Our Readers," ibid. 19, no. 6 (June 1855): 132.

52. James C. Jackson, "Dying," *Water-Cure Journal* 16, no. 1 (July 1853): 2 (emphasis in original); R. T. Trall, "July Meditations," ibid. 18, no. 1 (July 1854): 13 (emphasis in original); J. Berry, "Water and Its Effects"

[Excerpted from the *Massachusetts Cataract*], ibid. 8, no. 4 (October 1849): 107.

53. W. S. Bush, M.D., "Water-Cure at the West," ibid. 14, no. 1 (July 1852): 7–8; H. C. Foote, "Hygienic Law," ibid. 18, no. 5 (November 1854): 100.

54. R. T. Trall, "January Reflections," ibid. 9, no. 1 (January 1850): 17.

55. R. T. Trall, M.D., "The Unpardonable Sin," ibid. 10, no. 1 (July 1850): 24–26; Dr. [William A. Alcott], "Essays on Water-Cure, No. 1," ibid. 1, no. 6 (15 February 1846): 82; ibid. 2, no. 6 (15 August 1846): 93 (emphasis in original).

56. R. T. Trall, M.D., "July Sentiments," ibid. 16, no. 1 (July 1853): 13. (Emphasis in original.)

57. "Prospectus," *The Magnetic and Cold Water Guide* 1, no. 1 (June 1846): inside front cover; "Testimony of a Physician to the Benefits of Hydropathy," ibid., 7–8.

58. For an account of Andrew Taylor Still's activity as a magnetic doctor, see Norman Gevitz, *The D.O.'s: Osteopathic Medicine in America* (Baltimore: Johns Hopkins University Press, 1982), 12–15; and, for D. D. Palmer's work as a magnetist, see Vern Gielow, *Old Dad Chiro: A Biography of D. D. Palmer, Founder of Chiropractic* (Davenport, Iowa: Bawden Brothers, 1981), 35–76.

59. Will A. Potter, "Dr. Still and His Work," *Journal of Osteopathy* 4, no. 1 (May 1897): 18; "Vis Medicatrix Naturae," ibid. no. 6 (November 1897): 275.

60. A. T. Still, "What Can Osteopathy Give?" ibid. 4, no. 4 (August 1897): 186; A. T. Still, "Preparatory Studies Essential," ibid., 184; Still, "What Can Osteopathy Give?" 185–86.

61. "The Scope and Spirit of Osteopathy," *Journal of Osteopathy* 4, no. 1 (May 1897): 12.

62. Still, "Preparatory Studies Essential," 183–84; "Vis Medicatrix Naturae," 275.

63. "Dr. A. T. Still's Department," *Journal of Osteopathy* 4, no. 7 (December 1897): 315.

64. *Journal of Osteopathy* 5, no. 7 (December 1898): 322.

65. For a discussion of Still's possible spiritualism, see Gevitz, *The D.O.'s*, 13–14, 156 n52; and, for accusations of atheism, see, e.g., William Smith, "Success," *Journal of Osteopathy* 5, no. 1 (June 1898): 11. Nineteenth-century osteopaths, in general, battled claims that their system was allied with spiritualism. See, e.g., Helen de Lendrecie, "Around the Flag," *Journal of Osteopathy* 4, no. 1 (May 1897): 30.

66. De Lendrecie, "Around the Flag," ibid., 30.

67. "Commencement Exercises: Address of Dr. J. Martin Littlejohn, Ph.D., LL.D.," ibid. 5, no. 3 (August 1898): 115; Mason W. Pressly, "The March of Mind," ibid. 4, no. 1, 17 (uppercase in original); "Reported by Albert Fisher, Englewood, Ill.," ibid. 6, no. 5 (October 1899): 204 (the father was George H. Abbott of Chicago).

68. Daniel David Palmer, Journal, as quoted in Vern Gielow, *Old Dad Chiro,* 56.

69. D. D. Palmer, *The Chiropractor's Adjuster: Text-book of the Science, Art, and Philosophy of Chiropractic for Students and Practitioners* (1910; reprint, [Portland, Oreg.: Portland Printing House], 1966), 446, 542, 94, 399. For further discussion of chiropractic, see Catherine L. Albanese, "The Poetics of Healing: Root Metaphors and Rituals in Nineteenth-Century America," *Soundings* 63 (Winter 1980): 390–94.

70. This estimate was shared with me during the summer of 1982 by Vern Gielow, who for many years was associated with the Palmer College of Chiropractic in Davenport, Iowa.

71. Joy M. Loben [Loban?], "The Completeness of Chiropractic Philosophy," *The Chiropractor: A Monthly Journal Devoted to the Interests of Chiropractic* 4, nos. 7 and 8 (August and September 1908): 30–31. Vern Gielow, in *Old Dad Chiro* and in a photocopy of the article that he shared with me, identifies him as Joy Loban (Gielow, *Old Dad Chiro,* 121), but D. D. Palmer calls him Loben (*Chiropractor's Adjuster,* 725).

72. Loben, "Completeness of Chiropractic Philosophy," 31 (uppercase in original), 33.

73. Ibid., 33, 35.

74. Ibid., 35–36.

75. For interpretations of the role of romanticism in nineteenth-century popular healing movements in America, see Shryock, *Medicine and Society in America,* 119–26; and, more allusively, Whorton, *Crusaders for Fitness,* 29.

76. Palmer's pamphlets were Charles Bradlaugh and Anne Besant, *Fruits of Philosophy: A Treatise on the Population Question* (facts of publication unavailable); and N. C. [a medical theosophist; i.e., Fellow of the Theosophical Society, whom I have been unable to identify], *Psychometry and Thought-Transference, with Practical Hints for Experiments,* Introduction by Henry S. Olcott (Boston: Esoteric Publishing, 1887). I obtained photocopies of both pamphlets during a research visit to the Palmer School of Chiropractic in 1982. My information on chiromancy comes from perusal of occult periodical literature of the time. Palmer's patient/friend and Greek scholar was the Reverend Samuel H. Weed. See Palmer, *Chiropractor's Adjuster,* 104–5; and Gielow, *Old Dad Chiro,* 82–83.

77. For the best book-length study of the Theosophical Society, see Bruce F. Campbell, *Ancient Wisdom Revived: A History of the Theosophical Movement* (Berkeley: University of California Press, 1980).

78. Gielow, *Old Dad Chiro,* 121.

79. For accounts of the early history of quantum physics, on which this one is mostly based, see Gary Zukav, *The Dancing Wu Li Masters: An Overview of the New Physics* (New York: Bantam Books, 1980); and Victor Guillemin, *The Story of Quantum Mechanics* (New York: Charles Scribner's Sons, 1968). And see, also, George Gamow, *Thirty Years That Shook Physics: The Story of Quantum Theory* (Garden City, N.Y.: Doubleday, 1966).

80. See the discussion in Werner Heisenberg, *Physics and Philosophy: The Revolution in Modern Science,* World Perspectives, vol. 19 (New York: Harper, 1958), 159–60; see, also, Zukav, *Dancing Wu Li Masters,* 192–95; and Fritjof Capra, *The Tao of Physics: An Exploration of the Parallels between Modern Physics and Eastern Mysticism,* 2d ed. (Boston: Shambhala, New Science Library, 1985), 77–79.

81. For Heisenberg and his "unsharpness principle," see Guillemin, *Story of Quantum Mechanics,* 91–101; and see Heisenberg's own statements in Werner Heisenberg, *The Physical Principles of the Quantum Theory,* trans. Carl Eckart and Frank C. Hoyt ([New York:] Dover, 1930), 3, 20; and Heisenberg, *Physics and Philosophy,* 55–58.

82. The phrase "organic energy" is Zukav's in *Dancing Wu Li Masters,* 43, 45, passim. And, for "frozen light" and slower speed, see Richard Gerber, *Vibrational Medicine: New Choices for Healing Ourselves* (Santa Fe: Bear, 1988), 59.

83. Werner Heisenberg, *Natural Law and the Structure of Matter* (London: Rebel Press, 1970), 32; Heisenberg, *Physics and Philosophy,* 81, 205.

84. Aldo Leopold, *A Sand County Almanac and Sketches Here and There* (1949; reprint, Oxford: Oxford University Press, 1981), viii, 216.

Chapter Five

1. "Statement of Purpose," *Earth Nation Sunrise* 1 (Fall 1982): 2; "The Earth Nation Rises," ibid., 1. The "co-creators" of the tabloid were Douglas Bissell, Leanne Shank-Bissell, Stephen Hawkins, Rebecca Schenk, Daniel Cheeseman, and Carol Bridges.

2. For a striking case study of the evolution of suburb from camp meeting, see Ellen Weiss, *City in the Woods: The Life and Design of an American Camp Meeting on Martha's Vineyard* (New York: Oxford University Press, 1987).

3. Henry D. Thoreau, *Walden,* ed. J. Lyndon Shanley, The Writings of Henry D. Thoreau (Princeton: Princeton University Press, 1971), 17.

4. In this heterogeneous context, the names of Black Elk, Lame Deer, N. Scott Momaday, Leslie Marmon Silko, Russell Means, Sun Bear, Michael Harner, Carlos Castaneda, and Lynn Andrews come readily to mind. For Black Elk, see Raymond J. DeMallie, *The Sixth Grandfather: Black Elk's Teachings Given to John G. Neihardt* (Lincoln: University of Nebraska Press, 1984); and, with caution, John G. Neihardt, *Black Elk Speaks: Being the Life Story of a Holy Man of the Oglala Sioux* (Lincoln: University of Nebraska Press, 1961); for Lame Deer, see John (Fire) Lame Deer and Richard Erdoes, *Lame Deer: Seeker of Visions* (New York: Pocket Books, Washington Square Press, 1972); for a discussion of the work of N. Scott Momaday and Leslie Marmon Silko, see Alan R. Velie, *Four American Indian Literary Masters: N. Scott Momaday, James Welch, Leslie Marmon Silko, and Gerald Vizenor* (Norman: University of Oklahoma Press, 1982), 11–64, 105–21; for Russell Means and religious traditionalism, see the discussion in Vine Deloria, Jr., *God Is Red* (New York: Grosset & Dunlap,

1973), 256–58; for Sun Bear, see any of his works, esp. *Sun Bear: The Path of Power,* as told to Wabun and to Barry Weinstock (Spokane, Wash.: Bear Tribe Publishing, 1983); for Michael Harner, see his *The Way of the Shaman: A Guide to Power and Healing* (New York: Harper & Row, 1980); and for Carlos Castaneda and Lynn Andrews, see, esp., the first published work of each: Carlos Castaneda, *The Teachings of Don Juan: A Yaqui Way of Knowledge* (Berkeley: University of California Press, 1968); and Lynn V. Andrews, *Medicine Woman* (New York: Harper & Row, 1981).

5. "And Life Continues: An Interview with Sun Bear," *Earth Nation Sunrise* 3 (Spring 1983): 14.

6. The description of medicine wheels that is presented here is garnered from my own attendance at the Medicine Wheel Gathering held at Camp Kern, near Lebanon, Ohio, October 3–5, 1986; from the program for the 1986 East Coast Medicine Wheel Gathering at Camp Monroe, New York, the same autumn; and from information gleaned more informally concerning others.

7. Sun Bear, *Sun Bear: The Path of Power,* 179.

8. See, esp., Sun Bear, *Sun Bear: The Path of Power;* Sun Bear, *Buffalo Hearts: A Native American's View of His Culture, Religion, and History* (Spokane, Wash.: Bear Tribe Publishing, 1976); Sun Bear and Wabun, *The Medicine Wheel: Earth Astrology* (Englewood Cliffs, N.J.: Prentice-Hall, 1980); and Sun Bear, Wabun, and Nimimosha, *The Bear Tribe's Self Reliance Book,* rev. ed. (Spokane, Wash.: Bear Tribe Publishing, 1986).

9. Sun Bear, *Sun Bear: The Path of Power,* 131, 173.

10. Ibid., 181.

11. Ibid., 36.

12. See, e.g., ibid., 21–22; and Sun Bear's account of the same event, in ibid., 136–37.

13. Ibid., 174. In 1981, according to Sun Bear, he had still another vision of many-colored light, in which, as he pointed his finger outward on a dark hilltop, a light shone. As he recounted, when he repeated the process again and again, lights—different in size, shape, and color—"came on" in the darkness. For Sun Bear, the lights represented the many different people who would come to him, and he thought that the many colors were "an important part of my vision, because it confirmed my belief that those who would come to me to learn would be of all colors, of all races, and of many nationalities" (ibid., 195).

14. Ibid., 137.

15. Ibid., 155.

16. Ibid., 216, 245–46.

17. Ibid., 245–46. (Emphasis in original.)

18. Ibid., 225–26, 207–8 (emphasis in original).

19. Ibid., 209.

20. Sun Bear, Wabun, and Nimimosha, *The Bear Tribe's Self Reliance Book,* 58.

21. Ibid., 13–14, 143–46, 129–35.

22. See n. 4 above.

23. Annie Dillard, *An American Childhood* (New York: Harper & Row, 1987), 8, 61, 132–33, 171, 134, 151.

24. Ibid., 226.

25. Annie Dillard, *Pilgrim at Tinker Creek* (New York: Bantam Books, 1975), 1, vi.

26. Ibid., 13.

27. Ibid., 80, 87.

28. Ibid., 193, 195.

29. Ibid., 198–202.

30. Ibid., 6.

31. Ibid., 35.

32. Ibid., 35, 247.

33. Ibid., 247.

34. Ibid., 247–48; William James, *The Varieties of Religious Experience: A Study in Human Nature* (1902; reprint, London: Collier-Macmillan, Collier Books, 1961), 78–142.

35. Dillard, *Pilgrim at Tinker Creek,* 248, 279.

36. Ibid., 62–63.

37. Ibid., 63; Dillard, *An American Childhood,* 161.

38. Annie Dillard, *Holy the Firm* (1977; reprint, New York: Harper & Row, Harper Colophon, 1984), 24, 16.

39. Ibid., 17.

40. See Julian of Norwich, *Showings* (1393), available in Edmund Colledge and James Walsh, trans., *Julian of Norwich: Showings,* The Classics of Western Spirituality (New York: Paulist Press, 1978).

41. Dillard, *Holy the Firm,* 36, 41–42.

42. Ibid., 45–47, 65.

43. Ibid., 66.

44. Ibid., 68–70, 75–76.

45. See, e.g., Annie Dillard, "An Expedition to the Pole," in Annie Dillard, *Teaching a Stone to Talk: Expeditions and Encounters* (New York: Harper & Row, 1982), 17–52.

46. Stephan Bodian and Florence Windfall, "Seeing Green," *Yoga Journal,* no. 79 (March/April 1988): 57. The Bodian-Windfall article is, in general, a useful introduction to the Green movement and, especially, to its religious dimension.

47. For a helpful discussion, on which this sketch is based, see Charlene Spretnak and Fritjof Capra, in collaboration with Rüdiger Lutz, "Green Politics in the United States: 1986," in their *Green Politics* (Santa Fe: Bear, 1986), 227–40. The Macalester College meeting was held in August of 1984.

48. *Ten Key Values,* in Spretnak and Capra, *Green Politics,* 230 (emphasis in original), 232.

49. Bodian and Windfall, "Seeing Green," 77–78.

50. Ibid., 78; quoted in ibid.

51. Charlene Spretnak, *The Spiritual Dimension of Green Politics* (Santa Fe: Bear, 1986), 25, 27. (Emphasis in original.)

52. Ibid., 29–31.

53. Ibid., 32–33. Charlene Spretnak's first published book was *Lost Goddesses of Early Greece: A Collection of Pre-Hellenic Myths* (1978; reprint, Boston: Beacon Press, 1981).

54. Spretnak, *Spiritual Dimension,* 34, 37, 41.

55. Spretnak, *Spiritual Dimension,* 42. With regard to popular accounts of quantum theory, two works linking the new physics to religious cosmologies come immediately to mind: Gary Zukav, *The Dancing Wu Li Masters: An Overview of the New Physics* (New York: William Morrow, 1979); and, originally published a year later, Fritjof Capra, *The Tao of Physics: An Exploration of the Parallels between Modern Physics and Eastern Mysticism,* 2d ed., New Science Library (Boston: Shambhala, 1985). Capra is a collaborator with Spretnak in the Green political movement and is coauthor, with Spretnak, of *Green Politics* (op cit.).

56. Ibid., 49–50 (emphasis in original), 52–53.

57. Quoted from Spretnak, *Lost Goddesses of Early Greece,* in Spretnak, *Spiritual Dimension,* 63.

58. Ibid., 71. For "deep ecology," see the discussion in Bill Devall and George Sessions, *Deep Ecology: Living as if Nature Mattered* (New York: Peregrine Smith, 1985); and see, also, for a succinct treatment from a process theological perspective, John B. Cobb, Jr., "Ecology, Science, and Religion: Toward a Postmodern Worldview," in David Ray Griffin, ed., *The Reenchantment of Science: Postmodern Proposals,* SUNY Series in Constructive Postmodern Thought (Albany: State University of New York Press, 1988), 99–113.

59. See James Lovelock, *Gaia: A New Look at Life on Earth* (New York: Oxford University Press, 1979). For a brief and useful discussion of the Gaia hypothesis from the Green perspective, see Jonathan Porritt, *Seeing Green: The Politics of Ecology Explained* (New York: Basil Blackwell, 1985), 206–9.

60. Charlene Spretnak, ed., *The Politics of Women's Spirituality: Essays on the Rise of Spiritual Power within the Feminist Movement* (Garden City, N.Y.: Doubleday, Anchor Books, 1982).

61. Judith Todd, "On Common Ground: Native American and Feminist Spirituality Approaches in the Struggle to Save Mother Earth," in Spretnak, *Politics of Women's Spirituality,* 439–40. For additional insights on the development of ecofeminism, from a Neopagan perspective, see Margot Adler, *Drawing Down the Moon: Witches, Druids, Goddess-Worshippers, and Other Pagans in America Today,* rev. ed. (Boston: Beacon Press, 1986), 414.

62. Grace Paley and Ynestra King, quoted in Gina Foglia and Dorit Wolffberg, "Spiritual Dimensions of Feminist Anti-Nuclear Activism," in Spretnak, *Politics of Women's Spirituality,* 449. (Uppercase in original.)

63. Adler, *Drawing Down the Moon,* viii–ix, xi, 376.

64. Ibid., 108.

65. Ibid., 10–11.

66. Ibid., 418–19. Starhawk's three books are the following: Starhawk, *The Spiral Dance: A Rebirth of the Ancient Religion of the Great Goddess* (San Francisco: Harper & Row, 1979); Starhawk, *Dreaming the Dark: Magic, Sex, and Politics* (Boston: Beacon Press, 1982); and Starhawk, *Truth or Dare: Encounters with Power, Authority, and Mystery* (San Francisco: Harper & Row, 1987).

67. Starhawk, *Spiral Dance*, 1, 11, 188.

68. Ibid., 2–3, 18.

69. Ibid., 130, 195.

70. Ibid., 110, 9 (emphasis in original); Starhawk, *Dreaming the Dark*, 11.

71. Starhawk, *Spiral Dance*, 27–28.

72. Starhawk, *Dreaming the Dark*, 28, 136.

73. Ibid., 135, 134.

74. Starhawk, *Dreaming the Dark*, 143.

75. Starhawk, *Spiral Dance*, 67, 132.

76. Ibid., 112.

77. Starhawk, *Dreaming the Dark*, 155; Starhawk, *Truth or Dare*, 241. For brief descriptions of witchcraft rituals, see Starhawk, *Truth or Dare*, 100; Starhawk, *Dreaming the Dark*, 155; and, with attention to raising energy, Starhawk, *Spiral Dance*, 128–33.

78. Starhawk, *Dreaming the Dark*, 13; Starhawk, *Spiral Dance*, 129. For a good example of Starhawk as therapist/guide on a magical inner journey, see Starhawk, *Dreaming the Dark*, 45–71.

79. Ibid., 26. (Emphasis in original.)

80. For studies of the role of the Transcendentalists in introducing Eastern materials to other Americans, see Arthur E. Christy, *The Orient in American Transcendentalism: A Study of Emerson, Thoreau, and Alcott* (1932; reprint, New York: Octagon Books, 1978); and, more recently, Carl T. Jackson, *The Oriental Religions and American Thought: Nineteenth-Century Explorations*, Contributions in American Studies, no. 55 (Westport, Conn.: Greenwood Press, 1981).

81. Virginia Samdahl, "The Reiki Story," in Larry Arnold and Sandy Nevius, *The Reiki Handbook* (Harrisburg, Pa.: PSI Press, ParaScience International, 1982), 2. I have not checked old University of Chicago records to verify the claim; in any case, with the preponderance of "meaningful" numbers in the story as Samdahl tells it, the function of the information is mythic more than factual. For this reason, too, I have not sought to verify any of the material Samdahl has supplied.

82. Samdahl, "Reiki Story," 5.

83. Ibid., 9–10. This view of the master's lineage has not gone unchallenged. Barbara Weber Ray, head of the American-International Reiki Association, claims Hawayo Takata transmitted the "Radiance Technique" "intact and complete" to her (see Barbara Ray, assisted by Marvelle Carter, *The Official Handbook of the Radiance Technique*, rev. ed. [Santa Monica, Calif.: American-International Reiki Association, 1987], 4).

84. My understanding of Reiki is derived from conversations with Virginia Samdahl, with William and Zelda Sheline, second-degree initiates and later Reiki masters in Springfield, Ohio, and with other Reiki initiates. It is also derived from Arnold and Nevius, *Reiki Handbook;* Barbara Weber Ray, *The Reiki Factor: A Guide to Natural Healing, Helping, and Wholeness* (Smithtown, N.Y.: Exposition Press, 1983); Barbara Derrick Lugenbeel, *Virginia Samdahl: Reiki Master Healer* (Norfolk, Va.: Grunwald and Radcliff, 1984); and other Reiki publications.

85. Arnold and Nevius, *Reiki Handbook,* 13.

86. Ray, *Reiki Factor,* 30 (emphasis in original), 39. For a useful study of how late twentieth-century holistic healing appropriates new scientific paradigms, employing quantum physics and holograms as explanatory grids, see Richard Gerber, *Vibrational Medicine: New Choices for Healing Ourselves* (Santa Fe: Bear, 1988), esp. 39–90. Gerber is himself a medical doctor with theosophical views.

87. Aveline Kushi with Alex Jack, *Aveline Kushi's Complete Guide to Macrobiotic Cooking: For Health, Harmony, and Peace* (New York: Warner Books, 1985), xi. "One peaceful world," for example, was the theme for the 1988 Macrobiotic Summer Conference at Great Barrington, Massachusetts (August 8–14, 1988). Two years earlier, in 1986, Michio Kushi—Aveline Kushi's husband and leader of the movement—was responsible for a One Peaceful World Proclamation. At the same time, he began One Peaceful World, an educational organization to promote his macrobiotic approach to peace in the world. A year later a partly autobiographical book by Michio Kushi was published as *One Peaceful World.* See Michio Kushi with Alex Jack, *One Peaceful World* (New York: St. Martin's Press, 1987).

88. For an account of the incident, see Kushi with Jack, *One Peaceful World,* 20. See, also, Ronald E. Kotzsch, *Macrobiotics: Yesterday and Today* (New York: Japan Publications, 1985), 163. In general, my brief account of the history of macrobiotics follows Kotzsch. See, too, his dissertation (Ronald E. Kotzsch, "Georges Ohsawa and the Japanese Religious Tradition" [Ph.D. diss., Harvard University, 1981]), which is helpful from a number of perspectives.

89. Ronald Kotzsch, on the basis of macrobiotic periodical distribution, offers the estimate of one hundred thousand adherents. Michio Kushi himself, according to Kotzsch, judges that there are between three hundred thousand and five hundred thousand "true macrobiotics" in the nation and "some two million semi-macrobiotics." See Kotzsch, *Macrobiotics,* 183.

90. Information on which this and following paragraphs are based may be found in a number of Kushi- or Aihara-inspired books. See, e.g., Kushi with Jack, *Aveline Kushi's Complete Guide to Macrobiotic Cooking;* Michio Kushi with Stephen Blauer, *The Macrobiotic Way: The Complete Macrobiotic Diet and Exercise Book* (Wayne, N.J.: Avery Publishing, 1985); Michio and Aveline Kushi, *Macrobiotic Diet: Balancing Your Eating in Harmony with the Changing Environment and Personal Needs,* ed. Alex Jack

(New York: Japan Publications, 1985); and Herman Aihara, *Basic Macrobiotics* (New York: Japan Publications, 1985). Information also comes from conversations with members of the Midwest Macrobiotic Center in Cincinnati and Dayton, Ohio, the Santa Barbara Macrobiotic Community in Santa Barbara, California, and the 1988 Macrobiotic Summer Conference in Great Barrington, Massachusetts.

91. The anecdotal evidence for Michio Kushi's success in healing terminal cancer has received widespread attention, especially since 1982, when Houghton Mifflin published physician Anthony Sattilaro's autobiographical account of his use of macrobiotics for the remission of prostate cancer that had spread throughout his body. Sattilaro was president of Methodist Hospital in Philadelphia at the time. (See Anthony Sattilaro with Tom Monte, *Recalled by Life: The Story of My Recovery from Cancer* [Boston: Houghton Mifflin, 1982].) Kushi himself has worked with members of the medical community to assist the sick and has established considerable rapport with those in the health sciences. Like so many who teach that "new physics" supports their religious vision, he is convinced that his inherited, now expanded, teaching will be vindicated by modern science.

92. Michio Kushi, *The Book of Dō-In: Exercise for Physical and Spiritual Development* (New York: Japan Publications, 1979), 17.

93. Richard France and Jerome Carty, *Healing Naturally: The Commonsense Macrobiotic Approach to Cancer and Other Diseases,* 2d ed. (Boulder, Colo.: Amaizeing Books, 1982), 24. (Emphasis in original.)

94. Kushi with Jack, *Aveline Kushi's Complete Guide to Macrobiotic Cooking,* 230. Information on Aveline Kushi's cooking classes comes from a class held in Los Angeles, California, in January 1988.

95. John David Mann, "An Open Letter," *Macrobiotics Today* (June 1988): 6. (Emphasis and ellipsis points in original.)

96. Michio Kushi, "World Peace through World Health" (1980), in Michio Kushi, *Michio Kushi on the Greater View: Collected Thoughts and Ideas on Macrobiotics and Humanity,* comp. Editors of *East West Journal* (Wayne, N.J.: Avery Publishing, 1986), 79.

Epilogue

1. Sidney E. Mead, "History and Identity" (1971), in Sidney E. Mead, *History and Identity,* American Academy of Religion Studies in Religion, no. 19 (Missoula, Mont.: Scholars Press, 1979), 17–18. (Emphasis in original.)

Suggestions for Further Reading

Studying nature religion in America invites interdisciplinary work and the use of nontraditional sources. It means looking for religion outside of well-defined organizational contexts and exploring the writings of individuals who sometimes were not aware of the religious nature of what they were thinking and doing. In terms of secondary literature, it means turning to scholars whose primary interest is often not religious history or religious studies. And it demands that the broad base of popular religion throughout American history be examined.

Rather than attempt comprehensiveness for all of this in the suggestions that follow, I build on topics and themes that have been prominent in this book. I point here to the works that seem most useful in formulating a conceptual framework for nature religion. And I highlight the primary and secondary sources that have provided easiest entrance to the mentality—the thought and practice—of nature religion at different cultural moments. Like pebbles thrown in water, these sources will have, I hope, a ripple effect. Acquaintance with them should lead to acquaintance with other sources suggested by or in them. One good word leads to another; the network of "good words" grows.

Probably the best way to receive a first good word is to survey the history of the ideas and uses of "nature" in the West. Geographer Clarence J. Glacken, in his *Traces on the Rhodian Shore: Nature and Culture in Western Thought from Ancient Times to the End of the Eighteenth Century* (1967; reprint, Berkeley: University of California Press, 1976), offers a work of monumental scope in this endeavor. Lucid in its exposition and more modest in its proportions is Keith Thomas's *Man and the Natural World: A History of the Modern Sensibility* (New York: Pantheon Books, 1983), which argues for a marked shift in consciousness in England from the sixteenth to the eighteenth century. For a sweeping survey of the role of nature in the Judeo-Christian tradition, the strong suit is George H. Williams's *Wilderness and Paradise in Christian Thought: The Biblical Experience of the Desert in the History of Christianity and the Paradise Theme in the Theological Idea of the University* (New York: Harper, 1962). And, for a more episodic treatment of the Western tradition, one concerned with the human relationship to the natural world, there is the study by biologist Paul Shepard, *Man in the Landscape: A Historic View of the Esthetics of Nature* (New York: Alfred A. Knopf, 1967). Both Williams and Shepard bring their surveys eventually to America.

One can add to these volumes explicit treatments of nature in the American context. Here the work that comes most immediately to mind is Roderick Nash, *Wilderness and the American Mind*, 3d ed. (New Haven: Yale University Press, 1982). Also useful are Hans Huth, *Nature and the American: Three Centuries of Changing Attitudes* (Berkeley: University of

California Press, 1957); and Arthur A. Ekirch, *Man and Nature in America* (New York: Columbia University Press, 1963). A more recent work by Myra Jehlen, *American Incarnation: The Individual, the Nation, and the Continent* (Cambridge: Harvard University Press, 1986), explores the relationship between an American ideology of liberalism and the material fact of the land. Also written from specialized perspectives but still indicators of American attitudes toward nature are Peter J. Schmitt, *Back to Nature: The Arcadian Myth in Urban America* (New York: Oxford University Press, 1969); Henry Nash Smith, *Virgin Land: The American West as Symbol and Myth* (New York: Random House, Vintage Books, 1950); Arnold Smithline, *Natural Religion in American Literature* (New Haven: College & University Press, 1966); and Donald Worster, *Nature's Economy: A History of Ecological Ideas* (1977; reprint, Cambridge: Cambridge University Press, 1985), this last beginning with the eighteenth-century English background.

Before one engages the particulars of American responses to nature, though, it may be useful to explore theoretical frames that support religious inquiry concerning nature religion. In this context, classic works by Mircea Eliade dealing with mythic and symbolic structures are good places to begin. Probably most helpful are Eliade's *Cosmos and History: The Myth of the Eternal Return*, trans. Willard R. Trask (New York: Harper & Row, Harper Torchbooks, 1959); *Patterns in Comparative Religion*, trans. Rosemary Sheed (Cleveland: World Publishing, Meridian Books, 1963); *Myth and Reality*, trans. Willard R. Trask (New York: Harper & Row, Harper Torchbooks, 1968); and *The Sacred and the Profane: The Nature of Religion*, trans. Willard R. Trask (New York: Harcourt, Brace & World, 1959). The mythic power of a natural world untouched by human culture is suggested, too, by Claude Lévi-Strauss's *The Raw and the Cooked*, vol. 1 of *Introduction to a Science of Mythology*, trans. John Weightman and Doreen Weightman (New York: Harper & Row, Harper Torchbooks, 1970).

Understanding nature religion as an action system, however, means attending to its ritual dimension and seeing it as human work. Jonathan Z. Smith underlines these connections for religion in general in his incisive collection of essays *Imagining Religion: From Babylon to Jonestown*, Chicago Studies in the History of Judaism (Chicago: University of Chicago Press, 1982). So, from an anthropological perspective, does Pierre Bourdieu, with his concept of the habitus that prompts action according to particular and meaningful patterns. Bourdieu's *Outline of a Theory of Practice*, trans. Richard Nice, Cambridge Studies in Social Anthropology, no. 16 (Cambridge: Cambridge University Press, 1987), if difficult, is rewarding in its exposition of the habitus, as well as in its exploration of issues that surround the struggle for dominance in society.

Human work—even human work expressed in nature religion—means work fraught with status anxieties and the contest for mastery. This work puts religion squarely in an ordinary context even as it continues to point toward extraordinary concerns. The writings of Michel Foucault attend to the theme of dominance, especially as it arises out of the Enlightenment mentality inherited by the modern world. While almost any of Foucault's writings play out the theme with emphasis on one or another conceptualization of it, most useful here, with its graphicness and its call for a history of the present, is his *Discipline and Punish: The Birth of the Prison*, trans. Alan Sheridan (New York: Random House, Vintage Books, 1979). And one can gain a good sense of the range of critical perspectives on the work of Foucault in the recent volume edited by David Couzens Hoy, *Foucault: A Critical Reader* (Oxford: Basil Blackwell, 1986).

Meanwhile, a more general framework for understanding religion as a human construction, though without the concern for issues of dominance, is supplied by Peter L. Berger and Thomas Luckmann in *The Social Construction of Reality: A Treatise in the Sociology of Knowledge* (Garden City, N.Y.: Doubleday, Anchor Books, 1967); and by Berger, again, in *The Sacred Canopy: Elements of a Sociological Theory of Religion* (Garden City, N.Y.: Doubleday, 1967). An understanding of religion as both an ordinary and extraordinary phenomenon is suggested in the important essay by Charles H. Long, "Prolegomenon to a Religious Hermeneutic," originally published in the journal *History of Religions* 6, no. 3 (February 1967): 254–64, and reprinted more recently in Long's *Significations: Signs, Symbols, and Images in the Interpretation of Religion* (Philadelphia: Fortress Press, 1986), 27–37. Building on Long's work and language, I have discussed religion as ordinary and as extraordinary in Catherine L. Albanese, *America: Religions and Religion* (Belmont, Calif.: Wadsworth Publishing, 1981), 3–7, a work in which, in a cursory way, I have also explored the concept of nature religion (see 328–39).

The case study of nature religion through the Hutchinson Family Singers, with which this book begins, may be pondered at greater length with the help of John Wallace Hutchinson's *Story of the Hutchinsons (Tribe of Jesse)*, 2 vols. (1896; reprint, New York: Da Capo Press, 1977). Other published Hutchinson autobiographies, though less accessible, are [Asa B. Hutchinson?], *The Book of Brothers: History of the Hutchinson Family* (New York: Hutchinson Family, 1852); and Joshua Hutchinson, *A Brief Narrative of the Hutchinson Family: Sixteen Sons and Daughters of the "Tribe of Jesse"* (Boston: Lee and Shepard, 1874). Of even more importance is Dale Cockrell's now-being-published edition of the Hutchinson journals in *Excelsior: Journals of the Hutchinson Family Singers*, The Sociology of Music Series, no. 5 (Stuyvesant, N.Y.: Pendragon Press, 1989). And, for collections of the Hutchinsons' songs, see *Songs of the Hutchinson Family* (New York: Firth & Hall, 1843); and Asa B. Hutchinson, comp., *The Granite Songster; Comprising the Songs of the Hutchinson Family, without the Music* (Boston: A. B. Hutchinson, 1847).

Access to Native American religions as religions of nature must come from a variety of sources and traditions. One good introduction to the theme may be found in the collection of essays—a number of them either by Native Americans or containing Native American ethnographic material—edited by Dennis Tedlock and Barbara Tedlock, *Teachings from the*

American Earth: Indian Religion and Philosophy (New York: Liveright, 1975). General overviews of Native American religions are also quite useful, since nature provides the predominant symbolic center in Native American religious life. In this regard, Sam D. Gill's *Native American Religions: An Introduction,* The Religious Life of Man Series (Belmont, Calif.: Wadsworth, 1989) and his *Native American Traditions: Sources and Interpretations,* The Religious Life of Man Series (Belmont, Calif.: Wadsworth, 1983) come immediately to mind.

Beyond these, works specifically addressing environmental issues in connection with Native Americans are obvious choices. *American Indian Environments: Ecological Issues in Native American History* (Syracuse, N.Y.: Syracuse University Press, 1980), a collection of essays edited by Christopher Vecsey and Robert W. Venables, contains fruitful material, especially in essays by Christopher Vecsey, Calvin Martin, and Wilbur R. Jacobs (1–64). Kiowa author and literary scholar N. Scott Momaday contributes reflections on "Native American Attitudes to the Environment" to a collection edited by Walter Holden Capps, *Seeing with a Native Eye: Essays on Native American Religion* (New York: Harper & Row, Harper Forum, 1976), 79–85. More substantively, a challenge to the portrait of Native American as natural ecologist—at least in the case of Algonkian-speaking Eastern Canadian nations—comes from Calvin Martin, in *Keepers of the Game: Indian-Animal Relationships and the Fur Trade* (Berkeley: University of California Press, 1978), a work that generated a book-length response in *Indians, Animals, and the Fur Trade: A Critique of "Keepers of the Game,"* edited by Shepard Krech III (Athens: University of Georgia Press, 1981).

Perhaps as controversial, particularly with regard to the selectivity of its evidence, Sam D. Gill's *Mother Earth: An American Story* (Chicago: University of Chicago Press, 1987) argues against the historic presence of Mother Earth as long-standing Native American deity. On the other hand, there is no better way to come to terms with the centrality of earth symbolism than in collections of Native American myth. Christopher Vecsey's *Imagine Ourselves Richly: Mythic Narratives of North American Indians* (New York: Crossroad, 1988) is useful in this regard. Less technical and more accessible to beginners is the classic collection of myths by Alice Marriott and Carol K. Rachlin, *American Indian Mythology* (1968; reprint, New York: New American Library, Mentor Books, 1972). And, culturally closer, throughout, to Algonkian New England, there is William Jones's collection of texts from the Algonkian-speaking Ojibwa, which is available with an introduction regarding world view and narrative tradition, in Thomas W. Overholt and J. Baird Callicott, *Clothed-in-Fur and Other Tales: An Introduction to an Ojibwa World View* (Washington, D.C.: University Press of America, 1982). Also a clear choice for encountering Algonkian materials is the volume edited by Elisabeth Tooker, *Native North American Spirituality of the Eastern Woodlands: Sacred Myths, Dreams, Vi-*

sions, Speeches, Healing Formulas, Rituals, and Ceremonials, The Classics of Western Spirituality (New York: Paulist Press, 1979).

Secondary works regarding New England's Indian peoples are helpful in developing an interpretive perspective. Here anthropologist William S. Simmons's *Spirit of the New England Tribes: Indian History and Folklore, 1620–1984* (Hanover, N.H.: University Press of New England, 1986) is a solid contribution. Also of importance are Bert Salwen, "Indians of Southern New England and Long Island: Early Period," in Bruce G. Trigger, ed., *Northeast,* vol. 15 of *Handbook of North American Indians* (Washington, D.C.: Smithsonian Institution, 1978), 160–76; William S. Simmons, "Narragansett," ibid., 190–97; and Regina Flannery, *An Analysis of Coastal Algonquian Culture* (Washington, D.C.: Catholic University of America Press, 1939).

More introductory, but useful for reconstructing a precontact past, is Howard S. Russell's *Indian New England before the Mayflower* (Hanover, N.H.: University Press of New England, 1980). Insight may also be gained from the analysis of burial evidence in William Scranton Simmons, *Cautantowwit's House: An Indian Burial Ground on the Island of Conanicut in Narragansett Bay* (Providence: Brown University Press, 1970). In addition, works by seventeenth-century English colonists in New England, although heavily biased, can provide, when used judiciously, windows into the Algonkian world of the period. Most notable in this regard—and for their relative openness to the Algonkian world—are Roger Williams, *A Key into the Language of America* (1643), in *The Complete Writings of Roger Williams* (1866; reprint, New York: Russell & Russell, 1963); and William Wood, *New England's Prospect* (1634), ed. Alden T. Vaughan (Amherst: University of Massachusetts Press, 1977).

The encounter between native peoples and Europeans, in the case of French missionaries, is recorded at length in Reuben Gold Thwaites, ed., *The Jesuit Relations and Allied Documents: Travels and Explorations of the Jesuit Missionaries in New France, 1610–1901,* 73 vols. (Cleveland: Burrows Brothers, 1896–1901). Specifically New England records of the religious and cultural encounter may be found in Henry W. Bowden and James P. Ronda, eds., *John Eliot's Indian Dialogues: A Study in Cultural Interaction,* Contributions in American History, no. 88 (Westport, Conn.: Greenwood Press, 1980); and in Alden T. Vaughan and Edward W. Clark, eds., *Puritans among the Indians: Accounts of Captivity and Redemption, 1676–1724,* The John Harvard Library (Cambridge: Harvard University Press, Belknap Press, 1981), which contains, among others, the Mary Rowlandson captivity narrative. An older source for seventeenth-century captivity narratives is Charles H. Lincoln, ed., *Narratives of the Indian Wars, 1675–1699,* Original Narratives of Early American History (1913; reprint, New York: Barnes & Noble, 1959).

Secondary works that are especially helpful in detailing the New England encounter include William Cronon, *Changes in the Land: Indians, Colonists, and the Ecology of New England* (New York: Hill and Wang,

1983); Francis Jennings, *The Invasion of America: Indians, Colonialism and the Cant of Conquest* (Chapel Hill: University of North Carolina Press for the Institute of Early American History and Culture, 1975); and Neal Salisbury, *Manitou and Providence: Indians, Europeans, and the Making of New England, 1500–1643* (New York: Oxford University Press, 1982). For English missions to Indian peoples in the seventeenth century, the best short account is contained in Henry Warner Bowden, *American Indians and Christian Missions: Studies in Cultural Conflict,* Chicago History of American Religion (Chicago: University of Chicago Press, 1981), 96–133.

A good secondary source for launching an exploration of nature religion among the Puritans is Peter N. Carroll's *Puritanism and the Wilderness: The Intellectual Significance of the New England Frontier, 1629–1700* (New York: Columbia University Press, 1969). Conrad Cherry's essay "New England as Symbol: Ambiguity in the Puritan Vision," *Soundings* 58 (Fall 1975): 348–62, examines tensions within the Puritan theology of place. The relationship of Puritanism to environmental reform forms a prominent theme in Cecelia Tichi's *New World, New Earth: Environmental Reform in American Literature from the Puritans through Whitman* (New Haven: Yale University Press, 1979). Meanwhile, the study of Puritan figurative language in Mason I. Lowance, Jr., *The Language of Canaan: Metaphor and Symbol in New England from the Puritans to the Transcendentalists* (Cambridge: Harvard University Press, 1980) offers insights that are germane. So, too, does George H. Williams's *Wilderness and Paradise in Christian Thought* (cited above).

Eighteenth-century Puritan thought regarding nature, as exemplified in the writings of Cotton Mather and Jonathan Edwards, sets the stage for much that follows. In *The Christian Philosopher: A Collection of the Best Discoveries in Nature, with Religious Improvements* (1721; reprint, Gainesville, Fla.: Scholars' Facsimiles & Reprints, 1968), Cotton Mather studies the book of nature in ways that signal a new consciousness among the Puritans. Even more striking in this regard are Jonathan Edwards's writings. The collection edited by Clarence H. Faust and Thomas H. Johnson, *Jonathan Edwards: Representative Selections,* American Century Series, rev. ed. (New York: Hill and Wang, 1962), which includes Edwards's "Personal Narrative," is a good place to begin. Perry Miller's edition of Jonathan Edwards's *Images or Shadows of Divine Things* (1948; reprint, Westport, Conn.: Greenwood Press, 1977) contains a wealth of suggestive material for discovering Edwards's theology of nature. Still more in this vein may be found in Jonathan Edwards, *Scientific and Philosophical Writings,* ed. Wallace E. Anderson, The Works of Jonathan Edwards, vol. 6 (New Haven: Yale University Press, 1980).

Both the Miller and the Anderson editions contain lengthy and helpful introductions by the editors. In *The Language of Canaan* (cited above), Mason I. Lowance, Jr., offers correctives to the Miller reading of Edwards (258–72). More extensively, Clyde A. Holbrook supplies a personal and reflective essay on the meanings of nature for Edwards, in *Jonathan*

Edwards, The Valley and Nature: An Interpretative Essay (Lewisburg, Pa.: Bucknell University Press; London and Toronto: Associated University Presses, 1987). Conrad Cherry's sensitive treatment of Edwards's thought regarding nature is contained in *Nature and Religious Imagination: From Edwards to Bushnell* (Philadelphia: Fortress Press, 1980), 13–64, a work that, in general, deserves scrutiny for any study of theological construction in nature religion.

Study of the political uses of nature, on the other hand, leads away from the Puritan era and into the period of the American Revolution. No one work makes the nature religion of the Revolution its consistent theme and subject, but material that is relevant may be found in my own monograph, Catherine L. Albanese, *Sons of the Fathers: The Civil Religion of the American Revolution* (Philadelphia: Temple University Press, 1976). One gains a summary sense of the range of late-eighteenth-century popular opinion regarding nature in, on one side, the optimism of Royall Tyler's play *The Contrast: A Comedy in Five Acts* (1920; reprint, New York: AMS Press, 1970) and, on the other, the wilderness gloom of J. Hector St. John Crèvecoeur's *Letters from an American Farmer* (1782; Gloucester, Mass.: Peter Smith, 1968).

The Enlightenment background of the era receives definitive treatment in Henry F. May's *The Enlightenment in America* (New York: Oxford University Press, 1976). Also useful in view of their religious theme are G. Adolf Koch, *Republican Religion: The American Revolution and the Cult of Reason* (1933; reprint, Gloucester, Mass.: Peter Smith, 1964); and Herbert M. Morais, *Deism in Eighteenth-Century America* (1934; reprint, New York: Russell & Russell, 1960). Explicit linkage of the Enlightenment, politics, and nature is made in the essay by J. R. Pole, "Enlightenment and the Politics of American Nature," in *The Enlightenment in National Context*, ed. Roy Porter and Mikulas Teich (Cambridge: Cambridge University Press, 1981), 192–214.

Among primary sources, representative eighteenth-century English works that propound the religion of nature include Joseph Butler, *The Analogy of Religion, Natural and Revealed, to the Constitution and Course of Nation* (1736), Everyman's Library, no. 90 (London: J. M. Dent, 1906); William Wollaston, *The Religion of Nature Delineated* (London: Samuel Palmer, 1726); and Samuel Clarke, "A Discourse concerning the Unchangeable Obligations of Natural Religion, and the Truth and Certainty of the Christian Revelation" (1705), in *The Works of Samuel Clarke, D.D.* (1738; reprint, New York: Garland Publishing, 1978). Meanwhile, European—especially, English—conceptualization of nature during the eighteenth century is treated masterfully in Basil Willey, *The Eighteenth Century Background: Studies on the Idea of Nature in the Thought of the Period* (1940; reprint, Boston: Beacon Press, 1961).

The Freemasonic theme in the nature religion of the Revolution may be explored in Bernard Faÿ's *Revolution and Freemasonry, 1680–1800* (Boston: Little, Brown, 1935). For the English and European background of Freemasonry and revolution, there is Margaret C. Jacob's fine study *The Radical Enlightenment: Pantheists, Freemasons, and Republicans,* Early Modern Europe Today (London: George Allen & Unwin, 1981). And, for revealing primary sources from the late eighteenth and early nineteenth centuries, there are Captain George Smith's *The Use and Abuse of Freemasonry; A Work of the Greatest Utility to the Brethren of the Society, to Mankind in General, and to the Ladies in Particular* (1783; New York: Macoy Publishing & Masonic Supply, 1914); and Thomas Paine's, "Origin of Freemasonry" (1805), in *The Complete Writings of Thomas Paine,* ed. Philip S. Foner (New York: Citadel Press, 1945).

For nature as source of the sublime in the late eighteenth century, one should turn first to the classic English statement by Edmund Burke, *A Philosophical Enquiry into the Origin of Our Ideas of the Sublime and Beautiful* (1757), 2d ed. (1759), ed. J. T. Boulton (London: Routledge Kegan Paul, 1958). Characteristic late-eighteenth-century American expressions of the sublime may be found by perusing the works of William Bartram, in *The Travels of William Bartram,* ed. Francis Harper, Naturalist's ed. (New Haven: Yale University Press, 1958); Philip Freneau, in *The Prose of Philip Freneau,* ed. Philip M. Marsh (New Brunswick, N.J.: Scarecrow Press, 1955); and in *The Poems of Philip Freneau: Poet of the American Revolution,* ed. Fred Lewis Pattee, 3 vols. (New York: Russell & Russell, 1963); Timothy Dwight, in *The Major Poems of Timothy Dwight,* ed. William J. Mc Taggart and William K. Bottorff (Gainesville, Fla.: Scholars' Facsimiles & Reprints, 1969); and Joel Barlow, in *The Works of Joel Barlow,* ed. William K. Bottorff and Arthur L. Ford (Gainesville, Fla.: Scholars' Facsimiles & Reprints, 1970). A classic secondary source exploring a range of issues in which the concept of the sublime is embedded is Marjorie Hope Nicolson's *Mountain Gloom and Mountain Glory: The Development of the Aesthetics of the Infinite* (1959; reprint, New York: W. W. Norton, Norton Library, 1963).

Thomas Jefferson's attentiveness to the presence of the sublime in the American landscape deserves special attention, along with his embodiment of the other aspects of republican nature religion discussed in this book. Pertinent writings by Jefferson may be found in his *Notes on the State of Virginia* ([1784] 1861; reprint, New York: Harper & Row, Harper Torchbooks, 1964); in *The Portable Thomas Jefferson,* ed. Merrill D. Peterson (New York: Viking Press, 1975); and in *The Adams-Jefferson Letters: The Complete Correspondence between Thomas Jefferson and Abigail and John Adams,* ed. Lester J. Cappon, 2 vols. (Chapel Hill: University of North Carolina Press for the Institute of Early American History and Culture, 1959). For those who are ambitious there is the yet incomplete critical edition of Jefferson's writings, *The Papers of Thomas Jefferson,* ed. Julian P. Boyd and Charles T. Cullen, 21 vols. to date (vols. 1–20 edited by Boyd and vol. 21 edited by Cullen) (Princeton: Princeton University Press, 1950–).

The secondary literature regarding Jefferson is rich, and much may be gleaned from two works especially. These are Charles A. Miller's *Jefferson and Nature: An Interpretation* (Baltimore: Johns Hopkins University Press,

1988); and Charles B. Sanford's *The Religious Life of Thomas Jefferson* (Charlottesville: University Press of Virginia, 1984). An older work that is still helpful is Daniel J. Boorstin, *The Lost World of Thomas Jefferson* (1948; reprint, Boston: Beacon Press, 1960). Portions of Garry Wills's *Inventing America: Jefferson's Declaration of Independence* (Garden City, N.Y.: Doubleday, 1978) also deserve scrutiny for their bearing on the theme of nature religion in Jefferson's writing.

Far more boisterous in his embodiment of nature religion is David or Davy Crockett; his autobiographical work (with the help of Thomas Chilton) *A Narrative of the Life of David Crockett, of the State of Tennessee,* facsimile ed., ed. James A. Shackford and Stanley J. Folmsbee, Tennesseana Editions (Knoxville: University of Tennessee Press, 1973) already strains credulity. A sampling of the fictional Crockett of the Davy Crockett almanacs may be found in an enlarged facsimile edition with an introduction by Michael A. Lofaro, *The Tall Tales of Davy Crockett: The Second Nashville Series of Crockett Almanacs, 1839–1841,* Tennesseana Editions (Knoxville: University of Tennessee Press, 1987). The symbolic power of Crockett is explored in a collection of essays edited by Michael A. Lofaro, *Davy Crockett: The Man, the Legend, the Legacy, 1786–1986* (Knoxville: University of Tennessee Press, 1985), and also in a newer collection edited by Lofaro and Joe Cummings, *Crockett at Two Hundred: New Perspectives on the Man and the Myth* (Knoxville: University of Tennessee Press, 1989). Meanwhile, a useful compendium in sorting Crockett fact from Crockett fiction is Richard Boyd Hauck's *Davy Crockett: A Handbook* (1982; reprint, Lincoln: University of Nebraska Press, 1986).

Three of my own essays on Crockett—Catherine L. Albanese, "Citizen Crockett: Myth, History, and Nature Religion," *Soundings* 61 (Spring 1978): 87–104; Catherine L. Albanese, "King Crockett: Nature and Civility on the American Frontier," *Proceedings of the American Antiquarian Society* 88, pt. 2 (October 1979: 225–49; and Catherine L. Albanese, "Savage, Sinner, and Saved: Davy Crockett, Camp Meetings, and the Wild Frontier," *American Quarterly* 33 (Winter 1981): 482–501—are relevant to a study of nature religion. Especially valuable in its general treatment of the frontier hunter-hero is Richard Slotkin's *Regeneration through Violence: The Mythology of the American Frontier, 1600–1860* (Middletown, Conn.: Wesleyan University Press, 1973).

The study of Transcendentalism has yielded an abundance of resources for an exploration of nature religion. A work that gives access in one place to those Emerson and Thoreau primary texts expressing Transcendental spirituality and that also has a synthesizing general introduction is Catherine L. Albanese, ed., *The Spirituality of the American Transcendentalists: Selected Writings of Ralph Waldo Emerson, Amos Bronson Alcott, Theodore Parker, and Henry David Thoreau* (Macon, Ga.: Mercer University Press, 1988). Ralph Waldo Emerson's writings are available in the long-standard Centenary edition, *The Complete Works of Ralph Waldo Emerson,* ed. Edward Waldo Emerson, 12 vols. (1903–04; reprint, New York: AMS Press, 1968). Still being published, the new critical edition of Emerson's writings— *The Collected Works of Ralph Waldo Emerson,* ed. Alfred R. Ferguson et al., 4 vols. to date (Cambridge: Harvard University Press, 1971–)—contains the text of *Nature* and major essays and addresses.

The old standard edition—and still the most complete edition—of Henry David Thoreau's writings is the Walden edition, *The Writings of Henry David Thoreau,* 20 vols. (1906; reprint, New York: AMS Press, 1968). This edition is being superseded by a new critical edition of individual titles, including *Walden,* in the series The Writings of Henry D. Thoreau, ed. Walter Harding et al., 9 vols. to date (Princeton: Princeton University Press, 1971–). Thoreau's semicompleted but important "Huckleberries" is available in Henry David Thoreau, *Huckleberries,* ed. Leo Stoller (Iowa City: Windhover Press of The University of Iowa and The New York Public Library, 1970). And Thoreau's equally important essay "Walking" may be found in his *Excursions* (1863), with an introduction by Leo Marx (1962; reprint, Gloucester, Mass.: Peter Smith, 1975), 161–214.

Secondary works on Transcendentalism that may assist in exploring the presence of nature religion within the movement include Catherine L. Albanese, *Corresponding Motion: Transcendental Religion and the New America* (Philadelphia: Temple University Press, 1977); Paul F. Boller, Jr., *American Transcendentalism, 1830–1860: An Intellectual Inquiry* (New York: G. P. Putnam's Sons, 1974); Arthur E. Christy, *The Orient in American Transcendentalism: A Study of Emerson, Thoreau, and Alcott* (1932; reprint, New York: Octagon Books, 1978); Octavius Brooks Frothingham, *Transcendentalism in New England: A History* (1876; reprint, Gloucester, Mass.: Peter Smith, 1965); Philip F. Gura, *The Wisdom of Words: Language, Theology, and Literature in the New England Renaissance* (Middletown, Conn.: Wesleyan University Press, 1981), esp. 73–144; William R. Hutchison, *The Transcendentalist Ministers: Church Reform in the New England Renaissance* (1959; reprint, Boston: Beacon Press, 1965); Nathaniel Kaplan and Thomas Katsaros, *The Origins of American Transcendentalism in Philosophy and Mysticism* (New Haven: College & University Press, 1975); and Arnold Smithline, *Natural Religion in American Literature* (cited above). The artistic counterpart to Transcendentalism and American cultural romanticism in general is examined with lucidity in Barbara Novak, *Nature and Culture: American Landscape and Painting, 1825–1875* (New York: Oxford University Press, 1980).

Perry Miller's classic essay "From Edwards to Emerson," arguing for the role of nature in a mysticism that links Jonathan Edwards to Emerson, may be found in Perry Miller, *Errand into the Wilderness* (1956; reprint, New York: Harper & Row, Harper Torchbooks, 1964), 184–203. Sherman Paul's *Emerson's Angle of Vision: Man and Nature in American Experience* (1952; reprint, Cambridge: Harvard University Press, 1969) is still the best treatment, by a literary scholar, of themes of nature and correspondence. David Robinson's *Apostle of Culture: Emerson as Preacher and Lecturer* (Philadelphia: University of Pennsylvania Press, 1982) explores the theme of self-culture to good effect. Stephen E. Whicher's sensitive study

Freedom and Fate: An Inner Life of Ralph Waldo Emerson (Philadelphia: University of Pennsylvania Press, 1971) is a classic. And Sacvan Bercovitch has written with insight about Emerson and the myth of America, in *The Puritan Origins of the American Self* (New Haven: Yale University Press, 1975), 157–86. Bercovitch's brief treatment of Emerson and Thoreau in *The American Jeremiad* (Madison: University of Wisconsin Press, 1978), 182–90, is also worth reading for its linkage of nature to nation.

For Thoreau as individual author, Victor Carl Friesen's *The Spirit of the Huckleberry: Sensuousness in Henry Thoreau* (Edmonton: University of Alberta Press, 1984) is a clear choice for the study of nature religion. With some contrast, William J. Wolf stresses Thoreau's Puritan heritage as he studies the Transcendentalist's mystical and ecological insight, in *Thoreau: Mystic, Prophet, Ecologist* (Philadelphia: United Church Press, Pilgrim Press, 1974). Sherman Paul probes Thoreau's inner life masterfully in *The Shores of America: Thoreau's Inward Exploration* (1958; reprint, Urbana: University of Illinois Press, 1972). Still further, Frederick Garber connects nature and consciousness in Thoreau's work, in *Thoreau's Redemptive Imagination* (New York: New York University Press, 1977). Within the context of the symbolic function of Indians as equivalents in American culture for nature, Robert F. Sayre's *Thoreau and the American Indians* (Princeton: Princeton University Press, 1977) is worth reading. In similar vein, Richard F. Fleck has edited material from Thoreau's "Indian Notebooks," in *The Indians of Thoreau: Selections from the Indian Notebooks* (Albuquerque: Hummingbird Press, 1974). Fleck also offers a comparative study of Indian influence on Thoreau and John Muir, in *Henry Thoreau and John Muir among the Indians* (Hamden, Conn.: Archon Books, 1985).

John Muir himself is best introduced through his biographer Linnie Marsh Wolfe, in *Son of the Wilderness: The Life of John Muir* (1945; reprint, Madison: University of Wisconsin Press, 1978), and through the perceptive study by Michael P. Cohen, *The Pathless Way: John Muir and American Wilderness* (Madison: University of Wisconsin Press, 1984). The recent popular biography by Frederick Turner, *Rediscovering America: John Muir in His Time and Ours* (New York: Viking, 1985), is also a welcome addition; and, from a Christian theological stance, there is Richard Cartwright Austin, *Baptized into Wilderness: A Christian Perspective on John Muir,* Environmental Theology, Book 1 (Atlanta: John Knox Press, 1987).

Beyond these full-length works, Sandra Sizer Frankiel renders a brief but sensitive account of Muir and his religion of nature, in *California's Spiritual Frontiers: Religious Alternatives in Anglo-Protestantism, 1850–1910* (Berkeley: University of California Press, 1988), 120–25. And a special issue of *The Pacific Historian* 29 (Summer/Fall 1985), titled *John Muir: Life and Legacy,* includes essays by Ronald H. Limbaugh ("The Nature of Muir's Religion," 16–29); Paul D. Sheats ("John Muir's Glacial Gospel," 42–53); Richard F. Fleck ("John Muir's Homage to Henry David Thoreau," 54–64); Edmund A. Schofield ("John Muir's Yankee Friends and

Mentors: The New England Connection," 65–89); Kathleen Anne Wadden ("John Muir and the Community of Nature," 94–102); and Lisa Mighetto ("John Muir and the Rights of Animals," 103–112).

Selections from Muir's private journals are available in Linnie Marsh Wolfe, ed., *John of the Mountains: The Unpublished Journals of John Muir* (1938; reprint, Madison: University of Wisconsin Press, 1979). A useful autobiographical selection from Muir's letters, journals, and articles is contained in *To Yosemite and Beyond: Writings from the Years 1863 to 1875,* ed. Robert Engberg and Donald Wesling (Madison: University of Wisconsin Press, 1980). And Muir's published writings may be obtained readily in various editions, many of them published by the University of Wisconsin Press or the Sierra Club. Fruitful places to begin include John Muir, *The Mountains of California* (1894; reprint, New York: Penguin Books, 1985); John Muir, *Our National Parks* (1901; reprint, Madison: University of Wisconsin Press, 1981); John Muir, *My First Summer in the Sierra* (1911; reprint, Boston: Houghton Mifflin, n.d.); John Muir, *The Yosemite* (1912; reprint, Madison: University of Wisconsin Press, 1986); John Muir, *A Thousand-Mile Walk to the Gulf,* ed. with an introduction by William Frederick Badé (1916; reprint, with foreword by Peter Jenkins, Boston: Houghton Mifflin, 1981). In addition, Richard F. Fleck's brief anthology edition, John Muir, *Mountaineering Essays,* Literature of the American Wilderness (Salt Lake City: Gibbs M. Smith, Peregrine Smith Books, 1984), contains helpful material.

Muir's work in launching a conservation movement forms the theme for Stephen Fox's study, *John Muir and His Legacy: The American Conservation Movement* (Boston: Little, Brown, 1981). The translation of private sentiment into a political tool for conservation interests is treated perceptively in Christine Oravec, "John Muir, Yosemite, and the Sublime Response: A Study in the Rhetoric of Preservationism," *The Quarterly Journal of Speech* 67 (August 1981): 245–58. More generally, the nineteenth-century background for later preservation and conservation efforts is surveyed in Lee Clark Mitchell, *Witnesses to a Vanishing America: The Nineteenth-Century Response* (Princeton: Princeton University Press, 1981). The genesis of national parks is given specific attention in Roderick Nash, "The American Invention of National Parks," *American Quarterly* 22 (Fall 1970): 726–35.

Muir's greatest successor in the twentieth-century ecology movement is Aldo Leopold, whose classic work *A Sand County Almanac and Sketches Here and There* (1949; reprint, Oxford: Oxford University Press, 1981) demands serious attention. Leopold is now the subject of a full-length biography in Curt Meine's *Aldo Leopold: His Life and Work* (Madison: University of Wisconsin Press, 1988). Environmental philosopher and ethicist J. Baird Callicott has edited an important collection of essays on Leopold, with an introduction and two essays of his own, in *Companion to "A Sand County Almanac": Interpretive and Critical Essays* (Madison: University of Wisconsin Press, 1987). Leopold is also a continuing presence in Callicott's new collection of his own essays, *In Defense of the Land Ethic: Essays in Environmental Philosophy* (Albany: State University of New York Press, 1989). In an older study, Roderick Nash calls Leopold "prophet," in a chapter devoted to him in *Wilderness and the American Mind* (cited above), 182–99, while Nash's new work *The Rights of Nature: A History of Environmental Ethics* (Madison: University of Wisconsin Press, 1988) ranges in environmental discussion from the past into our own time.

Transcendentalism's other legacy, in the mind-cure movement, is explored in Gail Thain Parker's *Mind Cure in New England: From the Civil War to World War I* (Hanover, N.H.: University Press of New England, 1973). Also important, especially in its Part-One treatment of mind cure, is Donald Meyer, *The Positive Thinkers: Religion as Pop Psychology from Mary Baker Eddy to Oral Roberts*, 2d ed. (New York: Pantheon Books, 1980), 19–125. For the New Thought movement, the standard, though dated, resource is Charles S. Braden, *Spirits in Rebellion: The Rise and Development of New Thought* (Dallas: Southern Methodist University Press, 1963). An older work by Horatio W. Dresser, *A History of the New Thought Movement* (New York: Thomas Y. Crowell, 1919), may be used judiciously.

A complete—but not critical—edition of the writings of Phineas P. Quimby has now been published, as Phineas Parkhurst Quimby, *The Complete Writings*, ed. Ervin Seale, 3 vols. (Marina del Rey, Calif.: Devorss, 1988). This work should supplant the older, badly anthologized edition of Quimby's writings, in Horatio W. Dresser, ed., *The Quimby Manuscripts* (1921; reprint, Secaucus, N.J.: Citadel Press, 1969). Still, the readier availability and more compact size of the Dresser edition suggest that it may need to be reckoned with for some time to come. Short near-contemporary (1888) biographies of Quimby, by his son George Quimby and by an unnamed biographer, may be found in Quimby, *Complete Writings*, 1:19–29. Horatio W. Dresser also offers biographical reflections on Quimby, in his *Quimby Manuscripts* and in *Health and the Inner Life: An Analytical and Historical Study of Spiritual Healing Theories, with an Account of the Life and Teachings of P. P. Quimby* (New York: G. P. Putnam's Sons, Knickerbocker Press, 1906). A connection between Quimby and Transcendentalism is examined in Stewart W. Holmes, "Phineas Parkhurst Quimby: Scientist of Transcendentalism," *The New England Quarterly* 17 (1944): 356–80.

For a study of nature religion, the most relevant of Mary Baker Eddy's writings is the first edition (by Mary Baker Glover [Eddy]) of *Science and Health* (1875; reprint, Freehold, N.J.: Rare Book Company, n.d.). This work may be fruitfully compared with the final edition, in Mary Baker Eddy, *Science and Health with Key to the Scriptures* (Boston: Trustees under the Will of Mary Baker G. Eddy, 1906). Also a good source is Mary Baker Eddy, *Miscellaneous Writings, 1883–1896* (Boston: Trustees under the Will of Mary Baker G. Eddy, 1896). The best study of Eddy's thought as found in Christian Science is—by an academically trained insider—Stephen Gottschalk's *The Emergence of Christian Science in American Reli-*

gious Life (Berkeley: University of California Press, 1973). No completely satisfactory biography of Eddy is available, but Robert Peel's trilogy— *Mary Baker Eddy: The Years of Discovery* (New York: Holt, Rinehart and Winston, 1966); *Mary Baker Eddy: The Years of Trial* (New York: Holt, Rinehart and Winston, 1971); and *Mary Baker Eddy: The Years of Authority* (New York: Holt, Rinehart and Winston, 1977)—again by an academically trained insider, represents the best attempt.

The mesmeric background, both for mind cure and for the alternative-healing strategies of physical religion, deserves careful attention. The best current introduction to mesmerism is Robert C. Fuller's *Mesmerism and the American Cure of Souls* (Philadelphia: University of Pennsylvania Press, 1982). Fuller has also contributed an essay, "Mesmerism and the Birth of Psychology," in Arthur Wrobel, ed., *Pseudo-Science and Society in Nineteenth-Century America* (Lexington: University Press of Kentucky, 1987), 205–22. Franz Anton Mesmer's own writings, germane to the study of nature religion, may be found in George Bloch, trans. and comp., *Mesmerism: A Translation of the Original Scientific and Medical Writings of F. A. Mesmer* (Los Altos, Calif.: William Kaufmann, 1980). Charles Poyen, who toured New England in 1836 to bring the news of animal magnetism, recorded his experience in *Progress of Animal Magnetism in New England* (Boston: Weeks, Jordan, 1837). By a decade later, George Bush was linking Mesmer to Emanuel Swedenborg in *Mesmer and Swedenborg; or, The Relation of the Developments of Mesmerism to the Doctrines and Disclosures of Swedenborg* (New York: John Allen, 1847).

No critical biography of Emanuel Swedenborg exists in English, but George Trobridge's *Swedenborg: Life and Teaching*, 4th ed. (1935; reprint, New York: Swedenborg Foundation, 1962) can serve as a usable introduction. A more recent choice is Cyriel Odhner Sigstedt, *The Swedenborg Epic: The Life and Works of Emanuel Swedenborg* (1952; reprint, London: Swedenborg Society, 1981). Sig Synnestvedt's *The Essential Swedenborg: Basic Teachings of Emanuel Swedenborg, Scientist, Philosopher, and Theologian* (New York: Swedenborg Foundation, Twayne Publishers, 1970) contains a short account of Swedenborg's life, as well as excerpts from his copious writings, organized around a series of topics or themes. The materiality of Swedenborg's heaven is explored in Colleen McDannell and Bernhard Lang, *Heaven: A History* (New Haven: Yale University Press, 1988), 181–227.

Any study of Swedenborg's writings as they pertain to the theme of nature religion should include Emanuel Swedenborg, *Heaven and Its Wonders and Hell, from Things Heard and Seen*, trans. J. C. Ager (1852; reprint, New York: Swedenborg Foundation, 1964); Emanuel Swedenborg, *The Delights of Wisdom pertaining to Conjugial Love after Which Follow the Pleasures of Insanity pertaining to Scortatory Love*, trans. Samuel M. Warren, and rev. trans. Louis H. Tafel (1856; reprint, New York: Swedenborg Foundation, 1980); and Emanuel Swedenborg, *The True Christian Religion, Containing the Universal Theology of the New Church*, trans. John C. Ager, 2 vols. (1853; reprint, New York: Swedenborg Foundation, 1970).

The relationship of mesmerism, in turn, to spiritualism, is treated in a nineteenth-century work by William Carpenter, *Mesmerism and Spiritualism: Historically and Scientifically Considered* (New York: D. Appleton, 1889). The best recent account of spiritualism and the materialism of its theology is R. Laurence Moore, *In Search of White Crows: Spiritualism, Parapsychology, and American Culture* (New York: Oxford University Press, 1977). For an important new contribution written with a focus on the nineteenth-century women's movement, there is Ann Braude, *Radical Spirits: Spiritualism and Women's Rights in Nineteenth-Century America* (Boston: Beacon Press, 1989). R. Laurence Moore has also contributed an essay—"The Occult Connection? Mormonism, Christian Science, and Spiritualism"—linking Christian Science and spiritualism to Swedenborg's teachings, in *The Occult in America: New Historical Perspectives,* ed. Howard Kerr and Charles L. Crow (Urbana: University of Illinois Press, 1983), 135–61. Meanwhile, Robert S. Ellwood, Jr., discusses theosophy to advantage in his article "The American Theosophical Synthesis" in the same volume, 111–34. The best single book on theosophy is Bruce F. Campbell's *Ancient Wisdom Revived: A History of the Theosophical Movement* (Berkeley: University of California Press, 1980). Also informative in its accounts of spiritualism and theosophy is J. Stillson Judah, *The History and Philosophy of the Metaphysical Movements in America* (Philadelphia: Westminster Press, 1967).

Studies of physical religion in the nineteenth century must begin with some account of orthodox medical practice in the United States. Here John Duffy, *The Healers: A History of American Medicine* (Urbana: University of Illinois Press, Illini Books, 1979); Richard Harrison Shryock, *Medicine and Society in America, 1660–1860* (New York: New York University Press, 1960); and William G. Rothstein, *American Physicians in the Nineteenth Century: From Sects to Science* (Baltimore: Johns Hopkins University Press, 1972) are particularly useful. Good overviews of health reform and sectarian healing movements may be found in James C. Whorton, *Crusaders for Fitness: The History of American Health Reformers* (Princeton: Princeton University Press, 1982); and Harvey Green, *Fit for America: Health, Fitness, Sport, and American Society* (New York: Pantheon Books, 1986).

Norman Gevitz has recently edited a volume—*Other Healers: Unorthodox Medicine in America* (Baltimore: Johns Hopkins University Press, 1988)—which, in addition to essays on nineteenth-century health-reform and physical healing movements, includes essays on Christian Science healing, Protestant divine healing, and folk medicine in the twentieth century. Most germane to the study of alternative healing and religion is a new work by Robert C. Fuller, *Alternative Medicine and American Religious Life* (New York: Oxford University Press, 1989). And, exploring the alternative-healing movement in contemporary life more fully, there is Meredith B. McGuire, with the assistance of Debra Kantor, *Ritual Healing in Suburban America* (New Brunswick: Rutgers University Press, 1988). For the nineteenth century, John B. Blake's essay "Health Reform," in Edwin

Scott Gaustad, ed., *The Rise of Adventism: Religion and Society in Mid-Nineteenth Century America* (New York: Harper & Row, 1974), 30–49, is a solid contribution. Ronald L. Numbers's essay "Do-It-Yourself the Sectarian Way," in Judith Walzer Leavitt and Ronald L. Numbers, eds., *Sickness and Health in America: Readings in the History of Medicine and Public Health* (Madison: University of Wisconsin Press, 1978), 87–95, is also helpful.

The Leavitt and Numbers volume also contains James C. Whorton's article "'Tempest in a Flesh-Pot': The Formulation of a Physiological Rationale for Vegetarianism," 315–30, which summarizes the early vegetarian movement. It is fortunate, too, that a full-length study of Sylvester Graham and his work exists in Stephen Nissenbaum's *Sex, Diet, and Debility in Jacksonian America: Sylvester Graham and Health Reform* (Westport, Conn.: Greenwood Press, 1980). Also helpful for understanding Graham is the older essay by medical historian Richard H. Shryock, "Sylvester Graham and the Popular Health Movement, 1830–1870," *Mississippi Valley Historical Review* 18 (1931): 172–83. Beyond these, the millennial leanings of the other leading Christian physiologist, William Andrus Alcott, are studied in James C. Whorton, "'Christian Physiology': William Alcott's Prescription for the Millenium" [*sic*], *Bulletin of the History of Medicine* 49 (1975): 466–81.

The sectarian journals listed in the notes to chapter 4 offer some clues as to how to approach primary reading regarding individual healing movements. In the secondary literature, in addition to their treatment by scholars in general medical histories, William G. Rothstein writes on "The Botanical Movements and Orthodox Medicine," in Norman Gevitz, *Other Healers* (cited above), 29–51. Older essays by Alex Berman—"The Thomsonian Movement and Its Relation to American Pharmacy and Medicine" (*Bulletin of the History of Medicine* 35 [1951]: 405–28, 518–38) and "Neo-Thomsonianism in the United States" (*Journal of the History of Medicine* 11 [1956]: 133–55)—may also be consulted for background. Homeopathy receives the attention of Martin Kaufman, in *Homeopathy in America: The Rise and Fall of a Medical Heresy* (Baltimore: Johns Hopkins University Press, 1971), although Kaufman may have been premature in printing homeopathy's obituary. Kaufman recognizes the new state of affairs for homeopathy in his essay "Homeopathy in America: The Rise and Fall and Persistence of a Medical Heresy," in Gevitz, *Other Healers* (cited above), 99–123. Beyond this, two works with a contemporary holistic healing perspective offer representative documentation of the homeopathic revival; they are Richard Grossinger's *Planet Medicine: From Stone Age Shamanism to Post-Industrial Healing*, rev. ed. (Boulder, Colo.: Shambhala, 1982), 161–244; and Richard Gerber, *Vibrational Medicine: New Choices for Healing Ourselves* (Santa Fe: Bear, 1988), 71–90.

Water cure has recently been the subject of two studies that focus on women's health: Jane B. Donegan's *"Hydropathic Highway to Health": Women and Water-Cure in Antebellum America*, Contributions in Medical

Studies, no. 17 (Westport, Conn.: Greenwood Press, 1986); and Susan E. Cayleff, *Wash and Be Healed: The Water-Cure Movement and Women's Health* (Philadelphia: Temple University Press, 1987). Cayleff has also contributed the article "Gender, Ideology, and the Water-Cure Movement" to Gevitz, *Other Healers* (cited above), 82–98. A more general article by Marshall Scott Legan, "Hydropathy, or the Water-Cure," may be found in Arthur Wrobel, ed., *Pseudo-Science and Society in Nineteenth-Century America* (cited above), 74–99. Legan has also contributed "Hydropathy in America: A Nineteenth-Century Panacea" to the *Bulletin of the History of Medicine* 45 (1971): 267–80. In addition to these, an older study of water cure by Harry B. Weiss and Howard R. Kemble, *The Great American Water-Cure Craze: A History of Hydropathy in the United States* (Trenton, N.J.: Past Times Press, 1967), may be examined.

The most accessible historical work on osteopathy is Norman Gevitz's fine study *The D.O.'s: Osteopathic Medicine in America* (Baltimore: Johns Hopkins University Press, 1982). Gevitz has also contributed an essay, "Osteopathic Medicine: From Deviance to Difference," to his edited volume *Other Healers* (cited above), 124–56. The founder of osteopathy, Andrew Taylor Still, offers both autobiographical reflection, in *The Autobiography of Andrew Taylor Still* (Kirksville, Mo.: By the author, 1897; rev. ed., 1908), and other valuable insights regarding osteopathy, in *The Philosophy of Osteopathy* (Kirksville, Mo.: By the author, 1899). And one may also examine Arthur Hildreth's work *The Lengthening Shadow of Andrew Taylor Still* (Kirksville, Mo.: Journal Printing, 1942).

For chiropractic, there is no satisfactory overall study of its founder, D. D. Palmer, and the character of his work. The best treatment currently available, though, is Vern Gielow's *Old Dad Chiro: A Biography of D. D. Palmer, Founder of Chiropractic* (Davenport, Iowa: Bawden Brothers, 1981). Walter I. Wardwell's essay "Chiropractors: Evolution to Acceptance," in Gevitz's *Other Healers* (cited above), 157–91, mostly concerns the evolving social status of chiropractic. I have discussed chiropractic from a symbolic perspective, in Catherine L. Albanese, "The Poetics of Healing: Root Metaphors and Rituals in Nineteenth-Century America," *Soundings* 63 (Winter 1980), 390–94. D. D. Palmer intersperses technical data with philosophical reflection, in *The Chiropractor's Adjuster: Textbook of the Science, Art, and Philosophy of Chiropractic for Students and Practitioners* (1910; reprint, n.p., 1966). Also in a reflective vein, Joy M. Loben [Loban?] offers an important exposition of the "theology" of chiropractic, in "The Completeness of Chiropractic Philosophy," an article in *The Chiropractor: A Monthly Journal Devoted to the Interests of Chiropractic* 4 (August and September 1908): 30–36.

Moving from the aftermath of magnetism in nineteenth-century manipulative healing to the new electromagnetic model of the twentieth century leads into the world of the quantum. Probably the most lucid and succinct account of the history of quantum theory may be found in Victor Guillemin, *The Story of Quantum Mechanics* (New York: Charles Scribner's Sons, 1968). More indulgent and more protean is Gary Zukav, *The Dancing Wu Li Masters: An Overview of the New Physics* (New York: Bantam Books, 1980). An interest in Eastern mysticism marks Fritjof Capra's comparative study *The Tao of Physics: An Exploration of the Parallels between Modern Physics and Eastern Mysticism,* 2d ed. (Boston: Shambhala, New Science Library, 1985). Beyond these and somewhat more technical is George Gamow, *Thirty Years That Shook Physics: The Story of Quantum Theory* (Garden City, N.Y.: Doubleday, 1968). And, for the uses of quantum theory for the environmental movement, see J. Baird Callicott's essay "Intrinsic Value, Quantum Theory, and Environmental Ethics," in his *In Defense of the Land Ethic: Essays in Environmental Philosophy* (cited above), 157–74.

Protagonists of quantum theory have not been bashful in offering philosophical reflection. Although Albert Einstein and Max Planck might be cited, most significant here are a series of discussions by Werner Heisenberg: *Physics and Philosophy: The Revolution in Modern Science,* World Perspectives, vol. 19 (New York: Harper, 1958); *The Physicist's Conception of Nature,* trans. Arnold J. Pomerans (New York: Harcourt, Brace, 1958); *Natural Law and the Structure of Matter* (London: Rebel Press, 1970); and *Philosophic Problems of Nuclear Science,* trans. F. C. Hayes (New York: Pantheon, 1952).

In the late twentieth century, material for a study of nature religion is ready in abundance, and only works concerning the figures and movements explored in chapter 5 are cited here. The best introduction to Sun Bear is his autobiographical *Sun Bear: The Path of Power,* as told to Wabun and to Barry Weinstock (Spokane, Wash.: Bear Tribe Publishing, 1983). Also of value are Sun Bear, *Buffalo Hearts: A Native American's View of His Culture, Religion, and History* (Spokane, Wash.: Bear Tribe Publishing, 1976); Sun Bear and Wabun, *The Medicine Wheel: Earth Astrology* (Englewood Cliffs, N.J.: Prentice-Hall, 1980); and Sun Bear, Wabun, and Nimimosha, *The Bear Tribe's Self Reliance Book,* rev. ed. (Spokane, Wash.: Bear Tribe Publishing, 1986). In addition, the Bear Tribe Network magazine *Wildfire* is always a good source on Sun Bear, the Bear Tribe, and issues that concern them.

Annie Dillard's recent autobiographical reminiscences, in *An American Childhood* (New York: Harper & Row, 1987), provide useful entrance to her world. Dillard's *Pilgrim at Tinker Creek* (1974; reprint, New York: Bantam Books, 1975) is already a classic, the most important of her works. Her *Holy the Firm* (1977; reprint, London: Collier-Macmillan, Collier Books, 1961) forms a kind of sequel to the *Pilgrim* book. Important, too, is Dillard's collection of essays, *Teaching a Stone to Talk: Expeditions and Encounters* (New York: Harper & Row, 1982).

For Green politics and its environmental concerns, two useful books that survey the movement from its Western European origins and also include chapters on the United States are Jonathon Porritt, *Seeing Green: The Politics of Ecology Explained* (New York: Basil Blackwell, 1985), with

"The Greening of America," 224–40; and Charlene Spretnak and Fritjof Capra, in collaboration with Rüdiger Lutz, *Green Politics* (Santa Fe: Bear, 1986), with "Green Politics in the United States: 1986," 227–40. "Seeing Green," an article by Stephan Bodian and Florence Windfall, in the New Age *Yoga Journal*, no. 79 (March/April 1988): 56–59, 76–78, provides a helpful introduction to the Green movement, with special attention to its spiritual dimension. And a fuller account of Green spirituality is contained in Charlene Spretnak, *The Spiritual Dimension of Green Politics* (Santa Fe: Bear, 1986).

The concept of "deep ecology," which finds congenial reception among the Greens, is expounded in Bill Devall and George Sessions, *Deep Ecology: Living as if Nature Mattered* (New York: Peregrine Smith, 1985). Also favored by the Greens, the Gaia hypothesis—that the earth is a single living being—is argued in James Lovelock, *Gaia: A New Look at Life on Earth* (New York: Oxford University Press, 1979). At least two contributions in Charlene Spretnak, ed., *The Politics of Women's Spirituality: Essays on the Rise of Spiritual Power within the Feminist Movement* (Garden City, N.Y.: Doubleday, Anchor Books, 1982), express an explicit ecofeminist perspective: Judith Todd, "On Common Ground: Native American and Feminist Spirituality Approaches in the Struggle to Save Mother Earth," 430–45; and Gina Foglia and Dorit Wolffberg, "Spiritual Dimensions of Feminist Anti-Nuclear Activism," 446–61. In a more comprehensive statement of ecofeminism, the new volume edited by Judith Plant, *Healing the Wounds: The Promise of Ecofeminism* (Santa Cruz: New Society, 1989), contains contributions by a series of leading ecofeminists.

Ecofeminism blends with forms of contemporary American paganism and Goddess religion in Margot Adler's informative survey *Drawing Down the Moon: Witches, Druids, Goddess-Worshippers, and Other Pagans in America Today*, rev. ed. (Boston: Beacon Press, 1986). Probably the most visible follower of the Goddess currently is Starhawk, and she gives accessible accounts of her form of nature religion, in *The Spiral Dance: A Rebirth of the Ancient Religion of the Great Goddess* (San Francisco: Harper & Row, 1979); *Dreaming the Dark: Magic, Sex, and Politics* (Boston: Beacon Press, 1982); and, most recently, *Truth or Dare: Encounters with Power, Authority, and Mystery* (San Francisco: Harper & Row, 1987).

Female power predominates, too, in the form of energy healing with Japanese roots that is Reiki. For the best overall introduction, the choice is Barbara Weber Ray, *The Reiki Factor: A Guide to Natural Healing, Helping, and Wholeness* (Smithtown, N.Y.: Exposition Press, 1983). And, for the best introduction to the "traditionalist" perspective within the context of American Reiki, there is Larry Arnold and Sandy Nevius, *The Reiki Handbook* (Harrisburg, Pa.: PSI Press, ParaScience International, 1982). Virginia Samdahl, who is representative of the traditionalist view and who is also the first mainland American to be initiated as a Reiki master, is the subject of a popular account in Barbara Derrick Lugenbeel's *Virginia Samdahl: Reiki Master Healer* (Norfolk, Va.: Grunwald and Radcliff,

1984). On the other hand, emanating from the Ray organization are Barbara Ray, assisted by Marvelle Carter, *The Official Handbook of the Radiance Technique* rev. ed. (Santa Monica, Calif.: American-International Reiki Association, 1987); and Barbara Ray, assisted by Marvelle Carter, *The Expanded Reference Manual of the Radiance Technique: The Radiance Technique A to Z* (St. Petersburg, Fla.: Radiance Associates, 1987).

For macrobiotics, the other contemporary form of healing discussed in this book as an expression of nature religion, the literature is remarkably large. Perhaps the best comprehensive introduction to macrobiotics is Ronald E. Kotzsch's *Macrobiotics: Yesterday and Today* (New York: Japan Publications, 1985). Useful in underlining the movement's understanding of macrobiotics as a way of life are Michio Kushi with Stephen Blauer, *The Macrobiotic Way: The Complete Macrobiotic Diet and Exercise Book* (Wayne, N.J.: Avery Publishing, 1985); and Herman Aihara, *Basic Macrobiotics* (New York: Japan Publications, 1985). Michio Kushi, the acknowledged Japanese-American leader of the movement, contributes autobiographical reflections, historical theories, and long-range prognostications, in Michio Kushi with Alex Jack, *One Peaceful World* (New York: St. Martin's Press, 1987). Kushi's reflections on a variety of contemporary problems are gathered in a compilation by the editors of *East West Journal, Michio Kushi on the Greater View: Collected Thoughts and Ideas on Macrobiotics and Humanity* (Wayne, N.J.: Avery Publishing, 1986).

The best-known work by the Japanese founder of macrobiotics is Georges [the French form of his name] Ohsawa, *Zen Macrobiotics: The Art of Rejuvenation and Longevity,* rev. and ed. Lou Oles and Shayne Oles Suehle, The Philosophy of Oriental Medicine, vol. 1 (Los Angeles: Ohsawa Foundation, 1965). And, for a succinct expression of George Ohsawa's religious vision, there is his work *The Book of Judgment,* rev. ed., ed. Herman Aihara and Sandy Rothman (Oroville, Calif.: George Ohsawa Macrobiotic Foundation, 1980). The only scholarly study of Ohsawa is Ronald E. Kotzsch's Harvard dissertation, "Georges Ohsawa and the Japanese Religious Tradition" (Ph.D. diss., Harvard University, 1981), material from which is also available in Kotzsch's *Macrobiotics: Yesterday and Today* (cited above).

Among books focusing on macrobiotic diet, the cookbook by Aveline Kushi with Alex Jack, *Aveline Kushi's Complete Guide to Macrobiotic Cooking: For Health, Harmony, and Peace* (New York: Warner Books, 1985), should be consulted for Kushi's reminiscences regarding Japanese folk customs from her childhood, as well as for her articulation of macrobiotic food philosophy. Also valuable in this regard is Michio and Aveline Kushi, *Macrobiotic Diet: Balancing Your Eating in Harmony with the Changing Environment and Personal Needs,* ed. Alex Jack (New York: Japan Publications, 1985). Without a doubt, the most well-known story of healing through macrobiotics is the religiously sensitive account by Philadelphia physician Anthony Sattilaro with Tom Monte, *Recalled by Life: The Story of My Recovery from Cancer* (Boston: Houghton Mifflin, 1982). Also important as an expression of macrobiotic spiritual vision in the context of healing is Richard France and Jerome Carty, *Healing Naturally: The Commonsense Macrobiotic Approach to Cancer and Other Diseases,* 2d ed. (Boulder, Colo.: Amaizeing Books, 1982). Exercise becomes a particular and significant expression of nature religion in Michio Kushi's philosophical treatment *The Book of Dō-In: Exercise for Physical and Spiritual Development* (New York: Japan Publications, 1979). Finally, the periodicals *Solstice* (Charlottesville, Va.), *Macrobiotics Today* (Oroville, Calif.), and *Return to Paradise*—now *One Peaceful World,* a newsletter—(Beckett, Mass.), are good sources for information on the macrobiotic community.

Index